Bernhardt, Terry, Duse
The actress in her time

Bernhardt, Terry, Duse
The actress in her time

JOHN STOKES
MICHAEL R. BOOTH
SUSAN BASSNETT

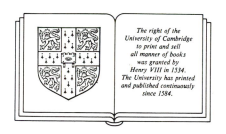

The right of the
University of Cambridge
to print and sell
all manner of books
was granted by
Henry VIII in 1534.
The University has printed
and published continuously
since 1584.

CAMBRIDGE UNIVERSITY PRESS

Cambridge
New York   New Rochelle   Melbourne   Sydney

Published by the Press Syndicate of the University of Cambridge
The Pitt Building, Trumpington Street, Cambridge CB2 1RP
32 East 57th Street, New York, NY 10022, USA
10 Stamford Road, Oakleigh, Melbourne 3166, Australia

First published 1988

Printed in Great Britain at
the University Press, Cambridge

British Library cataloguing in publication data
Stokes, John, *1943–*
Bernhardt, Terry, Duse: The actress in her time
1. Bernhardt, Sarah   2. Duse, Eleonora
3. Terry, Ellen
I. Title   II. Booth, Michael R.
III. Bassnett-McGuire, Susan
792'.028'0922   PN2638.B5

Library of Congress cataloguing in publication data
Stokes, John, 1943–
Bernhardt, Terry, Duse: The actress in her time /
John Stokes, Michael R. Booth, Susan Bassnett
p.   cm.
ISBN 0-521-25615-1
1. Actresses – Biography.   2. Bernhardt, Sarah, 1844–1923 – Biography.
3. Terry, Ellen, Dame, 1847–1928 – Biography.
4. Duse, Eleonora, 1858–1924 – Biography.
I. Booth, Michael R.   II. Bassnett, Susan.   III. Title.
PN2205.S76   1988
792'.028'0922 – dc19   87-16732 CIP

ISBN 0 521 25615 1

Contents

vvvvvvvvvvvvvvvvvvvvvvvvvvvvvvvvvvvvvvvvvvvvvvvvvvvvvvvvvvvvvvvvvvv

Illustrations

vvvvvvvvvvvvvvvvvvvvvvvvvvvvvvvvvvvvvvvvvvvvvvvvvvvvvvvvvvvvvvvvvvvvvvvvvvvvvv

Acknowledgements

vvvvvvvvvvvvvvvvvvvvvvvvvvvvvvvvvvvvvvvvvvvvvvvvvvvvvvvvvvvvvvvvvvvvvvv

For help with research in France, thanks are due to the librarians of the Bibliothèque de l'Arsenal, Mlle Guibert of the Comédie-Française archives, and M. Frères of the Musée du Théâtre at Couilly. Mme Gigou, Keeper of the collection of the Association de la Régie Théâtrale at the Bibliothèque Historique de la Ville de Paris, was patient with enquiries and generous with material. Administrators at the Théâtre Porte Saint-Martin, the Théâtre de la Renaissance and the Théâtre des Nations were uniformly enthusiastic in reconstructing Bernhardt's tenure of the buildings they now operate. Faith Evans participated both in the research and in the writing, and thanks are also due to the University of Warwick for granting the sabbatical leave in which the work was done. *John Stokes*

I wish particularly to thank for their assistance in research Molly Thomas, formerly Curator of the Ellen Terry Museum, Jennifer Aylmer and the staff of the Theatre Museum, whose help was especially appreciated during the trying period when the Museum was not open to the public, Alan Hughes and Tracy Davis. *Michael R. Booth*

I should like to thank Alessandro Tinterri of the Actors' Museum, Genoa for his considerable assistance, also Mirella Schino of the University of Bologna whose work on Duse has been invaluable. My co-writers, Michael Booth and John Stokes, have been exemplary for their patience and their shrewd, intelligent comments on my work. To both, much thanks. Irene Pearson, who typed the manuscript at great speed and with her usual great efficiency, deserves special praise. Finally, my thanks as always to my family for providing me with an environment in which to think and write creatively. *Susan Bassnett*

Thanks are due to the following for permission to reproduce photographs: Raymond Mander and Joe Mitchenson Theatre Collection (illustration 1);

Collection de l'Association de la Régie Théâtrale, Bibliothèque Historique de la Ville de Paris (illustration 4); Victoria and Albert Museum (illustrations 3, 11, 14, 16 and 17); Theater Arts Library, The Harry Ransom Humanities Research Center, University of Texas at Austin (illustrations 10, 12, 13 and 18); Fondazione Giorgio Cini, Venice (illustrations 19–26).

Introduction

ʏʏʏ

BERNHARDT, TERRY AND DUSE are the three most famous names in a long list of female performers who thrived between the mid nineteenth and early twentieth centuries. Their careers have been the subject of many books and films, and all three have had aspects of their lives fictionalized by historical novelists; Eleonora Duse even became 'La Foscarina', the heroine of D'Annunzio's novel *La fiamma*, during her own lifetime. In old age, all three actresses appeared on film and it is still possible to catch flickering images of them in the few remaining clips, though in the main our visual impressions derive from the surviving photographs of their greatest roles.

They were above all professionals and we have deliberately sought to emphasize that aspect in our accounts. The task that we have set ourselves has not been that of biographers; there are many books that give details of the extraordinary private lives. We have tried instead to show three working actresses: which is why we have sometimes questioned the assumptions made by others and explored gaps in the evidence. All three may have had celebrated love affairs, all three may have had a tendency towards behaviour typical of the *prima donna*, but all three were remarkably self-controlled when it came to their art. Bernhardt and Duse were managers besides being actresses, taking an active part in handling their business affairs, their publicity and their choice of roles, and though Terry was not so caught up in finance, she was nevertheless crucially involved in determining how she should perform. These aspects have often been minimized and we have sought to redress the balance.

And in offering an alternative version of their achievement, we have inevitably been drawn into reflections on the status of women at the end of the nineteenth century. Their careers span the years when a trans-European feminism emerged that manifested itself in some countries through suffragette movements, in others through the gradual penetration of women into areas of professional and intellectual life that had previously

I

been barred to them. In France, as in Italy, organized feminism had a strong anti-clerical bias, whilst in Britain it was closely linked to the growth of grass-roots socialism. In all three societies a central problem for feminists was the need to present a more affirmative view of woman in contrast to the passive notion of the angel of the house or the derogatory notion of the man-hating hysteric. In such a context the image of woman presented on stage assumed enormous significance.

But that image was by no means consistent. Paradoxically, the growth in importance of the female performer had developed parallel with the increased repression of women in society generally through the nineteenth century. The principal actress became a major box-office draw, and male performers, with a very few exceptions, such as Irving and Salvini, took second place. The number of paintings with women as subject is another notable feature of the period, and the common factor between the image of woman in paintings, in photographs and in the theatre was the use that could be made of her. As object of the gaze of the spectator, woman on stage or in a frame could be possessed vicariously, could be held in the mind's eye and enjoyed, could even be pasted into an album or hung on a wall for the continuing delectation of her admirer/owner.

Linked to this private act of possession was the low social status of the performer. That factor affected the career patterns of all three. Duse, with her *petit bourgeois* aspirations, perhaps felt the pressure more strongly than the other two, and her refusal to allow members of her own family to see her act shows how deeply she feared the taint of unrespectability. All three strove for an independence of image through the creation of particularly individualistic playing styles. Bernhardt, more successfully than either Terry or Duse, created an image of herself that allowed her to appear as the incarnation of theatricality. She aroused enormous animosity precisely through her outrageous brand of feminist behaviour – in a male-dominated society she exploited her privileged position as a *prima donna* to the maximum effect.

The story of an actress's struggle for success became emblematic and it recurs again and again in what amounts to a sub-genre within the nineteenth-century novel, offering a narrative trajectory of great fascination. This was partly because, as Christopher Kent has said,

to Victorians the profession of actress, like that of governess, had a symbolic importance as an occupation for women that transcended mere numbers. It offered striking opportunities for independence, fame and fortune, and even for those outside

2

it the stage incarnated fantasies providing vicarious release in the notion that there was an area of special dispensation from the normal categories, moral and social, that defined woman's place.[1]

Yet actress and prostitute remained almost synonymous at times, and there are endless accounts of the way in which relationships between actresses and members of the aristocracy developed through the sending of expensive gifts as part of the process of purchasing favours. The actress held a marginalized position in the hierarchy of sexual relations; she was independent in terms of her professional activity, something that most other women could never aspire to; she could become rich, famous and powerful, but at the same time she could only achieve that success by allowing herself to be bought by her public.

Making adequate allowance for a sociological potency beyond the official record is only another of the problems that historians of performance must face if they are to recapture an art that is, in any case, purely temporal. Previously, performance history when not simply biography, acting as a byproduct of 'personality', has been approached in two ways: in 'theory', meaning the old, still vexatious issues of 'identification' and 'impersonation'; or in 'theatre history', often so preoccupied with the reconstruction of whole productions that the performer is reduced to a mere component. No approach can be dismissed out of hand. After all, as much depends on the evidence available as on the project in mind. Biographers of Rachel and of Edmund Kean have not been inhibited by their subjects' comparative silence about their art – their contemporaries had enough to say. Perhaps the problem of writing about past performance only begins to feel pressing when there is such a wealth of documentation that the moment in question looks set to disappear in a welter of descriptive accounts in which the same terms continually recur in widely different contexts. It is certainly true that the careers of Bernhardt, Terry and Duse gain in complexity and in interest when one considers that they took place when the overwhelming change in international performance style was towards 'naturalism'.

It was often said at the time about each one of them that she was a 'natural' actress, but from our twentieth-century viewpoint it is difficult to imagine exactly what an audience may have seen that was 'natural', and how one kind of performance might have been characterized as being more 'natural' than another. What did Max Beerbohm mean when he described Terry as the 'incarnation of our capricious English sunlight' and what did

Arthur Symons mean when he described Duse as 'a chalice for the wine of the imagination'? What did audiences see when faced with performances that obviously stirred them profoundly but that reviewers have described with unhelpful poeticisms?

We are confronted here with the fundamental problem of historical analysis when it seeks to discover what was seen in an age when conventions of seeing were quite different. The riddle has attracted some distinguished theoreticians. Ernst Gombrich and Umberto Eco have both maintained that what is seen depends on the relationship between an image and some previously culturalized context.[2] In other words, a culture establishes certain codes of seeing which become the parameters for producing the reality of what actually *is* seen. Gombrich, for instance, cites Villard de Honnecourt, a thirteenth-century artist and architect, who claimed to copy a real lion yet reproduced that reality in terms of the heraldic conventions of his time.[3] Similarly, each of the actresses discussed in this book seems to have created her own sign conventions through which audiences perceived her. Bernhardt's carefully contrived passion, which she marketed through well-planned interviews, photographs and set and costume designs, became her dominant feature. Terry was able to project an image of spontaneous girlishness even whilst pinning up her inadequately remembered lines around the stage. Duse, who was seen by many colleagues skilfully applying powder, acquired the reputation of not using make-up, and generations of reviewers praised her naturalness with respect bordering at times on awe.

Today, in the post-realist theatre, audiences still expect performances to be measured by their verisimilitude to 'real life'. But cinema and television have given us a completely different notion of realism from that which existed in the pre-electronic age. Although all forms of realist acting have to begin with the intention of being believable at some level, there have been great changes in what audiences are accustomed to. An example of changing conventions could be seen in the staging of lyric opera over the past twenty years or so. Where once there was an acceptable gap between visual realism (Mimi, dying of consumption, could be happily fat and fortyish, wooed by a stout fiftyish student lover) and the requirements of the story line, that gap now has to be narrowed. The protagonists have come increasingly to resemble physically the characters they play, following the conventions established by the realist prose theatre in the age of cinema and television. That such a change can happen in such a short

4

space of time is an indication of the speed with which audience demands can be reshaped and redefined by new modes of seeing.

One such major shift involves audience response to demonstrable technical virtuosity in acting. To act in the nineteenth century involved participation in a conventionalized bravura display; its distance from 'real life' was an accepted part of the code, even though the emotions aroused in the spectators were assessed in terms of their closeness to reality. There were handbooks of poses, kinetic arrangements, voice projection; assessment was not made in terms of how close or distant the performance was to everyday life but rather in terms of its impact on the audience. Performers and spectators colluded in the arrangement of signs. With the advent of naturalism that conventionalized system was modified, but nevertheless re-established in other terms. Boundary lines between spectator and performer were not breached; what did change was the form of the convention pact between them.

Moreover, that pact was different in different cultural contexts. The Italian theatre, for example, gave great prominence to the prompter, who read the lines aloud throughout the performance. The prompter was not subdued until the 1920s and we can only imagine how audiences coped with hearing a ghostly voice, sometimes speaking more loudly than the actors on stage. When Pirandello came to London in 1925 with his Teatro d'arte company, critics complained about the insistent voice of the prompter above the actors' dialogue. Changing conventions of emotional behaviour in life also conditioned perception in the theatre. When Duse played Paula in *La seconda moglie* in London in May 1900, the reviewer in *The Stage* was already perturbed at the way in which her leading man, Carlo Rosaspina, played Tanqueray 'with Southern effusiveness, with tears, sobs, profound sighs and claspings of hands'.[4]

Variations between national cultures did little to inhibit the opportunities for export. Shaw, Archer, Symons and Walkley, the English observers, may have been over-quoted at the expense of local *cognoscenti* but they can hardly be held to blame for their privileged adjudications in London in 1895 when Terry was at the Lyceum, Duse at Drury Lane and Bernhardt at Daly's. At the very peak of their careers the great actresses demonstrated that the real strength of their individual style was its cosmopolitan appeal. And if the scale of their international success, popular as well as critical, is hard to credit now, that may be for one single overwhelming reason: the predominantly visual quality of their acting. At

5

times this has even caused doubts about the value of what they conveyed. So much so that in the 1950s, when Eric Bentley found himself unmoved by the great Greek actress Katerina Paxinou, he recalled the legend of Eleonora Duse. Recent experience, he said, had made him 'skeptical of all those critical pieces on Duse that were written in entire innocence of the Italian language. There are many things a woman can put across without words; dramatic literature is not one of them; and unintelligible words are not better than no words at all.'[5]

Max Beerbohm, who unlike Bentley actually saw Duse perform, would probably have agreed, though at the time his dissent from the general adulation was more consciously perverse. 'All the other critics understand the language perfectly,' he complained, 'else they would not be able to tell us unanimously that Duse's technique is beyond reproach. The technique of acting lies in the nice relation of the mime's voice, gesture and facial expression to the words by him or her spoken. Obviously, if those words are for you so much gibberish, you cannot pass any judgement on the mime's technique.'[6]

Bentley and Beerbohm, unlikely companions in almost every other respect, hold to the quite widespread belief that acting is primarily to do with giving meaning to words. There could be no stronger argument against their view than the careers of Bernhardt and Duse, and even of Ellen Terry.

Puzzling over pictures that are shamelessly posed, or struggling through reviews keener on itemizing what the actress wore than in analysing what she said, we have to remind ourselves that our feeling that the data has nothing to say may be because it is telling us something other than what we think we want to know. The evidence is in front of our eyes, but we have to learn to see it. Nineteenth-century theatre was 'visual' in the all-embracing sense that almost nothing occurred in the drama that could not be made visibly manifest. That principle applied even to actors and their bodies. An actor's 'presence' was quite literally that: a theatrical space physically occupied. Set and costume designs, promptbooks and rehearsal copies, have to be examined for the spatial patterns they imply. Then, at the points of intersection, we can discover the visible presence of the performance that really signified.

All of which means widening the boundaries of research. Historians of nineteenth-century theatre now know that they must look beyond the stage – to literature and to the fine arts – if they are fully to comprehend the conventions that operated upon it. Two recent books in particular have suggested the new approach: Michael Booth's *Victorian Spectacular Theatre*[7] and Martin Meisel's *Realizations*. In the nineteenth century the arts shared and exchanged with one another, and much that was exciting in the culture involved implicit combinations and comparisons between media. Interdisciplinary practice should not, however, be mistaken for homogeneity of intention. There were common codes at work, unquestionably, but they had to be flexible to a considerable degree. As Meisel puts it, nineteenth-century narrative in general involved 'not a fixed set of signs or a closed system of iconic representation, but an expanding universe of discourse, rule-governed but open, using a recognizable vocabulary of gesture, expression, configuration, object and ambiance'.[8] It was because they partook of that openness that the great actresses thrived.

'Nature' and 'woman' were closely related concepts in the 'expanding universe' of discourse, the actress a suitably illusionistic representation of the equation between two unstable ideas. The women who imitated other women (and sometimes even men) at once demonstrated and disturbed essential notions of the female. *Fin-de-siècle* audiences knew this themselves, and were not hesitant in applying explanations, but there were too many contending possibilities, and biology and history rivalled each other in their minds.

So important did he think the topic that Havelock Ellis, in his 1894 textbook *Man and Woman*, devoted a special section to the actress and her success.

There is at least one art in which women may be said not merely to rival but naturally to excel men: this is the art of acting . . . And if we look back at the history of the stage during the last two hundred years, against every famous actor whose name survives it seems usually possible to place a still more famous actress . . . It is not difficult to find the organic basis of women's success in acting. In women mental processes are usually more rapid than in men; they have also an emotional explosiveness much more marked than men possess, and more easily within call. At the same time the circumstances of women's social life have usually favoured a high degree of flexibility and adaptability as regards behaviour; and they are, again, more trained in the vocal expression both of those emotions which they feel and those emotions which it is considered their duty to feel. Women are, therefore, both by nature and social compulsion, more often than men in the position of actors. It is probable also that women are more susceptible than men to the immediate stimulus of admiration and applause supplied by contact with an audience.[9]

The connection between the kind of biological uncertainty and prejudice, exemplified by Ellis, and the contribution that theatre could make to prevailing sexual ideologies, was intricate and long-lasting. Pictorialism could make a spectacle of the human body; it could not, even in *tableaux vivants*, turn the body into an inorganic object – though the temptation was often there. As Michael Booth remarks in his essay on Terry, nineteenth-century theatre is full of statues turning into women and women turning into statues. 'Pygmalion and Galatea' was a favourite theme, and there was hardly an actress who was not at some stage in her career called 'statuesque', though in fact some were more marmoreal than others. Helen Faucit and Ellen Terry were at one pole; Rachel and, somewhat unexpectedly, Duse at the other. Sarcey said of Bernhardt's 1893 Phèdre that it had 'an artistic beauty that made one quiver with admiration, the look of a fine statue'.[10] A preoccupation with the impersonality of the body runs from the early Romantic period through to Symbolism, and even surfaces in Craig's *Übermarionette*. Craig designed symbolic sets in which both Terry and Duse were required to do little more than beautifully pose; none of his productions was a conspicuous success, but the style obviously came more easily to Duse than it did to Terry. Both Duse and Bernhardt were keen to play Anna, the blind soothsayer in D'Annunzio's *La città morta*, who responds to inanimate matter as if it were living and actually identifies with stone, and D'Annunzio was quite prepared to inscribe Bernhardt's copy, 'To Sarah Bernhardt who once displayed in her living eyes the blindness of a sacred statue',[11] even if the play had originally been intended for her rival.

Statues achieved a sublime fixity of attitude that acting could only try to imitate. But at the same time the statuesque style threatened to imprison the living potential of the performer. The conflict between organic and material representations of life obsessed nineteenth-century writing about the theatre and, whether as cause or as consequence, posed a challenge to sexual identity. Woman as statue might be placid, contained and inspiring, or intransigent, permanent, accusing and unanswerable.

In other words there was, at the deeper levels of sociological meaning, much more to the cult of the actress than her portrayal of the familiar syndrome of Madonna and whore – though that obviously contributed to style and repertoire. Why else was the range of plays available so comparatively limited, even when Ibsen had become international? Bernhardt threatened to learn English and to play Portia and Juliet. Fortunately the English language resisted her assault, perhaps because she only made herself available for instruction in the early hours of the morning. Duse felt obliged to have a stab at Théodora but, no doubt to her relief, found Sardou's lack of subtlety largely beyond her. Terry was somewhat luckier in Sardou's *Madame Sans-Gêne* but loathed the experience just as much.

Custom and the market required some show of jousting between the stars, and internationalism did nothing to weaken the impact of theatrical fashion; it simply made it international. For all their obvious and much vaunted differences, it is striking how all three were made party to the same trends. They were all said to be remarkable because of their disdain for corsets, their fondness for the flowing line. Duse made Fortuny famous but Bernhardt had long been insisting that her own dresses be continually remodelled until 'they become quite moulded to the line of my figure'. Terry was closely involved with the English 'dress reformers' of the 1880s. It did not take long, once Duse had set the pattern, for Bernhardt to boast that she too eschewed make-up. All three were likened to Pre-Raphaelite paintings; Terry had the best claim. None were said to walk so much as to 'float', 'glide', or execute some other superior form of progress. Publicity seized on the trivial detail because it guessed the underlying direction. The 'nature' of woman was changing – becoming, so it was said, more 'natural' all the time, ever closer to a modern ideal in which the glamour of unusual women would be held to depend upon their radiant transformation of the average female.

Bernhardt, for one, thought that it was in the 'nature' of women to be 'charming', which was why acting was such a feminine art: '. . . it contains in itself all the artifices which belong to the province of woman: the desire to please, facility to express emotions and hide defects, and the faculty of assimilation which is the real essence of woman.'[12]

Neither Terry nor Duse would have disagreed in principle though they all had reservations about each other's practice. Their comments carry professional insight and professional rivalry in about equal weight. When Terry said that Bernhardt 'always seemed to me a symbol, an ideal, an *epitome* rather than a woman',[13] she was hinting that foreigners still needed to rely upon the exotic. Bernhardt, for her part, said that Terry was 'as near absolute perfection as anyone can be. In her, English dramatic art has a splendid exponent', but she added, with devious French paradox, 'I'll tell you the difference between her and Monsieur Irving – she is an *artiste* first, an actress afterwards; he, on the contrary, is an *actor* first, and afterwards an *artiste*.'[14] For Bernhardt, it was Duse, the greater rival, who presented the easier intellectual problem: 'That disdainful mouth, those white teeth, those eyes smiling and wretched. And what charm! A great actress – a pity that she is such a *poseuse*.'[15] The ambiguous quality of 'charm' returns us once more to the 'natural', with all its uncertainties.

Anyone who attempts to examine the work of Bernhardt, Terry and Duse today is therefore faced with a multi-layered set of problems. There is the fundamental difficulty of trying to describe performances that have been recorded by reviewers and photographers who perceived the world in a completely different way, and there is the all-encompassing problem of the change in perception between the nineteenth and the late twentieth centuries. When we try to reconstruct performances, we utilize the perceptual and conceptual tools of our own time; yet when we come to look closely at the contemporary descriptions of the three actresses, it is clear that those tools are simply not adequate. What is required is an imaginative leap backwards in time, an excursion into the fictive world of another age, and that is fraught with difficulties. Moreover, all three actresses have passed into mythology and have created their own sign-system of legend. Ellen Terry lives on as the eternal girl-actress, the symbol of health, youth and energy, in contrast with Duse, the suffering, mature woman. Between them stands Bernhardt, the creature of passion and power, larger than life and dangerously unpredictable. We have taken these myths along with the biographies and have incorporated them into our view of their work, despite the altered historical contexts. All three myths survive because they derive from archetypal myths of femininity which are still alive in the theatre today, and which flourish particularly in the cinema.

Bernhardt, Terry and Duse worked in an age when mass communication was beginning to change the nature of an actor's reception. Other nineteenth-century actresses had toured extensively and had established reputations on both sides of the Atlantic, but by the end of the century the pattern of touring had accelerated. Actors could not only travel with far greater speed and convenience, but the development of cheap photographic reproduction techniques and the emergence of film as a medium for recording people and events marked the start of the internationalization of culture that has characterized so much of the twentieth century. Even Terry, who never toured Europe despite her American visits, acquired a significance far beyond the immediate British environment. As a symbol of youth and energy, she also represented a notion of Englishness, and her Shakespearean repertoire stressed the significance of continuity and tradition even in the New World.

All three myths, different though they were, derive from a specific moment in time when certain images of women filled a particular need. Audiences were changing rapidly as a whole new theatre-going class emerged in the second half of the nineteenth century. As Romanticism gave way to Naturalism, as the expanding bourgeoisie demanded more theatre and more from the theatre, so star performers came to acquire a compensatory function. In England, the British Empire flowered and became over-ripe; as a consequence, visions of youth and health such as that created by Terry proved that all was still well with the world. In Italy, the dream of the Risorgimento collapsed into provincial neo-fascist dullness, and the figure of maturity and fortitude supplied by Duse provided the focus for a generation without ideals. Duse the anti-star, as John Stokes has called her,[16] offered an image of the neurotic, troubled soul of an emergent nation. In France, which had suffered the crushing blow of defeat by the Prussians in 1870, Bernhardt's nationalistic flamboyance offered a contrast to complacency and provided a reminder that there was an alternative to the commercialized respectability that had come to substitute for patriotism.

Possessing any of these three actresses, audiences acquired something of value in their own age. Their gaze captured and held an image of femininity that was both immediately sensual and symbolic of something much larger. Writing in 1905, Martin Buber defines Duse as the voice of her Italian ancestors rather than as an individual. Dramatic tension, he argues, derives from the movement out of the security of the familiar into the threat of the infinite, where the abyss opens that robs the word of its power: 'For the word is never something for and in itself but only comes to completed reality through being received.'[17]

Whatever audiences perceived in the work of Bernhardt, Terry and Duse, it was clearly something that took them beyond the immediate and into wider, deeper areas of themselves. This special quality is forever inaccessible to us now, since it died with them and with the time in which they lived. It is also something that challenges historical analysis, just as it challenged description by those contemporaries who struggled to express the inexpressible in the restricting language of their reviews and articles.

Nevertheless, it is a mark of our respect for that specialness that we acknowledge not only its existence, but the inadequacy of our attempts to invoke it. Theatre scholarship, helpful, important and wide-ranging though it may be, has no language with which to define that relationship between an actress of genius and her audiences.

Sarah Bernhardt

ᵧᵧ

JOHN STOKES

WE KNOW MORE about Sarah Bernhardt than we do about any other nineteenth-century actress. We have paintings and photographs, recordings and films, reviews and memoirs. We have the texts of the plays in which she appeared and, in some instances, her own *livrets de scène*. If Bernhardt is misunderstood, it is not because she is under-documented, but because so much that we admire on our stage today has developed in direct reaction to all that she came to stand for.

History has passed harsh judgement on a career that was always directed towards public approval. Rightly or wrongly, it is Bernhardt we think of when Chekhov's egotistical Madame Arkadina, determined to take pride of place, obliterates her son's experiments in a new kind of drama.[1] It is Bernhardt who is accused of being the first actress to debase her profession by advertising pills and potions across the world; Bernhardt who has become one of the theatre's rueful jokes about its own pretensions – Noël Coward's lugubrious 'sheep in white lace'.

In reality her dominance over the theatre of her time was far less secure than either her adulatory biographers or her resentful critics would have us believe. When she conquered London as a rebellious member of the Comédie-Française in 1879, at least two in her audience – Matthew Arnold and Henry James – already saw her as a symptom of cultural decline.[2] Later, as an independent actress and manager in Paris, she struggled against the alternative theatres of Antoine and Lugné-Poe, and suffered some near defeats.

Some of the distrust she inspired resulted from the responsibilities she inherited and was said to have betrayed. In the nineteenth century, to an extent difficult to conceive of today, the Comédie-Française symbolized a high ideal of theatrical organization, its repertoire a model of cultural guardianship. The international impact of Rachel in the 1840s may have shown that it was possible to bring the classical French drama back to vibrant life almost single-handedly, yet the terms of Rachel's fame – a

13

1   Sarah Bernhardt as Théodora in *Théodora*, 1884

14

unique 'genius' who had nevertheless benefited from a corporate 'tradition' – were antithetical. Bernhardt, too, as she very well knew, had initially to prove herself within the institutional authority of the Maison de Molière. She also knew that only outside of its bounds could she ensure that she appeared in the plays that she believed to suit her best, and gain the financial rewards that she knew to be there. The result was the Bernhardt repertoire: commissioned vehicles, popular favourites from an earlier epoch, and Racine: an idiosyncratic but inherently Romantic combination that played a powerful but not unquestioned part in French theatrical history.

The pattern of her career was, then, determined by opposing forces: tradition and innovation, institutional power and personal ambition, national conventions and worldwide consumption. A distinction, sometimes adopted by literary sociologists, between the modernizing of communications and the aesthetics of 'modernism', helps focus its outlines. 'Modernization' is an acceleration of production and distribution. 'Modernism' is a response to that process, which tends to uphold authoritarian control and impersonal strength; with the resulting paradox that 'modernism' has frequently been hostile to 'modernization'. It was because Bernhardt's career simultaneously related to both capitalist expansion and aesthetic protest that she became, at least for a time, 'modern' in the synthetic sense that Arthur Symons had in mind when he wrote, in the mid 1890s, that

To be modern in poetry, to represent really oneself and one's surroundings, the world as it is to-day, to be modern and yet poetical, is, perhaps, the most difficult, as it is certainly the most interesting, of all artistic achievements. In music the modern soul seems to have found expression in Wagner; in painting it may be said to have taken form and colour in Manet, Degas and Whistler; in sculpture, has it not revealed itself in Rodin? on the stage it is certainly typified in Sarah Bernhardt.[3]

This is the modernity of 'impressionism', of 'total art', of the Symbolist movement: the quivering intensity, indefinite shapes, untranslateable moods and exotic locations that Bernhardt conveyed on a grand commercial scale.

The need to remain 'modern and yet poetical' underlay her whole career, producing a stage image that both concealed and displayed the true economic circumstances of her theatre.[4] That is why this essay begins with an investigation into her lifelong dealings with the city of Paris. When she set out on her own in 1880, Bernhardt intended to profit from the urban developments that, interrupted by the Franco-Prussian War and its aftermath, had begun with Haussmann. Hers was a Paris-based career, and concentration upon Bernhardt the international phenomenon has tended to obscure the continual battles that she was engaged in with her compatriots. Rapturous receptions in the Middle West of America or (rather less rapturous) in the West End of London have to be set against variable attendances and civic criticism at home.

'Contextualization' is also the guiding principle behind the second section, which attempts to reconstruct her performances in Hugo, in Sardou and in Racine, as ideological artefacts; leading in turn to a more generalized discussion of her place in the aesthetics of the *fin de siècle*. A third and final section reflects upon her historical demise in England, perceived some thirty years or so after her physical death in France. Like the career of Bernhardt itself, the essay journeys from one capital to another, from one audience to another. It reaches forward in time, aware that theatrical history is not to be measured by the activities of a single lifespan, and that professional goals, individually pursued, always end up in the public domain.

The manager

Launching herself as an independent artist in 1880, Bernhardt was going for broke. She already had a history of debt. Eight years earlier, she had been fined 6,000 francs for leaving the Odéon, a sum which amounted to the whole of her first year's salary at the rue de Richelieu. On becoming a *sociétaire* of the Comédie in 1875 she had *ipso facto* committed herself to a standard twenty-year agreement: her departure after only five provoked a demand for 300,000 francs damages for breach of contract. On 25 June 1880 the Tribunal de la Seine first heard her described as 'an assertive and calculating woman' and then reduced the penalty to the still considerable sum of 100,000 francs. They also allowed the theatre to confiscate the 49,000 francs she had contributed to the pension fund: a decision that they had reached by taking into account not only the actress's high standing and the theatre's consequent loss, but the fact that she had 'almost immediately seized the chance of an engagement abroad'.[5]

What the Tribunal was referring to was the contract that Bernhardt had signed on resignation: an American tour which offered huge financial prospects ($1,000 per show and 50% of receipts over $4,000), together with the freedom to choose her own company and repertoire.[6] Her private initiatives in London the previous year, as drawing-room performer and as sculptress, had opened economic opportunities irresistible and overdue – though it was not immediately apparent from her current roles exactly how she would exploit them.

In 1880 Bernhardt had been a professional actress for eighteen years. Her first, short-lived stint at the Comédie in 1862–3 had been followed by six years at the Odéon, where she had worked with the director Félix Duquesnel and had initially attracted attention for her *travesti* role in Coppée's *Le Passant* (1869). Her definitive Dona Maria in Hugo's *Ruy Blas* (1872) carried her back to the Comédie, where her second stay had been marked by graduation from Aricie to Phèdre (1874) and a further Dona Maria in 1879. She had also been acclaimed as Andromaque and had proved, despite some success as Mistress Clarkson in *L'Etrangère*, that she was less at home in contemporary plays and an actress for serious drama rather than comedy. All in all, these were precarious grounds on which to found an independent career.

Bernhardt's gift for publicity saw her through. The American and European tours of 1880–2 were a financial triumph. In the United States and Canada alone, her personal gain was said to have come to over 900,000 francs.[7] Not surprisingly, on her return to Paris she became fired with managerial ambitions. Within the space of two years she entered into negotiations for no fewer than three Paris theatres. Professionally, she was undoubtedly on the crest of a wave, but already one can see how the size of her reputation might falsely justify the scale of her ambitions – and of her outgoings. Records of theatre business in nineteenth-century France being very hard to come by, it is foolhardy to try to be precise about budgets. In Bernhardt's case, the situation is aggravated by contradictory press reports, the fabled sums earned on global tours, the legendary personal expenditure and her own insouciance. What is certain is that much was glossed over, not least by Bernhardt herself. Probably the most revealing sources for her early ventures into management, therefore, are the many court hearings which featured her name, or, for her last theatre at Châtelet, the records kept by the City of Paris.

From the start, she was surrounded by advisers, impresarios, protégés and relatives. This also makes it difficult to judge the true extent of her personal prerogative in carrying out decisions between 1882 and 1884. The press were quick to comment on her habit of buying theatres in her son

2 Cartoon from *Le Monde Parisien*, 19 August 1882, satirizing Bernhardt's business methods

Maurice's name, which they already saw as proof of her evasive ways of conducting business.

In the summer of 1882 Bernhardt and her Greek husband, Aristide (Jacques) Damala entered negotiations for the Théâtre des Nations. The venture came to nothing at the time but six years later, after the Damalas had separated and the owner had died, his heirs brought a claim for damages against the couple.[8] At the end of July 1882, Bernhardt did succeed in buying, in the name of seventeen-year-old Maurice, the lease of the Théâtre de l'Ambigu on the Boulevard Saint-Martin. The current owner was in financial trouble but two years later he too was instituting proceedings, claiming to have been paid less than a third of what was agreed.[9]

What had occurred in the interim was characteristic of Bernhardt's early financial recklessness and artistic misjudgement. Apart from providing a stage for the hapless Damala, she seems to have had no clear idea of what to do at the Ambigu. Catulle Mendès's *Les Mères ennemies* reached its hundredth performance, but the takings failed to justify enormous expenditure on décor, costumes, furniture and weaponry.[10] Damala, in the leading role, defected after a month. *La Glu*, by her new attachment Jean Richepin, ran for only fifty performances in spite of a cast which included Agar and the young Réjane. Bernhardt had almost certainly underestimated the power of her own presence.

For at the very moment when she was experiencing her first managerial disaster she was, at the nearby Vaudeville, having her first great triumph as a Boulevard actress. The play was *Fédora*, the author Victorien Sardou, and it heralded a long series of collaborations that was in turn to form the basis for Bernhardt's later work as a professional *metteuse-en-scène*. *Fédora* opened on 11 December 1882 and in its first run alone the receipts were said to have reached 100,000 francs with an average box-office daily taking of between 9,000 and 10,000 francs.[11] Bernhardt herself was being paid a widely publicized 1,000 francs a night for her performance as Fédora but this did little to reduce the debts she was building up at the Ambigu, where by the end of each month she was having to borrow in order to pay her company.[12] In February she was obliged to hold a public sale of her jewels, the proceeds of which (178,000 francs) were distributed by a Civil Tribunal. During the course of the hearing some unpaid suppliers to the Ambigu – architects, couturiers and so on – even tried to issue sequestration orders on her earnings from *Fédora*, but their demands were mitigated by a sympathetic judge.[13] In the spring she was forced to take the play on tour, in order, as one journalist put it, to 'repair the enormous holes made in her fortune by her luxurious tastes, her management of the Ambigu, and her carelessness in business matters'.[14] The many drains on Bernhardt's pocket included author's royalties of 12% – for this tour she had guaranteed Sardou a minimum return of 60,000 francs – and 10% to her administrator; the costs of travel, wages and rent of theatres amounting in all, it was surmised, to 60% of the takings.[15] In addition, she had just had to pay off a large slice of her debt to the Comédie-Française.[16]

In May 1883, when 'Maurice' officially ceded the direction of the Ambigu, the theatre had mounted only five plays and had lost over 400,000 francs.[17] But Bernhardt's failures there did nothing to quell her managerial aspirations, and later in the year she acquired the lease of the Théâtre de la Porte Saint-Martin, again nominally entrusting the direction to Maurice. She opened in September with the rather surprising choice of *Froufrou*, an intimate domestic drama.

The Porte Saint-Martin had always had a reputation for spectacle, recently reaffirmed by Sardou's *Patrie* (1869) but reaching much further back to its origins in the late eighteenth century, when it had been built to house opera. Later, in the 1830s, it was the site for many of the battles fought over the Romantic theatre of Dumas père and Victor Hugo. Mlle George, Frédéric Lemaître and Marie Dorval all acted there, bequeathing powerful associations that even survived the building's destruction by fire during the Commune.

The reconstructed theatre that Bernhardt acquired still retained much of the ambience of its predecessor. The interior, though it could seat 1800, was unusual: only 18 metres in depth from front of stage to back, against 26 metres in width and 22 metres in height, proportions that were said to give it 'much the look of a deep semi-circular well'.[18] *Froufrou* had been a success for Bernhardt in London; at the Porte Saint-Martin it seemed out of place. It was perhaps only intended as a fill-in for a new work by Richepin, *Nana Sahib*, a Hindu drama with distinct echoes of Bernhardt's own ménage, which was to occupy the Christmas season. In the event *Nana Sahib* had to be taken off after forty performances, and in January 1894 Bernhardt hastily recouped with *La Dame aux camélias*. This was the first, but by no means the last occasion on which Dumas's warhorse was to save her from catastrophe: she was to revive it no less than twenty-two times at various theatres in Paris over the next twenty years. The play's guaranteed appeal had already been demonstrated in America and throughout Europe, and she had given a sensational single performance at the Gaîté in May 1882 with Damala as Armand Duval.

A wildly successful run of more than a hundred performances temporarily restored fortunes and was a portent of future work at the Porte Saint-Martin. What *La Dame aux camélias* had indubitably shown was that this theatre would do best when its Romantic past was reinvoked with the help of modern resources. When Bernhardt's next production, a translation of *Macbeth* by Richepin, again failed to draw, she turned for help to her old mentor, Félix Duquesnel, who had had to resign from the Odéon because his spectacular productions were deemed unsuitable for France's second national theatre. On 15 September 1884 Duquesnel assumed direction of the Porte Saint-Martin, though Bernhardt was to retain a share in the profits. Sardou, who had always had the big theatre in mind for his next collaboration with Bernhardt, joined them, and it was this triumvirate of director, actress and playwright that was to bring about the *tour de force* of *Théodora* in the following year.

In 1884 Bernhardt was forty years old, and her capacity for attracting scandal had never been greater. In October, on her return from a summer season in London, the publicity campaign for the new production was soon underway in Paris. A rumour was spread that after a fatal revival of Richepin's *Macbeth* she had left for the country in a state of nervous exhaustion. Approached by *La Chronique Parisienne*, Sardou reported her to be disturbed, depressed, prostrate.

She exaggerates all aspects of her life, the pain as well as the joy; she conducts business, like everything else, at breakneck speed, letting herself be robbed left, right and centre, and taking on things that she cannot hold to. This leads to anger, rancour and hatred which is all the more destructive for not always having an outlet.

On hearing from Duquesnel that she was ill, Sardou had gone to her house, where he had found her in a state of 'violent over-excitement, writhing, rolling on and gnawing at the carpet, weeping in sheer exasperation'.[19]

However slender its basis in truth, this kind of knowing account of the star's febrile nature obviously made good copy. It was in everyone's interests, including Sardou's, to work anticipation up to fever pitch, to spread the teasing idea that Bernhardt might be too nervous to tackle the part of a legendary *nerveuse*. The strategy was undoubtedly successful, and *Théodora*, a text of calculated banality coupled with a *mise-en-scène* of extraordinary splendour, made it seem that Bernhardt had at last found a way of gratifying her personal ambitions and the Paris public at one and the same time. From its opening night on 26 December 1884 *Théodora* ran for 300 performances until Christmas Day of the following year, with a two-month break when it was taken to London. Sardou's *La Tosca*, also directed by Duquesnel, was to have a similar success in 1887 and 1888: 122 performances interrupted only by Bernhardt's decision to go on tour.[20]

The arrangements at the Porte Saint-Martin, which lasted for the rest of the decade, suited Bernhardt well in many respects: she could collaborate with her old friends Sardou and Duquesnel, learning their techniques while remaining free to absent herself for long stretches of international touring. The professional configuration, however, also brought with it certain disadvantages, not only artistic. After each tour she had to reingratiate herself with the Paris public, and there were many on hand to point out that by playing constantly to foreign audiences she had coarsened her talent. Nor could acting in Sardou be said to have developed her range. On the other hand, when she did attempt to renovate her Parisian repertoire, the ideas were often unfortunate. A lacklustre version of *Hamlet* in 1886, in which she played Ophelia in order to gratify Philippe Garnier's desire to perform the lead, made Sardou remark, 'It's Sarah, that's to say Garnier, who runs everything these days at that madhouse. Duquesnel thinks he's the director but he's much more like a *pensionnaire*.'[21]

By 1890 the partnership was unquestionably flagging with the failure of Sardou's *Cléopâtre*, about which it was agreed that only the death of the Queen saved the evening. It was to be Bernhardt's last play at the Porte Saint-Martin, and from 1891 to 1893 she busied herself with another world tour, the most lucrative of her life, which was said to have brought her a net gain of 3.5 million *francs d'or*.[22]

On her return to Paris Bernhardt modified her managerial tactics and acquired the Théâtre de la Renaissance, an elegant structure adjacent to the Porte Saint-Martin. The Renaissance was comparatively new, erected in 1873, a theatre for small-scale productions and intimate *soirées*. A civil engineer's report described it as 'a very pretty little interior, well appointed, very comfortable and very *coquette*'.[23] It was, and is, ornate and classical in style, with Corinthian columns, caryatids, cherubs and a gilded circular foyer: the whole cleverly confined within a space of 500 square metres, including dressing rooms, wardrobes, offices, even two cafés and shops. There were *loges* and *galeries* on four levels, with seating intended for up to 1,200. The stage, surmounted by a curved arch, was only 8 metres wide and 10 metres high. Twenty years after its construction, just before Bernhardt took it on, an American journalist conceded that the *salle* of the Renaissance was still 'one of the prettiest and least uncomfortable in Paris'.[24]

This, then, was an attractive property that suited Bernhardt's plans to establish herself as an efficient, creative actress–manager in a changed theatrical milieu. Antoine's Théâtre Libre (founded in 1887) and the Symbolist experiments that were to culminate in Lugné-Poe's Théâtre de l'Oeuvre in 1893 had placed a new emphasis on the need for modern plays, and on the possibilities of radical reform in *mise-en-scène*. While publicly discounting Antoine's experiments ('I was never a supporter of the Théâtre Libre and I think that it positively injured and retarded theatrical progress'), she was undoubtedly aware that reform was in the air, boasting that she had modelled her project on Irving's Lyceum, where 'much more attention is given to stage scenery and costume than with us, and this side of the drama should not escape the attention of the true artist, for a good *mise-en-scène* predisposes the public to listen favourably to the play, and makes the task of all concerned easy'.[25]

It was at the Renaissance that Bernhardt began to direct every aspect of rehearsal herself. Journalists described her as in constant attendance, scissors in hand, chopping up and pinning costumes, designing and redesigning mock-ups of the sets, always in search of new effects. She also claimed to have borrowed from English and American administrative practices to bring Paris theatre-going up to date. 'I have suppressed the *claque*', she told an English reporter in 1895.

It never saved a piece yet, and it is an unfair attempt to lead the opinion of the audience. I have, also, suppressed the *surtaxe* on tickets – the extra prices charged for booking seats in advance – and I have done away with the *ouvreuses*, those too-officious women attendants to whom foreigners object so strongly. In a word, I have formed the Théâtre de la Renaissance on the best English models.[26]

Although not all her grand claims were pursued, it is undoubtedly true that Bernhardt's five years at the Renaissance were the most innovative of her career, and that during this period she made a determined attempt to rejuvenate her image as an artist. With Rostand's *La Princesse lointaine* (1895) she aligned herself with the Symbolist theatre. With Sardou's *Spiritisme* and Rostand's *La Samaritaine* (1897) she tried, albeit unsuccessfully, to capitalize on the fashions for mysticism and religiosity. The first play she put on there in 1893, Jules Lemaître's *Les Rois*, and one of the last, Octave Mirbeau's *Les Mauvais Bergers* (1897), a play about striking factory workers so controversial that at the height of the Dreyfus affair the police requested her temporarily to close the theatre, show that she was prepared to experiment with the work of younger playwrights. Her brilliantly opportunistic response to Duse's sensational 1897 season at the Renaissance was to make the occasion a public contest and to poach, the following year, D'Annunzio's *La Vie morte* from her Italian rival. Moreover the employment of young actors – Lucien Guitry, de Max, Abel Deval – and the capture of Coquelin, another rebel from the Comédie Française, ensured that her surrounding company was of a consistently high standard. A new production of *Phèdre* (twenty exceptional *matinées* soon after she took the theatre in 1893) and a refurbished *La Dame aux camélias* (1896), indicated her desire to modernize an over-familiar repertoire. Drawing upon her favourite artists – Clairin, Abbéma and, a marvellous new find, Mucha – she projected in the 1890s a pensive grace that with its sinuous outline and elusive tints was irreproachably modern while discreetly appropriate for an artist who had been in the public eye for more than thirty years.

This was the Bernhardt who, in December 1896, was sufficiently powerful, or at least manipulative, to command a day of public recognition: the legendary 'Journée Sarah Bernhardt' when, after hosting a banquet for 500 people at the Grand Hotel, she performed in her own theatre excerpts from *Phèdre* and received the homage of twenty poets. 'When Sarah plays Phèdre, we are all incestuous', declaimed Rostand with unintentional honesty. Bernhardt herself was also uncomfortably close to the truth when she described the Renaissance as 'not so much a boutique . . . more of a temple'.[27] The economic foundations of the edifice were far from secure: continual foreign tours were needed to keep it erect and the only play to make a significant profit was Maurice Donnay's *Les Amants*, staged while Bernhardt was away. Sardou's *Gismonda* (1894), set in fifth-century Athens, made its hundredth but *Spiritisme* collapsed after only twenty. 'One recalls', wrote Catulle Mendès of the Renaissance Sardous, 'lamentable houses, almost empty, a few boxes occupied by *concierges*, in the weeks leading up to the obligatory *centième*.'[28] *La Princesse lointaine*, of which Bernhardt bragged, 'It's conceivable that the play won't make a sou, but that means absolutely nothing to me: I think it's marvellous, and I'll put it on in any case for my own pleasure',[29] did in fact lose her a fortune: 200,000 francs in thirty-one performances. And Musset's *Lorenzaccio* (1896), which she premièred sixty years after it had been written, may have helped her reputation as a patron of the obscure (Lugné-Poe had originally planned to present it) but meant little to the wider public. It is on record that in her five years at the Renaissance Bernhardt lost 2 million *francs d'or*.[30] Certainly she became tired of the risks of independent management on the Boulevard and began to prepare an assault on the city from within its own institutional framework.

In January 1899 Bernhardt took out a lease with the City of Paris on the Théâtre des Nations at Châtelet, one of the three theatres she had briefly considered in her flurry of lease-buying in the early 1880s. The move made sense for a number of reasons. Her granddaughter's husband, the play-wright Louis Verneuil, suggests that on the stage of the Renaissance she had found herself, at the age of fifty-five, 'in too close contact with the public',[31] and the new theatre, larger even than the Porte Saint-Martin, offered opportunities for productions on a monumental scale that would keep her at a safe and impressive distance from her audience. Then again, the Théâtre des Nations could seat 1,700, a great many more than the Renaissance, giving it a potential weekly profit of an additional 40,000 francs. As an experienced manager Bernhardt was well aware that costs did not directly accrue in proportion to receipts. Leading performers were not paid according to the size of the theatre in which they appeared, and overheads such as lighting and heating would only be marginally higher than before. Further, a lesson she had learnt from the Comédie-Française and the Odéon, the big stage would make it easier to keep several *décors* in operation at the same time, thus enabling plays to be alternated without the need for expensive removals. A flexible repertory might be possible, an answer to those who criticized her for long runs, while leaving her free rapidly to substitute in times of crisis.

All these considerations must have borne upon her decision, but the overriding factor was that the Châtelet building was a *municipal* theatre, owned by the City of Paris, though not formally subsidized like the state-funded Comédie-Française and the Odéon. Here there might be a sharing of financial responsibility between tenant and proprietors. In all her previous management ventures Bernhardt had been personally responsible for financial losses – hence the multitude of law suits for non-payment of rent, the sudden sales of jewellery and possessions. Now

25

she could, if in trouble, turn to the City councillors at the Hôtel de Ville and request deferral or even cancellation of debts without serious risk of the courts.

All that lay ahead, and the terms of her agreement with the City in 1898, widely reported in the Paris press, were demanding and confident on both sides. She was to pay 100,000 francs a year for a lease of up to fifteen years. The building was to be used only for theatrical purposes, and was to be open for at least nine months out of every twelve. It was to be available to the City four times a year; Bernhardt was to give one free matinée to schoolchildren and another on 14 July. She was to charge fixed prices and all costumes, décor and accessories were to be provided by Parisian suppliers. She was to pay a deposit of 150,000 francs into the City coffers and on top of this she was subject to a regulation requiring that 10% of receipts at all theatres be contributed to a government fund for the poor. Finally (the clause that was to be particularly irksome in the years to come), the agreement insisted that her lease was 'strictly personal, to be neither ceded nor sublet'.[32]

On the whole these were not arduous terms, and Bernhardt was probably speaking the truth when she told the journalist Alfred Delilia how she had been to the City 'to ask for help, and had received a charming welcome'.[33] Great hopes were invested in the new *locataire*. To understand why, we must go back to the Second Empire and to Haussmann's plans for the rebuilding of Paris, which had involved the demolition of the Boulevard du Temple with its melodrama houses and its outdoor shows of marionettes, mimes and acrobats. The 'Boulevard du Crime' (later to be famously reconstructed in Marcel Carné's film *Les Enfants du Paradis*) had for long provided a pleasure ground for *flâneurs* of all classes. Haussmann, anxious to fend off criticisms, hastened to suggest alternative plans for a new theatrical showplace near the Pont au Change on the Seine. Eventually it was decided to build four theatres: two in the Place du Châtelet and two opposite the Palais de Justice. Extraordinarily ambitious plans were drawn up which included not only theatres but cafés, fairs, markets and other places of entertainment. If the area was truly to compensate for the loss of the Boulevard du Crime, it was essential, declared the architects enthusiastically, that it should never be 'triste' by day or by night.[34]

In the event Haussmann's grand plans were never fully realized. Only two substitute theatres were built, both in 1862: the huge Théâtre de Châtelet and, opposite it, the *théâtre de luxe* originally named the Théâtre

Lyrique but holding a variety of different names and functions before Bernhardt took it over in 1899. In the interim the building passed through many different leaseholders, none of them conspicuously successful, and for eleven years housed the Opéra Comique as they awaited the rebuilding of their rue Favart home after a fire.

So it is hardly surprising that in 1899 Bernhardt found the theatre 'a little dishevelled, and showing traces of long service under different managements',[35] nor that the City was willing to pay for the structural renovation, though Bernhardt agreed to cover the improvements to the fabric. Touring the refurbished theatre in December 1899, Delilia was particularly impressed by the public foyer, which he described as 'virtually a museum, Madame Sarah Bernhardt's own little Louvre', containing seven large panels by Abbéma, Clairin, Louis Bernard and Mucha and depicting Bernhardt as La Samaritaine, Gismonda, Théodora, 'La Tragédie antique', La Dame aux camélias, Hamlet and La Princesse lointaine; an eighth, already commissioned from Mucha, was to show her as L'Aiglon.

The Théâtre Sarah Bernhardt, flamboyant monument to a unique career and, it was hoped, long-awaited answer to a civic embarrassment, was formally inaugurated on 16 December 1899 with Bernhardt as Hamlet, though it was *L'Aiglon*, which opened on 15 March 1900, that was to be the new theatre's greatest triumph.[36] The timing was opportune. 1900 was the year of the great Paris Exposition – bringing countless visitors to see a city that had transformed itself into theatre for the occasion. Magnificent pavilions, technological marvels, exotic displays ablaze with electric light, contributed to a mood of nationalistic euphoria that, in the wake of the Dreyfus affair, France was badly in need of. Even after 1900 Bernhardt would always be able to fall back on Rostand's play, along with *La Dame aux camélias*, if her theatre ran into trouble or was temporarily without a new production. Yet, also viewed in the long term, *L'Aiglon* was a catastrophe, confirming Bernhardt's belief that lavish historical dramas would continue to provide her with the best material. She never managed to find another play to repeat its colossal success, and Rostand never assumed for her the role of house dramatist once held by Sardou.

Acting in *La Tosca* in Rio de Janeiro in 1905 Bernhardt met with the accident to her knee that was to cause her obvious professional inconvenience as well as great pain. Her right leg was eventually amputated ten years later. Ironically, given her own obstinate patriotism, the climax of Bernhardt's personal physical crisis coincided with the outbreak of international hostilities. Between 1915 and 1920 she made only one appearance in her own theatre, playing the part of Strasbourg Cathedral in a dramatic poem, *Les Cathédrales*, though there were many patriotic appearances in England and America often rendered grotesque, if moving, by her age and disablement. She died in 1923 after a final heroic spasm of activity, including an extraordinary but brief run of Racine's *Athalie* in April 1920.

In effect, then, her creative participation in the Théâtre Sarah Bernhardt had lasted only fifteen years, during which time she engaged in all manner of heterogeneous projects whose main rationale was the need to fill a large stage with herself at its centre. Few of the contemporary plays she initiated there entered the popular repertoire. For the theatre historian, the most interesting production, despite the preponderance of historical melodramas, is probably Racine's *Esther* (1905), for which she reconstructed the original St-Cyr performance. The remainder, though notable for their expertise in the handling of large crowds, must stand as representative examples of the kind of meticulous spectacular staging perfected throughout Europe in the nineteenth century but now carried on beyond its natural life. Significantly perhaps, her more experimental work – Maeterlinck's *Pelléas et Mélisande*, for example – was carried out abroad. Nor is this just a summary judgement based on subsequent theatre history and a more recent set of aesthetic assumptions: the same criticisms were made, and vociferously, at the time.

In Paris, as everywhere in Europe, the theatre at the turn of the century was more factionally divided than it had been for decades, though in some instances the rebels were already being incorporated within the establishment. Antoine himself was to take on the directorship of the Odéon in 1906. From the very beginning of Bernhardt's reign at Châtelet, there were rumblings of discord at her anachronistic repertoire, the outmoded 'luxe' of her *mises-en-scène*, her star-centred groupings, her long runs, her expensive seats, her regular disappearances abroad. Although the complaints were not systematic, and even Antoine tempered his criticism with tributes to Bernhardt's past glories, she soon became the butt for advocates of 'popular theatre', who were particularly anxious to bring pressure upon the municipal authorities to provide suitable premises within the city. The formal statement of the new mood is Romain

Rolland's *Le Théâtre du peuple* of 1904, with its specific naming of Bernhardt as the symbol of outdated Romanticism.

I firmly believe that the Romantic drama is one of the most dangerous enemies of the popular theatre that we are trying to establish in France . . . One might even say that one performer has exerted a definitive influence on the shaping as well as the success of this art. It's her name – the name of Sarah Bernhardt – which best sums up this Byzantianized, or Americanized, neo-Romanticism: stiff and congealed, without youth or vigour, weighed down with ornaments, with jewels real or fake, bleak in its bluster, pallid in its glitter.[37]

In fact, apart from what was set out in the lease, it was difficult to say precisely what was expected of Bernhardt in her capacity as artistic director of a municipal theatre: she herself later claimed that she had never been given the 'cahier des charges', the document issued to state-subsidized houses, and was therefore under no obligation to anyone. Nevertheless there persisted a widespread feeling of unease that turned into outright political opposition on those occasions when Bernhardt was required to give public account of herself: her requests for extensions of her lease, first in 1909 and then again in 1921.[38]

In 1909 there were prolonged wrangles with the Paris Municipal Council. Eventually, having promised to enliven her programme and give up or renounce the foreign touring, the lease was renewed. The following summer she made her début as a music-hall artist at the London Coliseum and in the autumn embarked on a twelve-month tour of the Americas.

In 1921 Bernhardt confronted the bureaucrats for the last time, with motives that were obviously dynastic. It was, at the very least, an act of bravado to propose an extension of her lease on terms that would allow her to control the theatre, in association with her son Maurice and her granddaughter's husband Louis Verneuil, until 1943, when she would be very nearly a hundred years old. It was also, as it turned out, foolhardy, since it reinflamed many previous irritations. So bitter was the controversy that it was not entirely buried even by the plethora of praise that followed her death in March 1923. As *Paris Midi* pointed out, however outstanding her other achievements she could hardly be described as a good tenant.[39]

In her final negotiations, even Bernhardt had perhaps recognized that times were changing, offering to lend her theatre to Firmin Gémier (later to become first director of the Théâtre National Populaire), for twelve 'spectacles du théâtre populaire' a year, and to introduce at least four new works a year into her own programme. But the press attacks upon her had sometimes been violent. Hers had never been 'an art theatre', claimed one left-wing journal, but rather 'the cradle of a theatre that was already dead'.[40] Bernhardt countered with a writ but in the end the Municipal Council granted her only the six-year extension to which she was in any case entitled under French law. She had gained nothing except publicity, which for once in her life was entirely unwelcome.

The movement to reform Paris's municipal theatres, to make them, in one sense or another, more 'popular', finally put paid to Bernhardt's schemes to cling on to power from beyond the grave. The problems surrounding the Théâtre Sarah Bernhardt did, however, outlive her, and it says something for her public status that as an old woman, virtually retired from performance, she should still have been held accountable for the condition of the theatre in her native city. Throughout her career Bernhardt's exceptional individualism had provided scant protection from charges of public irresponsibility. The complaints were already being heard when she was a member of the Comédie-Française, they grew when she was at the Porte Saint-Martin in the 1880s, and were only countered by her brilliant orchestration of admiring voices during the time at the Renaissance. Her worst periods as a manager came when she was unable to reinvigorate the personality and techniques that had first marked her out as a unique performer. Underlying her whole career, its feats and its frailties, was her constant belief that the machinery of modern enterprise would always be driven by the waning flame of her irreproachably Romantic style.

The actress

Romantic revolutionaries in the first half of the nineteenth century had their ideals confirmed by the tragic intensity of Rachel which they felt as an awesome assault upon both role and audience. Rachel, they testified, left them exhilarated by her mixture of imaginative courage and intellectual control. By the 1870s, however, when Bernhardt started out, Romantic expectations had declined to the point where it was enough that a performer simply intoxicate with a display of emotional force, expressive range superseding, if necessary, textual opportunity. Out of this 'late Romanticism' came the Symbolist preferences which Bernhardt exploited in her middle and late career. For Symbolists the theatrical moment was elevated by a transparent purity of feeling between player and role that turned physical performance into ethereal manifestation and left the audience transfixed by yearning. Symbolism made the performer a possessor and giver of inspiration. Naturalism maintained, by contrast, that an audience would automatically respond when a performer respected the physical constraints of quotidian life – which is one of the reasons why it has been vigorously argued, throughout the twentieth century, that Naturalism is restricted to present imperatives. Bernhardt never took Naturalism very seriously, although she sometimes made misleading pronouncements about 'identification' which sound Naturalist on the surface.

In England, the later history of Romanticism was bound up with the development of melodrama. So it was in France, with this difference: whereas there were in England very few Romantic verse dramas thought suitable for revival, in France, in the early years of the Third Republic, the great Romantic pieces were being enthusiastically rediscovered some half a century after they had been written. It was as part of that process that Bernhardt made her name, revealing her distinctive qualities to revivals of Hugo: *Ruy Blas* in 1872 and *Hernani* in 1877. *Hernani* had been kept in the repertoire of the Comédie-Française from 1838 to 1851, and revived in 1867, but with nothing like the same *éclat* it achieved in 1877.[41] In Hugo, Bernhardt replaced memories, particularly of Mademoiselle Mars, and the playwright himself told her that she had surpassed Mars in the part of Dona Sol. Bernhardt's own accounts make it seem as if her personal style was entirely revolutionary and entirely of her own making. So for instance, in an interview of 1879, she insists that she has made an absolute break with tradition.

People come in your way with conventions, and you must have a will of iron to put them aside. When I went to the Française, I startled them by saying, '*Bon jour!*' in a modern comedy just as I should have said it in a drawing-room. I was told that it ought not to be said in that way. Why? Because there was a classic tradition – dating, perhaps, from the foundation of the house. They wanted more dignity; that is to say, more deliberation, solemnity, the pomp of the ancient manner. It was so all through. I dressed for my parts, according to my notions, solely with an eye to my personal advantages and defects. It was wrong. Why, again? Because Mdlle Mars had not dressed so. 'But Mdlle Mars was almost an old woman when she appeared in that character, and I am a young one.' 'That is no reason.' 'It shall be reason enough for me.' Now if you know the stage as I know it, you'll see where the need of my will of iron comes in. I insist; but my work is only half done. There is the public, likewise under the same absurd prepossessions. 'Things were not done like that in our day.' 'Probably; but the world has changed, what I am trying to show you is human nature as it has shown itself to me.' Humour them, conform to the tradition, and you may win some admiration. Dare to disregard it, and bear the chill of their temporary disfavour, and you will win all. It is the shorter if it is the harder road. To have made concessions in the hope of slowly revolutionizing their tastes would have been to take the longer one, and I really had no time for that. I wanted to *arrive*.[42]

This is a typical example of Bernhardt catching the individualistic mood of the time and presenting herself as a lone pioneer. The truth is more complicated. What 'human nature as it has shown itself to me' had amounted to in practice was an acting style notable above all for its control of gesture and pose and its emphatic deployment of emotion in the delivery of verse. The technique is known in the French theatre as 'détailler': adding subtlety to expression by precise inflection, throwing certain phrases into relief without losing sight of an underlying rhythm. Edmond Got, with whom Bernhardt trained at the Comédie-Française, is generally credited with mastery of this art, and is also said to have done a great deal to make the declaration of French verse less formal.[43] Nevertheless, whatever modifications Got made to tradition were relative. He is described, for instance, in 1879 as still insisting to his classes at the Conservatoire that tragic acting has a formal basis. Instructing an aspirant *tragédienne*, 'He beats the measure for her with his forefinger, exactly as if he were leading an orchestra – "Very good, mademoiselle, very good; don't forget it is pure music . . ." – while reproaching her for rushing the pace: "Think of the measure," he repeats, "Never go faster than your verse."'[44]

When young, Bernhardt was notorious for 'going faster than the verse', though her wild delivery was partly curtailed by the need to match speech with significant action – the effect of which was to *accentuate*, to vary the stages of anticipation and to delay the moment of release. The dramatic interest was therefore decisively shifted from content to delivery, bringing to Hugo's ponderous *coups de théâtre* a feverishness and a panache that brought out their inherent melodrama. Hugo gave Bernhardt a chance to display herself by elaborating basic confrontations, rather than by having to reconceive dramatic situations already burdened with complex meaning.

If an account of a rehearsal involving Mounet-Sully is anything to go by, she not only took every opportunity to draw attention to herself by subverting expectation, but was supported by Got in her attempts to imbue each and every exchange with as much nervous tension as possible.

3   Sarah Bernhardt as Dona Sol in *Hernani*, *c.* 1877

Here they are preparing the scene in which Ruy Blas's attack on ministerial corruption is followed by the unexpected appearance of the Queen.

The superb Sarah accordingly quits her tent, to place herself in very visible hiding, 'R.2.E'. Then her voice is heard, deep and sweet, with twice as much meaning in its lowest tones as in its highest.
    'O, merci!'

RUY BLAS. Ciel! (It is a start of surprise, and, as we may imagine, he is perfect here.)

LA REINE. Vous avez bien fait de leur parler ainsi.

> Je n'y puis résister, duc, il faut que je serre
> Cette loyale main si ferme et si sincère!

She darts out her hand, extending the arm at full length a gesture peculiar to her in private life as on the stage. She always shakes hands in that way.

GOT. I don't like that. You only give him your hand; you ought to take his.

SARAH BERNHARDT. I think my way is better; there is more *netteté* in the action.

She probably means that it is more statuesque, as it certainly is, but is perhaps unwilling to use an illustration from her favourite art. Her acting has always shown that she has a keen sense of the beauty of pose. She gets the full plastic as well as histrionic value of a situation.

PERRIN. But what does your text say? Look at the stage directions. *Reads.*
'She advances rapidly, and takes his hand before he can prevent her.'

SARAH BERNHARDT (*laughing*). Very well, then; give me your hand. (Mounet-Sully suffers her to take it.)

GOT (*to Perrin*). I think just where he wants most energy he shows least. (*To Mounet*) Your own movements there should be quick and decided, as full of nervous energy, as hers . . .[45]

Like *Ruy Blas*, *Hernani* gave her an opportunity to produce the unexpected, particularly as Dona Sol has very little to do in the first four acts but entirely dominates the fifth, which is in effect a prolonged death scene. Bernhardt played both roles in London in 1879, and it is the English critics, intent on educating their readers in the ways of French theatre, who give us the most detailed descriptions of her performances. They report that for the first four acts Bernhardt occupied herself by striking ostentatiously languorous poses. In the fifth act, though, everything changed. As Dona Sol prepared for her bridal night, her voice was at first little more than a whisper. But the sensual mood conjured up in lines like 'C'est la joie et je pleure!' was then dramatically broken by the appearance of her uncle, determined to destroy the marriage. Slowly Dona Sol awakened to the reality of her situation as she saw the poison vial in her husband's hand.

The *Daily Telegraph* gives a particularly attentive account of what followed.

Then begins the torrent of impetuous force that bursts out like a waterfall, and overflows the barriers of restraint. Dona Sol has declared herself to be fiercer than the tigress robbed of her young, and has hurled her defiance at the head of Don Ruy Gomez. She has flung herself before Hernani, and pointed to the dagger as her last protector, and then, with a sudden impulse, she changes to a despairing cry for mercy. This new key of passion was even more startling than the first. The words, 'Pitié! Vous me tuez, mon oncle, en le touchant! Pitié! Je l'aime tant!' echo with a sharp and resonant thrill, until, in a transport of baffled love, and with an access of supreme tenderness, she bends down the head of her lover and sobs out the words, 'Non! Non! Je ne veux pas, mon amour, que tu meures! Non! Je ne veux pas!' Sarah Bernhardt in all this wild delirium did nothing better than that one moment of concentrated love and despair . . . But even then the scene was not over. There was to follow the snatching of the poison vial, with the triumphant 'je l'ai', and all the intricate detail of the double death that is an echo, but not an imitation of the conclusion of *Romeo and Juliet*. With wonderful effect was given the quick, sudden, and terrible spasm as the poison works its way, that seems to tear and torture the fragile form; but again the violence changes into one more tender accent, 'Ne bois point! Oh! Je souffrirais trop!' It might have been thought that a scene so exhausting as this would have tired the voice, and that the intensity of the passion might have left no scope for yet another change. But, to the surprise of everybody, when every chord of hate, love, despair, threat, and pleading had been touched, there came a sweet and low murmur of exquisite resignation and most gentle content with the words

> Mort! Non pas! Nous dormons;
> Il dort. C'est mon époux, vois-tu, nous nous aimons,
> Nous sommes couchés là. C'est notre nuit de noce!
> Ne le réveillez pas . . . Il est las;

and then the rest was silence. We have spoken even now of the colour of the scene, of its rapidity, its intensity, and its brilliancy. But there yet remains to tell of the movement, and form, of the attitudes that result in apparently unstudied pictures, of the sinuous elegance and feathery lightness of Dona Sol as she insinuates herself in the arms of Hernani with all the confidence of affection, and finally sinks like some faint shadow upon the ground to catch his parting breath and pillow her head upon his dying breast.[46]

The *Telegraph* critic could hardly have known that he had here divined the foundation of Bernhardt's subsequent career as an actress: the sudden shifts in mood, the *ostinato* of the delivery, and the equally spasmodic movements of the body. Forty-four years later, at the time of her death, Shaw, her most unyielding critic, had absolutely no doubts about the importance of Hugo in the development of her subsequent, and in his view lamentable, mannerisms.

She had strength and temper enough to make a super-tigress of Dona Sol in *Hernani* for an unforgettable moment in the last act; and although this feat reappeared later on as a mechanical rant introduced *à tort et à travers* to bring down the house once in every play it was very astonishing at first.[47]

It may all have begun with Hugo, yet the same combination of restraint preceding release, of nervous impetuosity and graceful decline, informed her first assays at Phèdre, which she played in Paris in 1874 (between the first *Ruy Blas* and *Hernani*) and, sensationally, in London in 1879. Although Racine presented her with a far more formidable text than anything conceived by Hugo, it is nevertheless fair to describe Bernhardt's early Phèdres as being in the late Romantic mode. It certainly seemed obvious to observers at the time, even the most appreciative, that here was an actress determined to overwhelm the text through the charismatic intensity of her own theatrical presence. As Phèdre she combined the antique attractions of the *femme fatale* with the urgent dilemmas of a modern woman. Oscar Wilde caught something of the former in his poem 'Phèdre', dedicated to Bernhardt.

> Ah! Surely once some urn of Attic clay
>   Held thy wan dust, and thou hast come again
> Back to this common world so dull and vain,
> For thou wert weary of the sunless day,
>   The heavy fields of scentless asphodel,
>   The loveless lips with which men kiss in Hell.[48]

Zola, by contrast, felt that in *Phèdre*, as in Hugo, her 'modern flame' was dimmed. Nor had she done justice to herself in *L'Etrangère*, a play Zola considered simply absurd. But Zola's hopes that she might one day take 'a central role in a modern piece dealing with social reality'[49] was no closer to fulfilment in the plays she relied upon after leaving the Comédie. *La Dame aux camélias* and *Froufrou* were deliberate attempts to draw upon her proven capacity for romantic reversals, in which she disclosed strength in weakness and weakness in strength. With Sardou's help she soon concocted a theatrical mode in which the emotional patterns blue-printed by Hugo became the foundations of the drama as a whole.

Sardou's heroines (one should really say 'heroine', since they hardly change from one play to another) are women torn between uncontrollable impulses of power-hungry aggression and passive subservience. The plots are always designed to bring this divided nature to a crisis point by having the heroine fall in love with a man whom she must either sacrifice or destroy. Only the historical context changes. *Fédora* takes place in Nihilist

Russia, *Gismonda* in fifteenth-century Athens, and *Théodora* in sixth-century Byzantium. All draw upon the debased Romantic convention, most familiar in opera, whereby immediately comprehensible situations are inflated and glamorized through their displacement to exotic worlds.

It was in *Théodora* that the collaboration between Sardou and Bernhardt reached its *apogée*, impressing Emile Perrin, director of the Comédie-Française, as 'the greatest achievement in *mise-en-scène* of the nineteenth century',[50] and André Antoine, future founder of the Théâtre Libre, as a model for the staging of mass crowd scenes.[51]

For *Théodora*, Sardou provided a plot that was both crude and convoluted: while blatantly manipulative, it fought shy of precise significance; though loosely based on historical record, it progressed through a series of sensational incidents.

Théodora, once a circus performer, now the capricious and tyrannical wife of the Emperor Justinian, has taken to wandering the streets by night disguised as an innocent virgin named Myrtha. On one of her forays she meets and falls in love with a young Athenian, Andréas, who is involved in a conspiracy to overthrow the regime. Accompanied by his friend Marcellus, Andréas breaks into the Imperial Palace with the idea of assassinating Justinian. Marcellus is captured, and fearing that he may betray Andréas under torture, Théodora is obliged to kill him herself. Andréas escapes, but plots to insult Théodora publicly during a gala performance at the Hippodrome. Meanwhile his co-conspirators have come to suspect that the mysterious woman he meets at night is a spy. At the Hippodrome it belatedly dawns upon him that Théodora and Myrtha are one and the same. Justinian brutally quells the ensuing uprising but Andréas, though wounded, flees. A crazed Théodora visits him in secret, desperate to explain herself. Repudiated, she tries to drug him with an aphrodisiac which turns out to be a deadly poison. Justinian has learnt of his wife's infidelity in the interim, and the play ends with his order for her execution.

Sardou was one of the masters of spectacular theatre and, as this plot outline all too clearly shows, much of his skill as a writer lay in the provision of multiple opportunities for lavish *mises-en-scène* and virtuoso acting. Even before he began working with Bernhardt he was renowned for the care with which he researched his plays: prolonged reading in scholarly works and visits to the places he was evoking. In the case of *Théodora* there was a weighty backlog of scholarship for him to draw upon,[52] though his boasts of authenticity should not be taken entirely on trust. When *Théodora* was accused of being a somewhat inaccurate representation of Byzantium, he replied with a mixture of detailed refutation and a shrugging admission that he never allowed pedantry to stand in the way of dramatic effect. Moreover, he had another goal in view, in addition to historical verisimilitude, and that was the setting up of implicit parallels between Byzantium and modern Paris. There was in the first place a useful similarity between the central role and the actress for whom it had been written. Théodora has achieved fame and power without ever having lost sight of her origins, the warm 'Bohemian' world of performers – a sentimental legend with which Bernhardt would have been glad to be associated. And there were other ways in which the links between Byzantium and Paris were maintained. Sardou makes much of a choric figure named Caribert, a Gaul, who is seen early on in the play having the complexities of life in Byzantium explained to him. Caribert is a good-humoured innocent, somewhat at a loss amid the surrounding sophistication and brutality. Strangely, there were others in Sardou's Byzantium who seemed to be French, at least in their familiarity with modern French usage. One of the dressers at the circus referred to 'fricot', the colloquial French term for 'stew'. Accused in the press of having perpetrated an anachronism, Sardou replied, 'No . . . "fricot" isn't Byzantine but it is French, and that's enough, and sounds right coming from an old dresser at a circus.'[53] This is disingenuous, because *Théodora* continually plays rough Gallic honesty off against aristocratic corruption and, as Sardou must have known well, comparisons between the metropolitan mores of present-day Paris and the decadence of Byzantium were a staple in cultural polemic.[54]

Théodora was rather more involving than its text alone might suggest. The greatest impact came, of course, from the visual effects devised by Félix Duquesnel and some of the most prestigious stage designers of the time, men who had worked at the Comédie-Française and the Opéra. The scale of their ingenuity can now only be appreciated by examining the coloured illustrations and detailed descriptions produced at the time in magazines like *Les Premières Illustrées* for an audience habitually curious about the expertise and expenditure that went into archaeological spectacle.[55]

Théodora had eight *tableaux* in all (fewer in later revivals) which together composed a sequence of contrasting architectural and spatial moods.

1   *Justinian's Palace* (design by Carpézat). An immense room, its walls covered with mosaics. At the back, a golden gate through which could be seen the Palace Gardens and, further away, the town with its many domes and Santa Sophia, surmounted by a Byzantine cross. To the left, the door of an Oratory made of cedarwood encrusted with silver. Downstage, a large divan covered with Oriental materials, and cedarwood footstools, decorated with enamel and silver. At the back, an immense bronze peacock enamelled and enriched with precious stones.

2   *The Aisles of the Hippodrome* (by Rubé and Chapéron). Immense arcades barred by iron grilles through which could be seen part of the Hippodrome itself, with its columns, bronze elephants and triumphal arches.

3   *Andréas's House* (by Carpézat). A Greek interior of comparative simplicity, though with many domestic details.

4   *Justinian's Workroom* (by Robecchi). The walls entirely covered with mosaics representing sacred images on a gold base. Centre: a door leading to the oratory; left and right: doors leading to the Imperial apartments. These were of cedar encrusted with gold and silver and hung with Oriental drapes. To the right, a gallery lit by a large window of coloured glass patterned with golden roses.

5   *The Gardens of Styrax* (by Lemeusnier). Centre: a huge plane tree whose branches stretched out to cover virtually the whole of the stage. Other vegetation included pink laurel, tamarisks and mimosas. In the distance, a painted landscape showed forests and beyond them the distant blue of the Bosphorus.

6   *The Imperial Loge at the Hippodrome* (by Rubé and Chapéron). Gold throughout. At the back of the stage, two arcades. To the right, a staircase connected with the Imperial apartments; to the left, an iron gate looked on to the Hippodrome.

7   *Palace Room* (by Robecchi). Decorated with huge mosaic medallions, lit by a complicated triangular-shaped chandelier.

8   *Underneath the Hippodrome* (by Rubé, Chapéron and Yambon). A bare round room. Small windows let in a modicum of light.

These sets were like empty pictures waiting to be populated by an inherently pictorial kind of performance, and Sardou always made sure that his audiences had time to absorb them by opening each new phase of the drama with a delaying device. We can reconstruct the effect by combining the illustrative records of *Théodora* with a surviving *livret de scène*.[56] Like a promptbook, this handwritten document gives the play text with all the cues but without the bulk of long speeches. Beside the verbal cues are descriptions and diagrams of stage movements, with music cues where relevant, so that the *livret* gives an excellent idea of how Bernhardt's spectacular theatre was actually organized.

Her very first entrance, in act 1, scene 2 (*tableau* 1) demonstrates the method. The induction scene has been a conversation about the state of Byzantium between Caribert, the Gaul, and various courtiers which has allowed concentration on the set. A blast of organ music suddenly

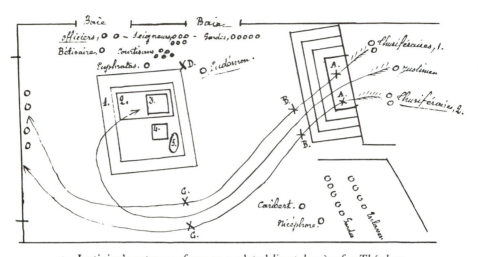

4 Justinian's entrance, from an undated *livret de scène* for *Théodora*

transfers attention to the Oratory. The doors open, the courtiers draw back, and Théodora appears, followed by women and eunuchs. She is wearing a gold robe embroidered at the hem with the heads of angels, a cloak of bright yellow satin, with gold thread and topaz, and a diadem of precious stones. The whole effect is like an icon and for full impact Théodora walks slowly to centre stage before descending to the waiting divan. As she does so the courtiers fall to their knees, heads bowed. A subsidiary movement of Théodora's handmaiden, Antonine, down to the divan establishes the Imperial party's final resting place and prepares a smooth transition to the next episode, which has Théodora in recline, hearing petitions from her subjects. Within the space of this entrance, then, we have moved from the comparatively static and verbal drama of the induction, through music and movement and a massive increase in stage colour and texture, to a focused stage picture with the star at its centre. This pattern is to be continually repeated throughout the production.

The most extended example is the processional entrance to the Hippodrome scene (*tableau* 6): a double entrance in which Justinian and Théodora appear successively. It begins with a group of slaves rolling open the bronze gates. A great murmur becomes audible off stage, accompanied by music. The Emperor is announced and Massenet's specially composed hymn strikes up: a verse from the chorus and the organ continues the theme. The court 'Usher' enters, stage right, and positions himself behind the throne with his back to the gates. The main procession arrives: first, the scholar-guards, who arrange themselves on either side of the main stairs, then two incense-bearers, who halt at the top of the stairs, turn round, swing their burners twice, descend, and repeat the action. This ceremony is duplicated by a second pair of incense-bearers, who pause in mid-stage yet again to swing their burners. Both pairs eventually position themselves in front of the gates, looking across the stage. After a pause Justinian appears, and a sign from the Usher brings everyone to their knees. Justinian descends, crosses the stage, climbs the dais, and halts in front of his throne. He is followed by various courtiers and courtesans, who group themselves, along with those already on the stage, behind the dais. Finally, four slaves join the scholar-guards downstage right. Throughout this entrance, everyone has joined in the Imperial hymn. As it ends, the organ music continues, but softly enough for dialogue to be heard. Justinian, wearing an Imperial cloak which spreads out behind him like a fan, gives his blessing to the left, to the right and to the front, each gesture accompanied by notes from the organ. The crowd rises, and Justinian, at last, sits.

A brief exchange between Caribert and his friends fills the gap before the entrance of Théodora. The whole procedure is about to begin all over again. The Usher announces her by recrossing the stage and taking up position near the scholar-guards. There is a new hymn, this time in praise of the Empress. A group of three eunuchs descend the stairs, and repeating the movement made earlier by the scholar-guards, join them on either side. Then come the flower-girls, who repeat the previous movement of the incense-bearers and end up alongside them, looking up at the thrones.

Only now does Théodora emerge. The Usher gestures and the whole company again fall to their knees. Théodora follows exactly the same route as Justinian, placing herself on her raised throne so that the train of her magnificent cloak falls to the lower level, where it is held in place by two attendants. Antonine follows her to a sitting position close by. With a final burst of the hymn everyone rises. There then follows a complex series of groupings and regroupings involving almost everyone on stage. The incense-bearers and the flower-girls intermingle to form a semi-circle which makes a background to the half-dozen principal characters stage centre. The scholar-guards seat themselves on the staircase while the eunuchs remain with the slaves.

All eyes are now on Théodora, who is enveloped in a costume inspired by the Byzantine mosaics in the church of San Vitale at Ravenna: her flower-patterned tunic set with precious stones, her blue satin cloak emblazoned with peacocks in sapphires, emeralds and rubies, her head covered by a bejewelled helmet, her face obscured by a yellow veil. A brief pause, and there is a roar from the Hippodrome, through which can be heard Andréas's call for her to remove the veil. She rises, does so, but the noise gets louder. Justinian, sensing revolt, leaps up, shouts to the guards to close the gates. The hubbub from the Hippodrome increases. Andréas is dragged on stage, Théodora rescues him, and, in a tumultuous climax, the rear curtains suddenly part to reveal a waiting army of Goths.

There could hardly be a better example of the techniques adopted by the triumvirate of Sardou, Bernhardt and Duquesnel, whereby massive display and extended movements, almost theatrically sufficient in themselves, were used to accentuate plot, nor of the gradual process by which they built up their stage pictures only to break them down. During Bernhardt's spendthrift period at the Porte Saint-Martin, the epic pretensions of spectacular melodrama became luxurious, ultimately degenerating into an orgy of profligate consumption.

Théodora obviously presages the bourgeois theatre so much derided by Brecht, what Roland Barthes has called the 'debauch of imitation', which 'achieved its culminating point in the baroque of the 1900s – a veritable pandemonium of costume'.[57] Yet Barthes's word 'pandemonium' is not entirely apt as a description of a spectacle that depended so greatly upon orchestration. Bernhardt's sets certainly quantified detail but always with an aim to concentration of view so that the pictorial values of the stage composition as a whole aided focus upon its volatile centre, Bernhardt herself. Slow and static effects contrast with the agitated moments that precede and follow them. Bernhardt was, after all, equally renowned for her rapidity, her impromptu responses to desperate situations. For example, the *livret* shows us clearly how she projected herself in *tableau* 4, when Théodora was required to improvise a diversion that would protect Andréas from discovery. Every move, every gesture, had to be alive with double meaning.

The scene begins in silence and in semi-darkness. The Oratory door quietly opens and Marcellus appears. He waits, listens, and gestures to his co-conspirator Andréas, who is visible in the doorway, to follow him. Marcellus disappears off stage, searching for the Emperor, and Théodora enters noisily from another door, stage centre. Antonine appears stage right. Marcellus cries out for Andréas to come to his aid. Théodora recognizes Andréas's name, and impetuously hurls herself across the Oratory door, preventing Andréas's entry. This is the moment commemorated in Nadar's famous photographs, which show Bernhardt spread-eagled across the massive wooden panels, her wild-eyed expression and the angular tension of her fragile body personifying her unnatural energy.

At the same time Théodora has to instruct Antonine to cry out that Marcellus is dead. The stratagem works. Andréas, trapped behind the door, has no option but to flee, though Marcellus, who has in fact only been wounded, is immediately dragged on stage by various Imperial aides, including the executioner equipped with his instruments of torture.

Later in the scene nervous agility is again required when Théodora has to carry out a surreptitious conversation with the wounded Marcellus virtually under the eyes of Justinian. Marcellus, aware that he might break down under torture and betray Andréas, shows Théodora how she might stab him with her gold pin. She hesitates, shuddering; he begins to shout Andréas's name; she strikes him in the heart. As the fatal gesture is rehearsed, rejected and then suddenly enacted all within a short space of time, so the simple dualities of Théodora's character – her protective instincts and her spontaneous violence – are reinforced.

In many respects the secret of Bernhardt's acting seems to have been the continual repetition of movements, gestures and expressions from a variety of stage positions, though always clearly visible to the audience. Even when Théodora is a victim of circumstance, she remains the initiator of action – a principle that infuses the play's *dénouement* which, like many of Bernhardt's death scenes, recapitulates character traits already thoroughly demonstrated.

In the final scene she pursues Andréas, anxious to convince him of her true intentions; and all her movements are designed to have him confront her face to face. She chases him within and between two acting areas: a table and two chairs to stage left, a bed slightly to stage right. When he sits on the end of the bed looking out to the audience, she performs a circular movement that takes her to a seated position behind him. She then slides round his back until she is lying alongside, her head towards the audience. Andréas briefly submits to this manoeuvre and for a second they are almost mouth to mouth, but at the line, 'Ah! Magicienne!', he recoils. Théodora gets to her knees, forcing him to rise and move across stage to the chairs.

Now crouching on the bed, she continues her imprecations, to no avail. Recalling the love potion in a flask around her neck, she leaves the bed and goes up stage so that she can prepare to slip it into his drink. With Andréas still refusing to look at her she moves round the back of the table to face him. Andréas rises and retreats across the stage; she stands, clinging to the table. As his insults continue, reaching a peak with 'Courtisane!', Théodora hurls herself at him, entwines his body with her own, and is repelled. While Andréas staggers from her assault she runs back to grab the cup, forces him to drink it, and tosses it away. The potion now burning inside him, Andréas lurches towards the bed, where he collapses, his body stretched diagonally but his head towards the audience. The movement is accompanied by three short near-rhyming words: 'Feu', 'L'amour', 'La mort', which makes Théodora realize that she has given him not a love potion but a poison. She screams and throws herself on top of his body. Failing to revive him, she runs to the door stage right, and cries for help. Yet again she crosses the stage and, kneeling by the bed, her face clearly visible, she lifts Andréas's head. He is dead. Again she screams, and again collapses upon him. At which moment the executioner and Justinian's aides arrive, slowly and silently moving up on her. At first only her sobs can be heard. Raising her head she sees the executioner produce a red silk cord. She asks him for respite, removes her jewelled collar, throws it to him, pushes back her hair, lifts Andréas's head on to her knees and in a final gesture rests her cheek on his, thereby offering the executioner her neck. The curtain falls on her final line – 'Go on then, I'm ready!' – as he throws the scarlet loop towards her.

When spectators recall 'feline suppleness'[58] and 'the windings of a snake'[59] this is the kind of thing they have in mind.

Théodora is a performer, by nature and by profession. She displays and dissembles simultaneously and the visually demonstrative style of Bernhardt's acting was thoroughly appropriate. As Théodora there was no question of Bernhardt having to imply more than she showed, so much depending upon the contrast between pictorial pose and expressive energy. In fact it may be that her ease in Sardou provides the essential clue to her failure seriously to attempt Ibsen who, particularly in his Naturalistic phase, never offered the kind of flamboyant and centred moments that she was used to. Sardou's deaths are glamorous – so much so that a fashion commentator could write of one of Bernhardt's dresses for *Fédora*, 'It's exactly the kind of dress in which a pretty woman would be happy to die.'[60] Ibsen's heroines die off stage, and though suicides are quite frequent (Hedda Gabler, Rebecca West), motivation remains enigmatic. For them, histrionic behaviour may be either a catalyst or a curse, never a fixed female characteristic. Nora Helmer's tarantella prepares the way for her final, more rational self-confrontation, and Hedda Gabler's taste for melodrama leads to disaster. But Bernhardt was prospering from her embodiments of performing women long before Nora and Hedda were seen to be suffering from their inability to stop acting, and some aspects of the Bernhardt style were preserved by Ibsenite actresses. Shaw understood as much, and went to some lengths to advise Janet Achurch that she must 'attain the force and terror of Sarah Bernhardt's most vehement explosions without Sarah's violence and abandonment, and with every appearance of having reserves of power still held in restraint'.[61] Like Achurch, Bernhardt's continental contemporaries, Duse and Réjane, managed to find the drama within Ibsen's determinedly bathetic structures. Bernhardt herself never could.

Moreover, although it seems unlikely that she would ever have espoused the feminist ideals that Ibsen's plays inspired and reinforced throughout Europe – believing, perhaps, that her career as a woman spoke for itself – her ideas of what constituted a 'psychological' drama were undoubtedly limited.

In 1894 she gave an interview to an English newspaper and found herself, not for the first time, questioned about Ibsen. As usual she took it in her stride.

'Ah! You in England are quite devoted to the northern dramatist, are you not? It is delightful to be popular on your side of the water,' she added prettily, 'for you all take things so intensely seriously. What do I think of Ibsen? I admire his Titanesque power, but I grieve at his obscurity and the cruelty we cannot but observe in his conception of life. When obscure, he is kind; when clear, cruel. Look at the *Doll's House* (a play, by-the-way, in which I should have acted over here had it not been that Réjane is going to show you her Nora Helmer) – can you imagine a more bitter story? I absolutely deny that Ibsen has "invented" the psychological play. Look at *La Femme de Claude*: it was one of Dumas fils's first comedies, yet it is intensely human and as absolutely unconventional as *Hedda Gabler*.'[62]

Bernhardt never did play Nora, of course – one wonders if she ever meant to. Her whole reply is suspect. For someone who specialized in murder by hat-pin and hatchet, who had made her name in Hugo and Racine, complaints about Ibsen's 'cruelty' are off the mark. We can guess, though, at what she had in mind when she spoke of the 'bitterness' of *A*

45

Doll's House. Bernhardt had been brought up in a theatrical tradition where plays tend to conclude either in sacrifice or in reconciliation, where the penalty for female separateness was death. Its master was Dumas fils, the agonist of adultery. *La Femme de Claude*, performed by Bernhardt in 1894, which she refers to as being as 'intensely human and as absolutely unconventional as *Hedda Gabler*', carried, in its later editions, a notorious preface in which the author justified his theme.[63] According to Dumas fils, his play was 'symbolic'. By which he meant that it was not about a particular woman, it was not really about women at all, it was about 'la bête': a creature below human dignity, the adulteress. When women stray from their wifely and maternal duties, said Dumas, they become literally inhuman. It was much the same argument as he had put forward in *L'Homme-Femme*, the outrageous pamphlet of 1872 in which he had suggested that a betrayed husband was morally entitled to kill his wife – 'Tue-la!'[64]

In many ways Bernhardt's melodramatic heroines (Sardou as well as Dumas fils) aren't 'women' either. Neither are they true monsters, but they do exist outside of the common order. Their eroticism is exceptional and Bernhardt needed that dimension because it suited the extravagant qualities of her acting style. Nor was she alone in broaching the comparison between Dumas fils and Ibsen, much debated in Paris in the early 1890s.[65] In the event, with the single exception of *La Dame aux camélias*, Dumas fils, the man whom Bernhardt implied had invented the psychological play, was routed. Bernhardt made a few tries – not unsuccessful – at the Naturalism of Sudermann's *Magda* and Mirbeau's *Les Mauvais Bergers*, but found salvation in Symbolism, and even tried out *The Lady from the Sea*. Like the Romantic style she knew best, Symbolist acting allowed for aesthetic display and perpetuated the idealization of the female that had accompanied the hysterical misogyny of Dumas fils.

The link was most neatly made by Oscar Wilde who, in his pseudo-Symbolist drama *Salomé*, has Herod echo Dumas fils in his concluding cry, 'Tuez cette femme!'. Had it not been for the intervention of the Lord Chamberlain, Bernhardt would probably have played the lead in Wilde's subversive drama in which it is an absurd man, Herod, who is intent upon adultery, and a judicious woman, Salomé, who kills first. Perhaps she was lucky to be released from a play that exploited the comic pretensions of sexual retribution.

The Symbolism that Bernhardt responded to was of a more sanctimonious nature, like Rostand's *La Princesse lointaine* (1895). This is middle-period Bernhardt, Mucha's Bernhardt, difficult to recapture in terms of actual performance because while the critical descriptions are more poeticized than ever, the physical image achieves new levels of commercial familiarity. The cultural moment is best summed up by the 'Journée Sarah Bernhardt' of December 1896, but more subtly conveyed by her revised *Phèdre* of November 1893, which helped to inaugurate her tenancy at the Renaissance.

As she had given no whole or consecutive performances of the part in Paris since her break with the Comédie Française, this new interpretation was seen as the culmination of all that she had learnt in the interim, and a reply to charges that her talent had become irredeemably debased. Certainly it was in that light that the dominant critics of the day, including Francisque Sarcey and Jules Lemaître, found themselves voicing unanimous enthusiasm. The wild abandon of the 1870s had now given way to a more mature conception that finally reconciled audiences to a playwright whose classical status had often seemed to be at odds with his limited theatricality.[66]

Sarcey's raptures in particular ('One of the most beautiful days of my life'[67]) are all the more remarkable when set in the context of his previous writings on Racine. In 1872 he had been thoroughly disappointed by *Britannicus*, and in 1873 had concluded that '*Phèdre* is more an admirable study of the female heart than it is good theatre'.[68] Later, though, in 1886, he was admiringly describing Bernhardt's Andromaque as a 'coquette'.[69] Her rendering had fitted neatly into his developing thesis that Racine's theatricality was best perceived alongside more modern kinds of theatre. By 1887 Sarcey didn't hesitate to compare *Bajazet* with Dumas fils's *La Princesse Georges*.[70] He was, in short, only able to accept Racine according to the familiar conventions of 'the well-made play' – the mode that had produced an image of woman with which Bernhardt was indelibly associated.

And Sarcey's eventual acceptance of Racine comes very close to the developed opinions of Lemaître. In a *conférence* delivered at the Renaissance, and in a *feuilleton* published at the same time, Lemaître expounded the thesis, apparently confirmed by Bernhardt's performance, that the trembling sensuality of Racine's masterpiece marked its author's return to Jansenism.

Never has a woman appeared more beautiful in the eyes of an assembled crowd – a beauty at once physical and 'spiritual'. Never has an artist conveyed with such inventive, harmonious and strong gestures, with such noble and purely expressive diction, with such an overwhelming charm, poignant and all-embracing, such a dolorous martyr of passion . . . What a wonderful crucifixion![71]

According to Lemaître, the modernity of Racine lay in his appalled realization of the voluptuous delights that could be discerned within an image of spiritual transgression. Fearing the precedent he might have created with *Phèdre*, Racine forsook the theatre; nevertheless, contended Lemaître, his apprehensions had been borne out by the neo-Catholic decadence of moderns like Barbey d'Aurevilly, who spiced religion with sensuality.

Sarcey and Lemaître were at one in their belief that *Phèdre* is about the theatrical possibilities of guilt, a resource recently exploited by the school of Dumas fils, which had prospered through replays of the 'endless battles between damnation and salvation to which women are condemned'. Both critics turned Racine's drama into an analysis of the female condition that derived transhistorical power from the aesthetic pleasure of seeing its pathos so perfectly conveyed.

To understand how Bernhardt's Phèdre came to be perceived in this way we must grapple with the primary evidence, and, in particular, with the sequence of publicity photographs reproduced alongside an article by Adolphe Brisson in the *Revue Illustrée* of 1895.[72] As these show a rather plump middle-aged woman swathed in gauze, surrounded by the potted palms and plaster pillars of some resort hotel, they will probably seem utterly remote from the imaginative stimulus that we know Bernhardt to have inspired. The photographs are important, though, not least because they are reminders of how much of her interpretation depended upon a number of key points in the play.

They begin with the famous first entrance, and it is immediately apparent that Bernhardt's open arms will be a crucial index of meaning. Here they express vulnerability, while physical balance is ensured by Oenone's supporting hand. Poise will be of the essence, even at such critical moments as the reprimand to Oenone in act III, scene 3.

Examining these pictures one has the sense of being systematically led through the drama, as if Bernhardt's Phèdre is somehow in control despite what she undergoes. That may well be an accurate impression because by this time Bernhardt was accustomed to roles specifically created with her

N'allons point plus avant; demeurons, chère Œnone.
Je ne me soutiens plus, ma force m'abandonne,
Mes yeux sont éblouis du jour que je revoi,
Et mes genoux tremblants se dérobent sous moi.
(Ac. I, sc. III.)

5 *Phèdre*, act I, scene 3

Ce n'est plus une ardeur en nos veines cachée,
C'est Vénus tout entière à sa proie attachée.
(Ac. I, sc. III.)

6 *Phèdre*, act I, scene 3

Que diras-tu, mon père, à ce spectacle horrible?
...Je crois te voir cherchant un supplice nouveau,
Toi-même de ton sang devenir le bourreau...
Pardonne!

(Ac. IV, sc. vi.)

7   *Phèdre*, act IV, scene 6

.. Et la mort, à mes yeux dérobant la clarté,
Rend au jour qu'ils souillaient toute sa pureté,

(Ac. V, sc. vii.)

in mind. Moreover, in order to demonstrate her concept of Phèdre, she drew upon familiar iconographic traditions of religiosity. At some points, the sensual content of Racine's lines seem actually to be countered by the sanctified gesture. The famous crux, 'C'est Vénus tout entière à sa proie attachée', is accompanied by an outstretched arm, which invites rather than resists heavenly power, while the confession of guilt from act III, scene 3 ('Je sais mes perfidies') is physically rendered by a hand-clasp over the breast indicative of absolute sincerity. She is on her knees for the appeal to Minos in act IV, scene 6, turning what might be a moment of total despair into one of entreaty. At the very end of the play she is clearly reinstated, perfectly serene, seated rather elegantly upon her throne, the neat folds of her gown and the graceful droop of her hand establishing her interior harmony.

At no point do Bernhardt's features seriously betray violent feelings: the mouth rarely twists, and the eyes are usually uplifted. To a modern observer, what might come forcefully to mind is a pictorial code that Barthes finds in Balzac and elsewhere – *'the Madonna with Raised Eyes'*:

This is a powerful stereotype, a major element in the Code of Pathos (Raphael, El Greco, Racine's Junie and Esther, etc.). The image is sadistic . . . it describes the pure, pious, sublime, passive victim (Sade's Justine) whose eyes raised heavenward are saying quite clearly: see what I will not see, do as you like with my body, I am disinterested, pursue your interest.[73]

This may seem far-fetched, less so if set against the testimony of contemporary observers. Brisson, probably writing with Bernhardt's approval, maintained that her instinct for gesture linked external grace with a more intimate and sophisticated quality. It was as if she had managed, through the careful arrangement of her veils, the exquisite lassitude of her bearing, and the expression in her 'dying eyes' to add 'a touch of modern, perverse coquettishness'. Her modernity was even alluded to by the set, with its tiger-skins, its purple cushions, its ivory statuettes set among greenery. Brisson was reminded of 'our beautiful society women', with their passion for collecting. It was also reminiscent (though Brisson doesn't make the point) of Bernhardt's own extravagant tastes in interior decoration. The Symbolist Phèdre – Lemaître's 'dolorous martyr of passion' – also matches her environment in Naturalistic fashion, making her a doubly determined creature.

Though Bernhardt often said that she identified with all her parts, Phèdre was undoubtedly a special case: 'The moment I have put on the veils of Phèdre I think only of Phèdre, I am Phèdre and I am left shattered by the performance.'[74] Following the 'emotionalist' theory of acting, Brisson connected this with her improved vocal control. No longer was she prone to *déblayage* (accelerated delivery), she modulated, she added vocal colour and sonority. With simple inflections of the voice she hinted at a variety of unexpected meanings: 'Love sensual and tender, hope, shame, hurt pride, anger, despair, dejection, bitter jealousy and, finally, resignation.'[75]

Yet a positive element of Christian acceptance was apparently there even at the start. Brisson noted the way in which she breathed the line, 'Dieu! Que suis-je assise à l'ombre des forêts!' (act I, scene 3), as if the eternal 'freshness' of the woods could purge her of her guilt. And while he did acknowledge the violence of Phèdre's passion for Hippolyte, he was always anxious to show how Bernhardt conveyed an underlying tenderness, even when it involved finding meanings not obviously contained within the verse. He remarks, for instance, that her rendering of the lines, '. . . au comble de misère,/Mes yeux le trouvaient sous les traits de son père', betrayed the protective and maternal side of Phèdre, and that only when her advances were repulsed did she show signs of the fury of which she was capable. Ever prone to remorse, her rage on learning of the love between Hippolyte and Aricie is, even so, a sudden storm followed by calm. 'A new Phèdre appears, resigned, generous, elevated by sacrifice, victorious over herself – a Christian Phèdre.'[76] Brisson concludes by describing Bernhardt's delivery of the famous 'Tu le savais!'. She gathered her forces, paused, looked directly at Oenone, and after a silence slowly released the three words as a profound reproach.[77]

The idealized Phèdre at the Renaissance heralded Bernhardt's middle or 'iconic' period, as much a part of her Symbolist experimentation as *La Princesse lointaine* and some explicitly religious dramas. No longer the impersonation of characters so much as of presences, her performances were increasingly viewed as ritualized events. At the same time, because of the economic scale of her undertakings – her management at the Renaissance coupled with the global tours – she proffered the spectacle of her unbroken body like a rare relic. The advance in impersonal authority would eventually allow her to return to *travesti* roles: her Hamlet certainly had Symbolist antecedents, reminiscent of Delacroix in its visual style, but probably directly inspired by Maeterlinck, who had recently identified Hamlet as the type of the modern tragic hero.[78] In *L'Aiglon* she was to symbolize the troubled *gloire* of post-Revolutionary France, bringing a double perspective to history: the living image revivifying a timely historical legend. In the same year (1900) the Symbolist periodical *La Plume* devoted a whole issue to Bernhardt, full of apostrophes to her as 'the personification of the beauty that she loves above all else; she is Art'.[79]

We may speculate as to her own involvement in the process whereby she became a truly sacred monster, but her aura will remain hard to penetrate. More enlightening than the florid tributes of minor poets and the indulgent prose of aggrandising critics are the unguarded comments of her unprofessional audiences. These often reveal nothing so much as curiosity – an element that contributed much to the prolonged *dénouement* of her career. By allowing for the factor of curiosity, we may even unlock the mystery of *La Dame aux camélias*, always the most phantasmal display of her physical presence.

Writing of the very first Marguerite Gautier, Mlle Doche, Jules Janin explained her success on the grounds that 'respectable women want to know how the other kind live and die; the other kind want to see their own private lives portrayed on stage'.[80] This element of inquisitiveness only increased as the play's subject matter became more and more anachronistic. Dumas fils himself conceded in a later preface that it belonged to the 1840s and 1850s when, as he put it, bourgeois values had triumphed and 'a woman had become a luxury item on display, like hounds, horses and carriages'.[81] But when Bernhardt brought the play into her repertoire in the early 1880s, the object of Parisian curiosity was highly contemporary: Jacques Damala, Bernhardt's young Greek husband who played Armand Duval. *La Dame aux camélias* might offer, it was thought, insights into a much publicized relationship. Damala had little talent and was probably lucky to get off as lightly as he did in a production carefully designed to give him the best possible opportunities to point up the contrast between the impetuous cruelty of Armand and the self-sacrificing beauty of Marguerite.

In the 1890s, the challenge for Bernhardt was Duse. Sarcey's view, widely shared, was that whereas Doche had remained a courtesan to her last breath, and Duse had breathed innocence from her first entry, it was only Bernhardt who managed to bring the two elements together: to make of Marguerite 'an Imperia of superior nature, agitated and feverish, no doubt, but capable of kindness and tenderness and enveloped by a perfume of poetry', so that when she does fall in love, 'she becomes

transformed, idealized'.[82] That was in 1897, and Bernhardt's interpretation was no longer what it had been in the 1880s. Perhaps it was seeing
Duse as Marguerite in London in 1894 that had prompted her to mount a
revised production at the Renaissance in 1896, in which she took the
unusual step of costuming the play in its original period style. By
recapturing a previous era she found a way of reviving herself.

Mme Sarah Bernhardt, rejuvenated by new *mises-en-scène* and contemporary costumes, has once again incarnated this delightful and legendary consumptive. Surrounded by gentlemen in corsets and pale frock-coats like figures in a Gavarni, she has
triumphed again. In the flowing, flat-bodiced dresses of 1855 she has the sad and
innocent look of a street-girl – no dandy of the time could ever have dreamed of
better.[83]

In fact the use of contemporary costume also showed Bernhardt to be up
to date in her methods, almost Naturalistic. Antoine himself, despite his
contempt for what he saw as a mediocre play, admitted that Bernhardt
deserved her continuing success because of the emotion she always
managed to inject, these days helped by the facelift of historical reconstruction.[84] Others said that it was Antoine's example that was responsible
for Bernhardt's innovation.[85]

As it turned out, nothing could have suited the middle-aged Bernhardt
better than the role of Marguerite Gautier. But then the character has
always been full of surprises. Bemused by her extraordinary longevity on
stage and screen, Roland Barthes, writing in the 1950s, could only
conclude that it was because Marguerite allows herself to become the
victim of a 'mythology of love' that her 'alienation from the class of her
masters is not fundamentally different from that of today's petit bourgeois
woman'. Were she not so 'patently stupid' and so 'touching', she might
have opened the eyes of her audience to the reality of their condition.[86]
This is an attractively sceptical idea of the role that suffers from the
weakness, common to many semiotic readings of popular images, of
presuming a uniformly passive audience. Its inherently patronising nature
can at least be qualified by the historical observation that Bernhardt's
version of *La Dame aux camélias* continued to provide a trigger for
Romantic recreations of a distant period.

Marguerite Gautier became, like the consumption that struck her down,
a cultural memory and a shining object of Romantic fantasy. How else do
we excuse a young English provincial, D. H. Lawrence, responding to
Bernhardt in 1908 with something close to hysteria? So disturbed was

Lawrence by the climactic scene of *La Dame aux camélias* that he rushed from his seat and battered on the door of the theatre until an attendant let him out. A few days later, still caught up in the experience, he wrote to a friend that

Sarah Bernhardt was wonderful and terrible. She opened up the covered tragedy that works the grimaces of this wonderful dime show. Oh, to see her, and to hear her, a wild creature, a gazelle with a beautiful panther's fascination and fury, sobbing and sighing like a deer sobs, wounded to death, and all the time with the sheen of silk, the glitter of diamonds, the moving of men's handsomely groomed figures about her! . . . She represents the primeval passions of woman, and she is fascinating to an extraordinary degree.[87]

A slow death

La Dame aux camélias was the most enduring of the 'wonderful dime shows', in which, amid glittering luxury and morbid emotion, Bernhardt sank helplessly towards death. So long-lasting was her tinselled vision of what the young Lawrence called the 'primeval passions of woman', particularly in England, that it deserves, even now, an extended post-mortem.

We can begin with Henry James writing about Rostand in 1901, after *L'Aiglon* but with *La Princesse lointaine* in mind.

M. Rostand was romantic because Mme Sarah Bernhardt is so. Interesting enough thus, if we had time, to trace the influence of a particular set of personal idiosyncrasies, the voice, the look, the step, the very *physique* of a performer, with all its signs, upon literature, and curious thereby to see once more how closely in France literature is still connected with life. The theatre there is a part of life. A given actress may be a part, an immense part, of the theatre; and, as literature has also its share in the same, the performer passes more or less into the sphere of the eternal.[88]

James had been hesitant about Bernhardt from the start and, over the years, the actress had done little but confirm his initial distrust. In Rostand, James believed, she had found her level, and his essay is subtly designed to put both actress and playwright in their proper place. Whatever corner of eternity Bernhardt may be entitled to she will inhabit it only for as long as *La Princesse lointaine* is read, which may not be long at all.

James's exceptional francophilia made him an avid observer but a harsh critic of what passed on the Parisian stage. There were others in England who, less reverent of French tradition, were prepared to be much more scathing in their criticisms of its modern manifestations; and there were yet others who, lacking James's knowledge of the past, were able to see vestiges of ancient convention even in Bernhardt. The 'English Bernhardt' was a protean phenomenon with all manner of disparities between her reputation and her influence, a salutary example of how, in the theatre, one thing can lead to quite another.

So that while James may have seen Bernhardt as a symptom of the unholy alliance between Romanticism and internationalism, a few could still glimpse in her, despite the ravages inflicted by years of Sardou and Dumas fils, something of the authoritative French tradition preserved, or so they believed, at the Conservatoire and the Comédie. When Irving came under renewed attack, in 1892, for having put spectacle before verse-speaking in his productions of Shakespeare, it was still Bernhardt who was cited as a contrasting model for respectful delivery.[89]

In journalistic polemic, she was credited with the double talent of imbuing the threadbare rhetoric of Sardou with emotional richness and, conversely, of showing humility before the disciplined verse of Racine or, more controversially, imaginative bravura when confronted by the metrical freedom of Hugo. This was obviously a muddled defence, but it served to draw attention to the value of the training that Bernhardt had received in Paris, and about which she was ambivalent, when not downright contradictory, herself. According to English advocates of the Conservatoire system, what an institution failed to provide in creative stimulus, greatly gifted performers would supply from their own resources, but what even the most intuitively expressive temperament required first of all was grounding in tradition. When Bernhardt came out well in comparisons between English and French acting, it was when she was measured against a national legacy she had often publicly disparaged. The journalist who compared Irving unfavourably with Bernhardt in terms of their verse-speaking also admitted that she sometimes 'treats the carefully weighed and balanced lines of Racine and Hugo as though they were prose, heaps together word upon word, till we are no longer able to tell that we are listening to poetry'.[90]

Throughout the 1880s and 1890s arguments about the respective merits of English and French acting were commonplace; and Bernhardt became caught up in discussions more wide-ranging than anything her performances invited. Shaw gives the best example. His attacks on her self-exhibitionism in Sardou are renowned as the quintessence of witticism; it is not always realized that they were underwritten by a dislike of French rhetorical acting that Shaw had long felt. 'The French actor is no actor at all,' he declared pseudonymously in 1889, 'but only that horrible speaking automaton, an elocutionist, and his proceedings on the stage represent not life, but an empty simulacrum called a style. In genuine Art, *le style, c'est l'homme*. On the French stage, *l'homme, c'est le style*.'[91] In Shaw's view the priority given by French acting to mere elocution went with its predilection for over-symmetrical groupïngs (straight lines, in fact), and for the direct address: the stilted conventionality that made it, in contrast to English practice, seem inflexible and unchanging.

In 1889, though, Shaw had allowed for one unlikely exception to the general rule: 'Imagine, if you can, even the roughest English company making *Hernani* like a superior Madame Tussaud's, as the Comédie-Française did in spite of the passion of Sarah Bernhardt.' His later irritation at Bernhardt's reliance upon Sardou was perhaps fired by the impossible demand that she revivify a style of acting he had already decided was defunct. What Shaw was looking for was Naturalistic acting, in his own special sense: acting born of a work 'in which there is no verse to guide the voice and no dance to guide the body, in which every line must appear ponderously dull and insignificant unless its truth as the utterance of a deeply moved human soul can be made apparent'.[92] Disliking French drama of most periods, Shaw was predisposed to dislike French acting of almost every kind. Good plays, he believed, produced good acting; bad acting resulted from bad plays; and, in Shaw's view, many bad plays were written in verse, some of the very worst in French verse.

Shaw's prejudice against poetic rhetoric sets him quite apart from those of his contemporaries who were ready to respect or even to admire Bernhardt primarily for her vocal qualities. Wilde, who was extremely interested in the possibilities of verse drama, thought that English actors equalled the French but that 'they act best between the lines. They lack the superb elocution of the French – so clear, so cadenced, and so musical. A long sustained speech seems to exhaust them. At the Théâtre Français we go to listen, to an English theatre we go to look . . .'[93]

Wilde of course was well aware of Symbolist theory and had more than an inkling of the dramatic tension that could result when measured words governed intermittent action. *Salomé* is the proof.

Accused of having undervalued verse declamation, Henry Irving replied, with some justice, that even Bernhardt had needed to break away 'from certain cramping conditions of French art', that the history of French theatre throughout had been one of protest against the tendency (mocked even by Molière) of tragic actors to rely upon a monotonously repetitive and bombastic delivery.[94] But the arguments about French acting, in which Bernhardt played an important part, were not only about current practice at the Lyceum, they touched a deeper issue: the claims of language against spectacle in any theatrical art. When Irving maintained that the modern manager had an absolute responsibility to use modern scenic techniques unavailable to Shakespeare (an historical principle with which, incidentally, Bernhardt would probably have agreed), his detractors insisted that even to make that point was a sign of priorities gone grievously wrong. For them, the essence of theatre was speech, and what mattered above all else was 'poetry', the elevating tones they sometimes heard from Bernhardt.

By the turn of the century a small group of intellectuals, who wished to advance the cause of verse drama in England, had turned French acting into something of a cult. Arthur Symons was happy to indulge Bernhardt's opportunistic repertoire so long as he could still discern in her performances some element of the thaumaturgical power of recitation. He continually set the French against the English as instructive examples of how physical restraint was essential were the poetry to be released – praising not just Bernhardt but Coquelin, Réjane, Antoine and Lugné-Poe in this respect.[95] As a result Bernhardt became, even in her decline, an unexpected influence upon English Modernism. Coerced into providing a memorial epitaph in 1923, Shaw blankly and inaccurately asserted that 'Bernhardt made no contribution to the modern theatre.'[96] There was perhaps no reason for him to know of the entirely unconscious contribution she had made to the Irish dramatic movement of the early twentieth century.

It was on the advice of an amateur actor in Dublin, a devotee of French acting called Frank Fay,[97] that Yeats made a point of seeing Bernhardt and de Max play *Phèdre* in London in 1902, an experience he approached with the double advantage of absolute commitment to poetic drama and limited knowledge of French tradition. What he saw in Bernhardt was an endorsement of the ideal of rhythmic delivery and minimal movement that, in conjunction with Fay, he had been reaching towards with the productions of his own plays.

For long periods the performers would merely stand and pose, and I once counted twenty-seven quite slowly before anybody on a fairly well-filled stage moved, as it seemed, so much as an eyelash. The periods of stillness were generally shorter, but I frequently counted seventeen, eighteen, or twenty before there was a movement. I noticed, too, that the gestures had a rhythmic progression. Sara [sic] Bernhardt would keep her hands clasped over, let us say, her right breast for some time, and then move them to the other side, perhaps, lowering her chin till it had touched her hands, and then, after another long stillness, she would unclasp them and hold one out, and so on, not lowering them till she had exhausted all the gestures of uplifted hands. Through one long scene De Max, who was quite as fine, never lifted his hands above his elbow, it was only when the emotion came to its climax that he raised it to his breast. Beyond them stood a crowd of white-robed men who never moved at all, and the whole scene had the nobility of Greek sculpture, and an extraordinary reality and intensity.[98]

Yeats apart, Bernhardt's influence upon theatrical experiment outside France was considerable. The actress Florence Farr, who was close to Yeats and took part in Gilbert Murray's versions of Greek tragedy at the Court Theatre, certainly studied her delivery closely, as did many others. Modernism was on the lookout for archetypes, and Bernhardt fulfilled the need in more than one way. Even Ezra Pound respected her.[99]

In the 1930s and 1940s, the tide turned, and mythologized memories of Bernhardt as a Romantic actress served to buttress conventional, if not downright conservative views. The main culprit was the man who prided himself on being the foremost English critic of the era: James Agate. Whether anyone other than Agate himself seriously believed that he stood in the tradition of Hazlitt, Lewes, Shaw, even Archer or Walkley, is probably to be doubted. Agate was publicly mocked and privately disliked by many who worked in the theatre. His snobbery, philistinism and blindness to many kinds of innovation, seemed to be summed up in his unwavering dedication to the French theatre and the interminable offerings he laid on the altar of French tradition. Week after week, book after book (often it was much the same book), Agate reiterated his devotions, handing on the mania to his *protégé* Alan Dent.[100] In 1941 they amused themselves by reconstructing the London *début* of Rachel a century earlier. They loved making lists of definitive theatrical moments and they always included Rachel in London in 1841, Bernhardt in London in 1879.

Young actresses were invariably subjected to the invidious comparison with Bernhardt. Mary Pickford, Elisabeth Bergner and Sybil Thorndike were all put through the mill and generally found wanting. Perhaps Agate was merely trying to ratify his own origins. He was, as he boasted, a professional anachronism himself, having come to dramatic criticism late in life. And he was also, to be fair, as the brother of May Agate, indirectly connected with the French theatre. May trained with Bernhardt, who became a friend of the Agate family. James saw Bernhardt perform in Paris and in London. Yet for all the rhapsodizing, he had surprisingly little interest in the French classical texts. His short book on Rachel (1928)[101] which he considered to be his finest achievement, is not notable for original research, though it does make a great deal of Lewes's famous criticisms of Rachel and Charlotte Brontë's invocation of her as Vashti in *Villette*.[102]

Nevertheless, it was James Agate whom Kenneth Tynan first courted when he was a Birmingham schoolboy in the mid 1940s. Agate had something that Tynan was attracted by: a journalistic bravado that, in Tynan's hands, became a dandyish love of the *outré*. What Tynan did not take from Agate was his reverence for the French and for the Romantic tragedy queen. In his earliest writings Tynan is deliberately rude about the French stage, upsetting Orson Welles with his unmoved response to *Les Enfants du Paradis*. French theatre, Tynan believed, was at heart effeminate, its characteristic scenario requiring the hero willingly to place himself in the hands of a tyrannical female of the Bernhardt type who would then perversely demonstrate her power by dying at interminable length.

Death, or rather the representation of death on stage, is the self-conscious theme of Tynan's criticism, and he continually compares the maudlin nineteenth-century depictions of the subject with its Elizabethan counterparts. For Tynan, Bernhardt and the Bernhardtian tradition were part of that Victorian taste for the morbid which turned death into a prolonged spectacle that the watcher could indulge without fear. What he personally admired was the kind of heroic acting that conveyed through performance a sense of the reality of death, and he often drew comparisons between the art of the actor and that of the matador. So it is no surprise that in the preface to his book on bullfighting he should fall with delight on the celebrated passage from *Villette* in which Charlotte Brontë likens theatre to a *corrida*: 'Swordsmen thrust through, and dying in their blood in the arena sand; bulls goring horses disembowelled, made a meeker vision for the public – a milder condiment for a people's palate – than Vashti, torn by seven devils . . .'[103] Tynan's ideal of Romantic acting harked back to its origins rather than to its subsequent degeneration.

By contrast, Tynan's opposing number in the 1950s and early 1960s was (still is) devoutly attached to all periods of French theatre. Sir Harold Hobson has had no qualms in continuing the francophilia of Agate, though he has brought his own values to bear. In 1957, when Edwige Feuillère performed *La Dame aux camélias* and *Phèdre* in London, Tynan and Hobson were utterly divided in their feelings about the Bernhardtian tradition she espoused. Tynan recalled the advice given to Bernhardt when she had first played Phèdre – "Poussez le rôle vers la douleur et non vers la fureur"', complaining that 'Since Sarah . . . the "douleur" interpretation has been in vogue', and making it clear that he would have preferred Madame Feuillère to have drawn on the precedent set by Rachel, at least as Lewes recorded it. 'Without the tigress, the play has no motive force', Tynan said of Feuillère; 'this actress is wanting in the majestic attack that should compel awe.'[104]

On the same day Hobson, in the *Sunday Times*, was recalling Jules Lemaître's theory, thoroughly confirmed by Bernhardt's interpretation, that *Phèdre* 'shows us a woman oppressed by a feeling of mortal sin', and enthusing over Feuillère's performance.[105]

One way of accounting for the changes that took place in the English theatre in the 1950s might be to say that it finally rid itself of its humility before the French. Tynan's mixture of admiration for heroic acting coupled with his liking for Brechtian cool and his scepticism towards Feuillère mark the belated divestment of the cult of Bernhardt which had hung like a shroud over the English theatre for too many years. But while Tynan was looking for existential heroism, Hobson was championing Beckett for his pseudo-Christian stoicism. And there had been, in fact, one performance in Bernhardt's career which might have appealed to both. In 1920, seventy-six years old, unique and unipedal, Bernhardt had acted Athalie in the theatre that bore her name. She was carried on in a litter looking, according to Antoine, like a polychrome statue,[106] according to someone else, like a Rembrandt.[107] She then delivered her lines as if in a dream, effortlessly switching from bloody revenge to seductive charm. Academic critics often like to point out that a line runs from Racine to Beckett, a connection that they explain according to the formal constraints of the French theatre. For more human evidence of the link, they have only to remember Bernhardt's Athalie and her awesome last days when, like Winnie in *Ah! Les Beaux Jours*, she sat immobile under the lights, at the behest of a bell, terrifying her audience with her antique charm. Like

9   Sarah Bernhardt with Marguerite Moreno in *Athalie*, 1920

Winnie, Bernhardt always clung to the facile optimism of the future perfect – the 'this will have been' that blindly preempts the ravages of time. In the end the very fact of her reappearance came to resemble the nightmare vision of endless repetition that Freud called 'the Uncanny'.

10   Ellen Terry as Beatrice in *Much Ado About Nothing*

Ellen Terry

vvvvvvvvvvvvvvvvvvvvvvvvvvvvvvvvvvvvvvvvvvvvvvvvvvvvvvvvvvvvvvvvvvvvvvvvvvvvvvvv

MICHAEL R. BOOTH

UNLIKE ELEONORA DUSE and Sarah Bernhardt, both her immediate contemporaries, Ellen Terry was never a truly international star, nor the actress–manager of a company which toured internationally. Her one brief venture into management was financially unfortunate, and although she visited America seven times with Irving's Lyceum company and twice on her own account, she never made a European appearance, and lacked the mystery and glitter of Bernhardt and the dedication to high modern dramatic art of Duse. Unlike either of them she remained an actress – although a leading one – for the significant part of her career in the shadow of a dominant and powerful actor–manager at the head of his profession, Henry Irving, and she never really emerged into the light of her own day. She may have been incapable of doing so, and she may well have needed an Irving to create for her a stage career as distinguished as it was; and a place in public esteem and affection unmatched by any other actress in the history of the English stage.

Like Duse, but unlike Bernhardt, Ellen Terry was born into the theatre; in fact her mother and father established one of England's greatest theatrical dynasties. Her sisters Kate, Marion, and Florence, and her brother Fred went on the stage, and Ben and Sarah Terry were on the road in Coventry when their daughter Alice Ellen was born on 27 February 1847. Like all children born into theatrical families she received her earliest practical instruction from her parents; she remembered that her father was a charming elocutionist and her mother read Shakespeare beautifully. No doubt she received instruction from them over a period of years, since she went on stage at the not exceptionally early age – for one born into the profession – of nine, as Mamillius in Charles Kean's production of *The Winter's Tale* at the Princess's in 1856. The Keans were kindly but hard taskmasters. Ellen Kean strictly supervised the little girl in rehearsal and performance, as well as teaching her the art of throwing her voice to the gallery. At the Princess's rehearsals were lengthy and methodical, and the actress recalled that they 'often used to last till four or five in the morning. What weary work, it was to be sure! My poor little legs used to ache, and sometimes I could hardly keep my eyes open when I was on the stage.'[1] However, the leading lady of the Lyceum never forgot the value of the discipline and training she received under the Keans; it was her introduction to the wearing grind of the theatre but also to the dramatist in whose service she achieved the most and was loved the best, Shakespeare.

After leaving the Princess's in 1859, Ellen Terry toured for two years with her older sister Kate in a drawing-room entertainment of two short plays, and then for a season joined the company of Madame de Rhona at the Royalty Theatre in London, followed by a season in Bristol. Her parts in these years, except for Puck in *A Midsummer Night's Dream*, which she had played before with the Keans, were confined to light comedy and melodrama. A further season at the Haymarket was interrupted by her marriage, a week short of her seventeenth birthday, to the painter George Frederic Watts, thirty years her senior. It was a short-lived marriage, the disparity in age and personality being simply too great to sustain it. Within a year Ellen Terry was back with her parents. She returned to the stage in 1866 in Sheridan Knowles's *The Hunchback*, and joined the management of the Wigans at the Queen's Theatre in 1867 to act in Tom Taylor's *Still Waters Run Deep*, an engagement terminated by setting up house with the architect E. W. Godwin in Hertfordshire, where her children Edith and Gordon Craig were born. She acted no more until 1874, when financial difficulties forced her to accept the offer of Charles Reade to act and tour in his own play, *The Wandering Heir*. She was a great success as Portia in 1875 under the Bancroft management at the Prince of Wales's, and acted there until 1876 when she joined John Hare at the Court, especially distinguishing herself in 1878 as Olivia in W. G. Wills's adaptation of *The Vicar of Wakefield*. By this time Godwin had left her, she had obtained a divorce from Watts, and married an actor, Charles Kelly, from whom she separated in 1881.

At the end of 1878 Ellen Terry was engaged by Irving at the Lyceum, and the best-known and most illustrious years of her acting career followed. A string of Shakespeare plays succeeded the initial *Hamlet*: *The Merchant of Venice* (1879), *Othello* (1881), *Romeo and Juliet* (1882), *Much Ado About Nothing* (1882), *Twelfth Night* (1884), *Macbeth* (1888), *King Henry VIII* (1892), *King Lear* (1892), *Cymbeline* (1896), and *Coriolanus*

(1901). Interspersed with the Shakespeares were romantic dramas like Tennyson's *The Cup* (1881) and *Becket* (1893), and Wills's *Faust* (1885). She repeated her success as Olivia, and a revival of a third Wills play, *Charles I* (1879), offered her yet another good pathetic part as Henrietta Maria. *Coriolanus* was her last new production with Irving, and in 1902 she played at the Lyceum for the last time.

At the age of fifty-five Terry still had twenty-four new stage parts and roles in four films to undertake between a highly successful Mistress Page with Beerbohm Tree in 1902 and her final appearance in Walter de la Mare's *Crossings* in 1925. She also managed briefly in 1903, and toured America twice and Australia once. Naturally, these years did not contain the acting highlights of the Lyceum period: Mistress Page with Tree, Hermione in *The Winter's Tale* (1906, also with Tree at His Majesty's), Alice Grey in Barrie's *Alice-Sit-by-the-Fire* (1905), Cecily Waynflete in Shaw's *Captain Brassbound's Conversion* (1906), and the Nurse in *Romeo and Juliet* (1919) stand out from the other parts. She married for the third time, to the young American actor James Carew, in 1907, a marriage that endured little longer than the others, until 1910. Her last years were darkened by ill health but lightened by a great swell of public affection evident earlier in the Jubilee benefit at Drury Lane in 1906 and officially recognized in the New Year's Honours List for 1925. She died at her home in Smallhythe, Kent, on 21 July 1928.

When she finally retired in 1925, Ellen Terry had been on the stage for sixty-nine years. She died a Dame Grand Cross of the British Empire, only the second actress to be made a Dame (the first was Geneviève Ward). Her career had been in decline for some years, but when she died she was everywhere remembered and everywhere tribute was paid. Her merit as an actress had given her this position of eminence, and it had been confirmed by the double accolade of public loyalty and official recognition. Or so it would seem, but the truth is more complicated. We must turn to the cultural context of her performances as well as to the stage to seek the reasons for her success and early and almost immediate enthronement as queen of English actresses. As was the case with Sarah Bernhardt, acting alone did not make Ellen Terry what she was in public favour; like Bernhardt, but in a less flamboyant way, she became in certain circles a cult figure. Such a status was bestowed on her by the world of art and literature as well as by the production practices of the theatre, her own appearance, stage personality, and acting style.

In 1863, when Ellen Terry acted at the age of sixteen in a brief season at the Haymarket Theatre, Clement Scott was one of the young men, among them painters and poets, who came to worship at the shrine of this new stage goddess. Scott recalled her as 'ideal, mystical, and medi-aeval'; her appearance glowed in his remembrance like a vision: 'I never saw a more enchanting and ideal creature. She was a poem that lived and breathed, and suggested to us the girl heroines that we most adored in poetry and the fine arts generally.'[2] Among the parallels that occurred to Scott were Tennyson's Elaine, the Lily Maid of Astolat; Morris's Rapunzel; Browning's Porphyria; Undine; and a crowned queen in the *Morte d'Arthur*. Scott also specifically identified the later Pre-Raphaelite movement, especially the work of Rossetti, and the illustrated periodical *Once a Week* as among the major influences upon this circle of acolytes. According to Scott *Once a Week* 'cultivated what I may call modern mediaevalism, and we seemed to see Ellen Terry's face, or something like it, on almost every page'.[3] *Once a Week*, which was published from 1859 to 1880, certainly contained articles on art, but it was more of a literature magazine than an art journal. Among the many short stories and serialized novels which can be found in its pages in the early 1860s is *Eleanor's Victory*, by Mary Elizabeth Braddon. Her description of the heroine is apropos:

She was very pretty: so pretty that it was a pleasure to look at her, in her unconscious innocence, and to think how beautiful she would be bye-and-bye, when that bright, budding, girlish loveliness bloomed out in its womanly splendour. Her skin was fair but pale, – not a sentimental or sickly pallor, but a beautiful alabaster clearness of tint. Her eyes were grey, large, and dark, or rendered dark by the shadow of long black lashes. I would rather not catalogue her other features too minutely; for, though they were regular, and ever beautiful, there is something low and material in all the other features as compared to the eyes. Her hair was of a soft golden brown, bright and rippling like a sunlit river. The brightness of that luxuriant hair, the light in her grey eyes, and the vivacity of a very beautiful smile, made her face seem almost luminous as she looked at you. It was difficult to imagine that she could ever look unhappy. She seemed an animated, radiant, and exuberant creature, who made an atmosphere of brightness and happiness about her.

In both appearance and appealing personality traits, this could virtually be a description of the young Ellen Terry. One of her biographers remarked her 'stately head, mantled with golden hair; a countenance of piquant charm and exquisite mobility; the grey eyes of genius'.[4] Eleanor Vane is in many respects the physical ideal of young womanhood replicated in so much Victorian magazine fiction and popular illustration.

She appears in poetry as well. Tennyson's gardener's daughter is a poetic image of the ideal:

> One arm aloft –
> Gowned in pure white, that fitted to the shape –
> Holding the bush, to fix it back, she stood,
> A single stream of all her soft brown hair
> Poured on one side: the shadow of the flowers
> Stole all the golden gloss, and, wavering
> Lovingly lower, trembled on her waist.[5]

Ellen Terry continued to remind spectators of stories, legends, and illustrations. Joseph Knight thought that her Pauline in *The Lady of Lyons* at the Princess's in 1875 could have illustrated an old Border ballad or a legend of the Round Table.[6] As late as 1896, and for once swept away by the actress, Henry James declared that she was exactly the sort of heroine demanded by an old-time story told round the fire.[7]

Since Terry made relatively few stage appearances in the 1860s, withdrawing from the theatre twice for domestic reasons and reappearing only in the next decade, her impact upon theatre-goers of artistic and literary sensibilities was made all over again when she returned to the stage, especially as Portia and Ophelia. She was ten years older but still a young woman. Upon the occasion of Sarah Bernhardt's success in London in 1879, *The Times* (11 June) commented:

In the absence of that highest genius which throws sex, as all besides, into the background, the British public asks, first, and above all things, to be interested in the woman who presents herself before it as an actress. For this purpose, the specially feminine elements of grace, fragility, physical delicacy, a slender figure, a sweet voice, whatever most suggests purity, tenderness, even weakness and the need of protection – all the points, in short, that most distinguish woman from man are of paramount effect.

In many parts she played, Ellen Terry was the stage embodiment of this ideal. In 1881 James described her as 'something wholesome and English and womanly'.[8] Review after review stressed her sweetness, femininity, grace, delicacy, and tenderness; together with 'charm', 'grace' and 'tenderness' were the three most common nouns applied to her performances by reviewers in search of an appropriate vocabulary. *The Times* did not mention a sense of humour or the spirit of laughter, and these were not aspects of the feminine ideal. Nevertheless Terry possessed them in abundance; they suffused roles with a strength, warmth, and attractiveness which partly constituted her 'charm' and which the more passive and supposedly feminine qualities did not in combination possess. Her ability always to remain young was a vital part of her image and seemed in some way to preserve her on stage, fixing her in beautiful maidenhood or wifely devotion as a painting fixes a lovely model in oils. She retained this power until very late in her career. James remarked it in writing of her Imogen, which she played when she was nearly fifty: 'Her performance is naturally poetic, has delightful breadth and tenderness, delightful grace and youth. Youth above all – Miss Terry has never, without effort, been so young and so fresh.'[9] This youthfulness often expressed itself as a girlishness which was much admired, although James rebuked it when he found it in Portia. Several critics noted that although the fearful imaginings and dark terror in Juliet escaped her, Ellen Terry perfectly caught what they saw as Juliet's 'sweet girlishness' in the earlier scenes. Arthur Symons called her 'the eternal girl who could never grow old'.[10] A typical view which emphasises this quality and is implicitly referential of a feminine ideal is of Terry's Ellaline, the heroine of *The Amber Heart* (1888), a poetic legend by Alfred Calmour:

With her delicate art she endowed Ellaline with all the buoyancy and ingenuous simplicity of the freshest maidenhood. The slightest hint of affectation or dissimulation would have been ruinous. But her light-hearted, frank, and guileless girlishness was so natural, her manner so sprightly, free, and joyous, that it was easy to believe in the efficacy of her amulet.[11]

The fact that Ellen Terry was so strongly feminine, natural, girlish, warm, and appealing, the embodiment of young English womanhood, placed her in a very real sense almost beyond criticism. Unless one were unusually acerbic how could one be critical of an ideal, an icon of Victorian femininity graciously decorating and humanizing the stage? This was a real problem for reviewers and surely explains the general tone of uncritical adulation in both press and theatre-going public alike, at least for much the greater part of her career. Charles Hiatt summed it up:

Ellen Terry's buoyancy, her all-pervading gracefulness, the charm of her singular voice, in which laughter and tears seem to be in everlasting chase, the innate femininity of all she attempts, do in fact to some extent disarm cold and searching criticism. She possesses that magnetic personality which compels sympathy in spite of oneself and makes one almost insensitive to small shortcomings. One's reason is at the mercy of one's sympathy; in the eagerness of admiration, one forgets to analyse and is content merely to enjoy.[12]

After she had left the Lyceum, Max Beerbohm tried to explain the secret of Ellen Terry's success. He attributed it to her 'sense of beauty' and her 'buoyant jollity', going on to ask, 'Was ever a creature so sunny as she?

Did ever anyone radiate such kindness and good humour?' Her power of endearing herself to the audience was in itself an indisputable title to greatness, whether or not she was a great actress. This was her appeal to the general audience; to painters and other artists 'her primary appeal has been through the quality of her face, and through the sense of beauty that is evident in all the inflexions of her voice, and in every movement, pose, or gesture'.[13]

It is certainly true that all these qualities were part of Terry's *acting*, as such, of her technique, of her attitude to dramatic character and interpretation. But they were also a part of her personality; in ways essential to interpretation and performance she 'played herself', as we shall see, a fact that critics recognized, which defined and limited her range while strengthening her appeal. They were also part of a social and artistic image which transcended her acting.

There was another, possibly darker and more mysterious side to the image, of which the actress may have been well aware. She was not only the sweet, virginal delicate being of Victorian fancy and Victorian myths of womanhood; paradoxically, she also possessed a sensuality, a seductiveness, a sense of moral and sexual danger – important aspects of the images of Victorian women created by the painters – which were apparent in certain stage roles. John Martin-Harvey thought Ellen Terry's first Ophelia in 1878 remarkable:

Physically, the actress was absolutely irresistible. Her long virginal limbs, her husky voice, her crown of short flaxen hair, her great red mouth, an inability to stand still for a moment, a mentality which could never have risen into her Prince's spiritual atmosphere, a poise so frail that one trembled for her sanity, a physical attractiveness which gave an ample excuse for Hamlet's 'Get thee to a Nunnery,' as for her father's and even the Queen's fear for her honour – all these qualities prepared one's mind for the pitiful direction taken by her thoughts when she could no longer control them.[14]

Others viewed Terry's Ophelia differently. From his own account, Charles Hiatt could have been watching another actress. Ophelia was 'a girl rather than a woman',[15] a girl in mind and body, gentle, tender, and completely innocent. Terry herself saw Ophelia as 'pathetically weak' in brain, soul, and body,[16] and most critics praised her for tenderness, grace, picturesqueness, and pathos – a painter's Ophelia, in fact, for the subject of Ophelia, mad or drowning, was a popular one with Victorian painters, among them Watts, Millais, and Arthur Hughes. These feminine qualities of Ophelia accord admirably with the necessary qualities of womanhood as seen by Anna Jameson in *Characteristics of Women* (later titled *Shakespeare's Heroines*), a widely read and influential book, a copy of which Ellen Terry possessed and profusely annotated. Mrs Jameson believed that in Ophelia (and Miranda) 'the feminine character appears resolved into its very elementary principles – as modesty, grace, tenderness. *Without* these a woman is no woman, but a thing which, luckily, wants a name yet; *with* these, though every other faculty were passive or deficient, she might still be herself.' Shakespeare has shown that these 'elemental feminine qualities' when expanded under genial influences, 'suffice to constitute a perfect and happy human creature'.[17]

It seems hardly possible that Martin-Harvey's Ophelia and Hiatt's Ophelia could coexist in the same actress, but such a coexistence is one of the most interesting aspects of, for instance, Victorian art; innocence and potential corruption, beauty and moral degradation, the unblemished surface and the spotted soul – one sees these oppositions twinned again and again in Victorian painting, and why not on the stage? The fusion of a sexually and dangerously attractive Ophelia and an innocent Ophelia weak in mind and soul, very much in need of male protection, is characteristic of the way women were often seen in art and literature. Oscar Wilde, who knew more about corruption and sexual danger than many poets and painters, saw this twinning of 'passionate ecstasy' and virtuous uxoriousness in Ellen Terry's portrayal of Queen Henrietta Maria in *Charles I*. Wilde addressed a sonnet to her in tones of equally passionate ecstasy, culminating in the address:

> O Hair of Gold! O Crimson Lips! O Face
> Made for the luring and the love of man!

Terry played another loyal and virtuous wife, Camma, in the classically set *The Cup*, a performance that drew another sonnet from Wilde in which the poet turns from the vision of the actress standing 'antique-limbed, and stern' and calls for her to play

> That serpent of old Nile, whose witchery
> Made Emperors drunken, – come great Egypt, shake
> Our stage with all thy mimic pageants! Nay,
> I am grown sick of unreal passions, make
> The world thine Actium, me thine Antony![18]

There is more than a hint of Cleopatra in the sensuous evil of Sargent's famous portrait of Ellen Terry as Lady Macbeth, with a dark slash of red mouth and a green dress wickedly glinting with beetle wings, lifting the

11   Ellen Terry as Henrietta Maria in W. G. Wills's *Charles I*

crown to her head, her expression mingling triumph and degradation in
equal parts. She did not play Lady Macbeth as a villainess, and the
painting was not based upon any incident in the production; nevertheless,
she said cryptically that it contained "all that I meant to do".[19]
    Eleanor Vane's hair of 'soft golden brown', the 'golden gloss' of the

12 and 13   Ellen Terry as Iolanthe in W. G. Wills's *Iolanthe*

gardener's daughter's hair, and Wilde's 'Hair of Gold' are all part of a Victorian artistic and literary obsession with golden hair. This hair is treated in a context of deep sensuality like Wilde's view of Terry as Henrietta Maria, like Porphyria:

> She put my arm about her waist,
> And made her smooth white shoulder bare,
> And all her yellow hair displaced,
> And, stooping, made my cheek lie there,
> And spread, o'er all, her yellow hair.[20]

or like the women in Rossetti's later paintings, such as 'Monna Vanna', 'Fazio's Mistress', and the models in 'The Blue Bower' and 'Morning Music'. Rossetti's Blessed Damozel, it may be remembered, had long hair 'yellow, like ripe corn', and Swinburne's Madonna Mia 'curled gold hair' and a hood to draw over it 'wrought with strange gold'. Golden hair was also indicative of unblemished youth and innocence, like Eleanor Vane's, the gardener's daughter, or Rossetti's Virgin Mary in 'Ecce Ancilla Domini' and Millais's 'The Bridesmaid', an aesthetic and moral object to be admired in its own right.

Ellen Terry's hair was not the pure gold colour of Rossetti's models, but it was gold enough for the same aesthetic response to be made. In Victorian painting the gold of the hair is frequently complemented by gold in the costume, and so it was on stage. Tom Taylor, writing to thank the actress for sending him photographs of her as Portia in the Lyceum production of 1879, said, 'I like the profile best. It is most Paolo Veronesish and gives the right notion of your Portia, although the colour hardly suggests the golden gorgeousness of your dress and the blonde glory of the hair and complexion.'[21] In another sonnet, 'Portia', Wilde rhapsodized on the costume and made the same pictorial connection:

> For in that gorgeous dress of beaten gold
> Which is more golden than the golden sun
> No woman Veronese looked upon
> Was half so fair as thou whom I behold.[22]

The artist Graham Robertson greatly admired Ellen Terry's Portia, not least for the colouring. The memory of it 'is like a dream of beautiful pictures in a scheme of gold melting into one another; the golden gown, the golden hair, the golden words, all form a golden vision of romance and loveliness'. Robertson was also struck by her loveliness as Rosamund in *Becket*, 'especially in the rich gown of her first entrance, a wonderful

Rossettian effect of dim gold and glowing colour veiled in black, her masses of bright hair in a net of gold and golden hearts embroidered on her robe'.[23] Wearing costumes like this, looking as she did, carrying on to the stage all the complicated associations of innocence, temptation, and the feminine ideal, of legend and poetry, of art and decoration, of symbol and romance, of the medieval, the Venetian, and the Victorian, all before she even opened her mouth to speak her lines, it is surely true that Ellen Terry expressed a meaning and a significance to her audience, a quality of being, over and above her performance as an *actress*, however meritorious that was.

In descriptions such as Robertson's, Ellen Terry assumes the status of an art object, and from the beginning of her career she was an artistic creation as well as an actress. Clement Scott's appreciation of her in the 1860s was that of a lover of popular art and literature rather than as a connoisseur of performance; in the next decade Henry James, rarely an admirer of her acting, said in his first notice of her as Lilian Vavasour in a revival of Taylor and Dubourg's *New Men and Old Acres* at the Court in 1877 that she was picturesque: 'she looks like a Pre-Raphaelite drawing in a magazine – the portrait of the crop-haired heroine in the illustration to the serial novel'.[24] Writing of her in *The Lady of Lyons* at the Lyceum in 1879, James commented that 'she belongs properly to a period which takes a strong interest in aesthetic furniture, archaeological attire, and blue china. Miss Ellen Terry is "aesthetic"; not only her garments but her features bear the stamp of the new enthusiasm.'[25] When she arrived in New York for the first time in 1883 and was interviewed by a curious press, the *Tribune* reporter (21 October) found that her face 'seems to have been modelled on that of some sort of Pre-Raphaelitish saint – an effect heightened by the aureole of soft golden hair escaping from under the plain brown straw and brown velvet hat'. The aura of Pre-Raphaelitism and Aestheticism emanated from Ellen Terry until the end of the century; Max Beerbohm noticed it in 1901 when she played Volumnia.[26] The explanation of how she passed from a sixteen-year-old actress, young and beautiful and capable of inspiring literary and artistic men to heights of poetic sensibility, to an idealized star and cult figure of Aestheticism must be found in her private and artistic life as well as in public reaction to her performances.

During Ellen Terry's first marriage to the painter G. F. Watts, she was exposed for the first time to the world of high Victorian art and to the admiring artistic ladies and painter friends who comprised her famous husband's inner social circle. Watts's relationship with his young wife may have been unhappily abortive, but it produced an artistic relationship altogether, in the long term, far more important: she sat for at least five of his paintings – 'Watchman, What of the Night?', 'The Sisters', 'Choosing', 'Ellen Terry', and 'Ophelia' – this last fifteen years before she first played the part in 1878. There was also a 'Madness of Ophelia' based on the Lyceum performance – Watts retouched the earlier 'Ophelia' at this time – and a pencil drawing from 1878–9, 'Ellen Terry as Ophelia'.[27] Except for this drawing and the 'Madness of Ophelia', all the paintings depict their subject as unformed, beautiful, and chaste – there is nothing here, nor could there be, of the temptress, of the sensual appeal of Aesthetic decadence.

Already then, before she had even embarked upon a significant stage career, she had been created in art, and her next close personal relationship, with E. W. Godwin, placed her firmly in the Aesthetic movement as well as directly relating her to late Pre-Raphaelitism.

Godwin was a man of many talents: architect, theatre critic, historian, amateur archaeologist, journalist, essayist, aesthete, designer of furniture, costumes, and interiors. He was much older than Ellen Terry, and must have been substantially influential, after Watts, in forming her taste, not for paintings but for decoration, design, fabrics, and *objets d'art*. He too moved in a cultural and artistic circle, but one more Aesthetic and avant-garde than Watts, more concerned with beauty as an end in itself, not only in art but also in daily living. Before Ellen Terry left the stage for Godwin, she had met many of the leading poets, aesthetes, and artists of the day, and she was a visitor to Tudor House in Cheyne Walk, Chelsea, Rossetti's palace of Aesthetic decoration and a social centre for an advanced artistic and literary circle. Her own tastes in clothing and interior decoration were established by this period in her life, and they are well documented in interviews and personal memoirs. After her return to the stage and their separation, Godwin designed costumes for her, a function eventually taken over in the 1880s by Alice Comyns-Carr, the wife of Joseph Comyns-Carr, a member of the Aesthetic movement who was a director of the Grosvenor Gallery and editor of the *English Illustrated Weekly*. When Terry undertook the role of Camma, Henry Labouchère complimented Irving upon understanding the spirit of the age.

At a time of affected aestheticism, of rapture and intensity, of sad wall paper and green dados, what a stroke of diplomacy it was to engage Ellen Terry. This graceful and

14   Ellen Terry as Camma in Tennyson's *The Cup*

picturesque creature is the high priestess of the enthusiasts. She suits the dreams of the idealists. The age that gave us a Grosvenor Gallery must necessarily adore an Ellen Terry, for she is the embodiment of the aspirations of modern art. With her waving movements and skill in giving life to drapery, she is the actress of all others to harmonize with gold backgrounds and to lounge under blossoming apple trees.[28]

Harmonizing with gold backgrounds and lounging under apple trees brings to mind the paintings of Aesthetic artists; it is interesting how, as we have seen already, there was a continued correspondence in critical and artistic opinion between actress and painting, between Ellen Terry playing a character on stage and Ellen Terry playing a character in a painting, between the performer on stage and a central female figure in a painting incarnated as actress, as Ellen Terry.

The relationship between painting and the stage, and the significant effect of this relationship upon acting and production, is much older than Victorian Aestheticism, although the pictorialization of both acting and production reached its peak in the middle and late Victorian period. Not only painting is important here; so is the art of the sculptor. Quintilian advised Roman orators to model their physical techniques upon the attitudes of statues; the very word 'attitude', commonly applied to the actor in the eighteenth and nineteenth centuries, is derived from statuary and painting. Advice of this kind was regularly given to actors in eighteenth- and early nineteenth-century stage manuals and books upon acting, and no less a personage than Goethe recommended that the actor should properly go to school to a sculptor and a painter. In England in the 1820s the equestrian and mime Alexander Ducrow was playing in an act called 'Grecian Statues', in which he posed behind a picture frame in a series of famous statues from antiquity; at about the same time the *tableau vivant*, which combined elements of both statuary and painting in a pictorial representation of a subject from art, myth, or history, passed from the drawing-room to public performance. Critics writing about the great French *tragédienne* Rachel, a popular visitor to the London stage in the 1840s, often used the terminology of statuary to describe her performance. In the role of Hermione, a Shakespearean conjunction between statue and performer – Galatea was also transformed several times from statue to actress in eighteenth- and nineteenth-century drama – English actresses were complimented for their resemblance to statues.

In J. R. Planché's burletta, *The Court Beauties* (1835), paintings of the beauties of the court of Charles II come to life, as does Peg Woffington in Taylor and Reade's comedy, *Masks and Faces* (1852), assuming a position behind a picture frame as her own portrait. The same sort of thing happens in *Ruddigore*, when all the ancestors of Sir Ruthven Murgatroyd step out of their portraits to urge the recalcitrant baronet to desperate deeds of crime. The actor, as or in a picture, descending to the stage as a character, is a striking instance of the pictorialization of the stage in the nineteenth century, a phenomenon that linked actor and production technique in a strong visual image, sometimes in tableau, sometimes in motion. Such a phenomenon insofar as the actor was concerned has its roots in the much earlier pictorialization of the passions in tragedy (and later in melodrama) through a stylized language of gesture, facial expression, and attitude that rendered emotional response in a pictorial manner understood by the audience and corresponding to the emotions expressed at the same moment by speech. Thus did the actor convey meaning and feeling by pictures as well as words. Indeed, in early English melodrama the regulations of the Licensing Act governing minor theatres required him to act by dumbshow only; the picture therefore had to carry the full weight of passion and narrative, a development that vitally affected the course of melodramatic acting and was no small part of the continued pictorialization of acting style. The tableau act ending of melodrama, in which, arranged carefully in significant stage positions, actors froze into attitudes indicative of their reactions to the climactic events of the scene, was a group expression of emotion in the form of a 'picture', the term commonly used in stage directions to denote this technique, a technique of production as well as of acting. Another method of pictorial production principally but not solely used in melodrama was the 'realization' of a contemporary painting well known to the audience by means of a tableau combination of actors, properties, and scene painting. Such a method was employed until the twentieth century. In the 1820s scene painters like David Cox, David Roberts, and Clarkson Stanfield embarked upon careers of easel painting that would bring election to the Royal Academy for Roberts and Stanfield and great distinction as a landscape painter for Cox. Many scene painters of the eighteenth and nineteenth centuries followed this course. Later in the nineteenth century Irving and Tree asked painters of reputation like Alma Tadema, Burne-Jones, and Ford Madox Brown to design scenes, costumes, and properties for productions at their theatres.

Increasingly, then, in the nineteenth century, the arts of painting, acting, and stage production moved closer together, until in some productions, especially those of Irving at the Lyceum, they almost merged. Two years after Irving assumed the management of the Lyceum, Squire Bancroft took over the Haymarket in 1880 and installed a real picture frame 2 feet in width, moulded and gilded, right round the proscenium arch, which was flush with the front of the stage. The stage became a kinetic painting in three dimensions – Irving's scenic work at the Lyceum was frequently compared to old-master paintings – and the actor became a part of that painting. A pictorial style of acting was dictated by production circumstances as well as by the classical tradition of the tragic and melodramatic actor. Irving himself said that 'it is most important that an actor should learn that he is a figure in a picture, and that the least exaggeration destroys the harmony of the composition'.[29] Beauty was also a conscious aim of the actor, as it was of scene painting, and such an aim was both appropriate and strongly marked during the Aesthetic period. The creation of beauty by scenic pictures was paralleled by the beautiful pictures created by the actor through body line, gesture, movement, and the use of costume.

The actor, then, at this unique juncture in the history of the theatre, became a statue and a painting, or a subject in a painting, as well as a player. It is not possible fully to understand the arts of the nineteenth-century stage, whether in England or in Europe, without understanding their relationship to painting and – to a lesser and decreasingly important degree – to statuary. An actor or actress truly became a work of art in his or her own right, which Ellen Terry was. Henry James described her as having 'a face altogether in the taste of the period, a face that Burne-Jones might have drawn . . . she makes an admirable picture'.[30] Writing of her from the point of view of an artist, Graham Robertson said that 'her charm held everyone, but I think pre-eminently those who loved pictures. She was *par excellence* the Painter's Actress and appealed to the eye before the ear; her gesture and pose were eloquence itself. She was a child of the studio . . . She had learnt to create Beauty, not the stage beauty of whitewash and lip salve, but the painter's beauty of line, harmony, and rhythm.'[31] When the actress first appeared as Beatrice in 1880, in a provincial tour of *Much Ado About Nothing*, Davenport Adams noted that 'somehow or other Miss Terry always is a perfect vision of the picturesque . . . no lady on the modern stage is so much of a picture in herself, or falls so readily into the composition of the larger picture formed by the combinations of a drama'.[32]

It is interesting that Davenport Adams saw *Much Ado* (among other plays) as a 'larger picture' on whose canvas the actress took her compositional place. The Victorian fashion of producing Shakespeare, from Macready to Tree, was to 'illustrate' him as if he were a book; the nineteenth century was of course the great age of illustrated editions of Shakespeare. This pictorial treatment was felt necessary in order to actualize the text and the scene in life-like images of poetic beauty, to recreate the historical environment archaeologically and spectacularly, to leave nothing to the imagination of the audience.[33] Since Ellen Terry achieved much of her reputation in playing Shakespearean roles, she perforce appeared in elaborate and highly pictorial productions. The treatment of Shakespearean character as picture is evident in the innumerable paintings of characters and scenes in the plays, a movement which really gathered momentum with the Boydell Gallery in 1789 and extended all through the nineteenth century, especially in the annual exhibitions of the Royal Academy. Commentators upon Shakespeare could think in the same terms as painters. Cordelia, for instance, reminded Anna Jameson of a Madonna in an old Italian master.[34] Writing of Macbeth, she believed that Shakespeare's 'blackest shadows' are like Rembrandt's, and contrasted Lady Macbeth with Medea as works of art: 'For gothic grandeur, the rich chiaroscuro, and deep-toned colours of Lady Macbeth, stand thus opposed to the classical elegance and mythological splendour, the delicate yet inflexible outline of the Medea . . . there exists the same distinction between the Lady Macbeth and the Medea, as between the Medusa of Leonardo da Vinci and the Medusa of Greek gems and bas reliefs.'[35] For Mrs Jameson, Shakespeare's heroines and the heroines of other seventeenth-century dramatists could also be regarded as comparative statuary. 'The Cleopatra of Fletcher reminds us of the antique colossal statue of her in the Vatican, all grandeur and grace. Cleopatra in Dryden's tragedy is like Guido's dying Cleopatra in the Pitti palace, tenderly beautiful. Shakespeare's Cleopatra is like one of those gracful and fantastic pieces of Arabesque . . .'[36]

Ellen Terry had also been a Shakespearean statue. Christopher St John described her attitude in *The Winter's Tale*, where in the trial scene, the actress, clothed in white samite draperies, 'recalled the Niobe of the Louvre. Every gesture seemed a memory of the sorrow and dignity written by sculptors in marble, of those long lines of statues stolen by Europe from Greece.'[37] Comment of this kind not only related to Shakespeare; another writer said of her Camma in *The Cup* that 'aided by draperies arranged with the most singular skill, the figure, in its freedom and suavity, recalls the Elgin Marbles'. The critic went on to say that Terry as Camma also called to mind the painter who had learnt most from the Elgin Marbles, Albert Moore; thus 'in hue and line the actress is a realization of Mr. Moore's paintings'.[38] Moore was a leading Aesthetic painter almost exclusively concerned with a subject matter of languid young ladies elegantly posed in beautiful draperies in classical settings with lovely and delicate touches of colour in the background or foreground harmonizing with the same colour in their dresses. Henry Labouchère was thinking of both Moore and Rossetti when he referred to Terry as the actress to harmonize best with gold backgrounds and 'to lounge under blossoming apple trees'.

The sheer pictorial strength and pictorial beauty of Ellen Terry on stage could sometimes be abstracted from a part, detract from the acting of it, and be used, consciously or not, as a substitute for strength of character. A deficiency of this kind is implicit in much of Henry James's criticism of her and was apparently evident, for instance, in her playing of Pauline, the heroine of Bulwer-Lytton's *The Lady of Lyons*, who is furious and embittered by the marital trick played upon her by the fake aristocrat, Claude Melnotte, and the two conspirators who put him up to it. According to Charles Hiatt, 'fascinated by the picturesque appearance of the actress, and watching her power of assimilating herself to the decoration of a scene, the audience was content to accept for a proud Pauline, a tender, tearful and sympathetic lady, who has no heart to rail and no strength to curse'.[39] Joseph Knight also thought the actress's Pauline in 1875 'comprised a series of pictures each more graceful than the preceding', and that 'the long tender lines of a singularly graceful figure add wonderful picturesqueness to the illustrations Miss Terry affords'. However, 'in the short scene in the third act, in which Pauline chides her lover for treachery, the actress scarcely rises to the requisite indignation'.[40] As we shall see, Ellen Terry did not easily encompass power and tragic strength on stage, and to seek refuge in pictorialism may also have been an aspect of her Lady Macbeth, if Sargent's portrait is any indication of what she intended to do in the part.

Ellen Terry's pictorialism was most appropriate – for a Victorian actress – and most strongly marked in Shakespeare. As might be expected, her Ophelia created a pictorial as well as a theatrical stir. The Pre-Raphaelite qualities of her portrait of the character are evident in Henry James's description of 'a somewhat angular maiden of the Gothic ages',[41] and Hiatt's comparison with a Pre-Raphaelite saint or a madonna by Giovanni Bellini[42] – a clear pictorialization of the innocence and purity in Ophelia. George Bernard Shaw took the view that a picture had come to life; the actress had added what she learnt in the studio to what she learnt on the stage so successfully that 'it was exactly as if the powers of a beautiful picture of Ophelia had been extended to speaking and singing'.[43]

The high point of Ellen Terry's Shakespearean pictorialism seems not to have been Ophelia – although this character meant more to the age and more to artists – but Portia, which she first played in an archaeologically pictorial production by the Bancrofts at the Prince of Wales's in 1875, and again for Irving in 1879.

Even though Irving was not as ardent a theatrical archaeologist as Charles Kean or the Bancrofts, he nevertheless subscribed to the Victorian principle of the full pictorial and frequently spectacular replication, based on available authorities, of all Shakespeare's settings. In the case of *The Merchant of Venice* much information was derived from the detail of the Venetian masters; Venetian dress, Venetian manners, and Venetian life were recreated before the eyes of the audience. Percy Fitzgerald noted that the effect of the costumes was just as impressive as the beauty and splendour of architectural settings such as the Doge's court and the colonnades of his palace, which were achieved mostly by scene painting rather than by built-up sets. 'The pictures of Moroni and Titian had been studied for the dove-coloured cloaks and jerkins, the violet merchant's gown of Antonio, the short hats . . . and the frills. The general tone was that of one of Paolo Veronese's pictures – as gorgeous and dazzling as the *mélange* of dappled colour in the great Louvre picture.'[44] According to contemporaries, Veronese was the artist in whose paintings Ellen Terry could be found. Tom Taylor's view of Portia's profile as 'most Paolo Veronesish' has been mentioned above, and Joseph Knight said that the actress had been 'got up in exact imitation of those stately Venetian dames who gaze down from the pictures of Paolo Veronese'.[45] Portia's first dress was gold satin, which was appropriate, Dutton Cook thought, to 'the look of a picture by Giorgione';[46] Clement Scott commented that she could have 'stepped out of a canvas' – this phrase was in common use among critics of Ellen Terry – by Frederick Leighton.[47] Whether it was a specific painter who had been deemed the creator of a pictorialized Portia, or whether it was a matter of a generalized 'dream of beautiful pictures' (Graham Robertson's words), it is indisputably true that for the aesthetically inclined public Ellen Terry existed in art as well as upon the stage.

As actress rather than art object, closely though her own sense of aesthetics linked the two roles, Ellen Terry had thought long and carefully about the nature of her own art. Going on stage at such an early age and learning the fundamentals of acting from her parents and then from Mrs Kean did not prevent her from more mature reflection, especially in her autobiography and her lectures on Shakespeare, the former written after she had left the Lyceum and the latter toward the end of her stage career. She was a sensitive critic of her own acting and the acting of her colleagues (especially Irving), and commented intelligently and with discrimination upon a wide variety of contemporary performances. In general she stressed the importance of the imagination in approaching a character, and of beauty in playing it, as well as underlining the necessity of identifying herself with a role. Of the first essential quality she wrote, 'Imagination, imagination! I put it first years ago, when I was asked what qualities I thought necessary for success upon the stage. And I am still of the same opinion. Imagination, industry, and intelligence . . . are all indispensable to the actress, but of these three the greatest is, without any doubt, imagination.'[48] In order for the imagination to work freely, the actor must come to a part unhindered by any advance conception of how to play it, and unencumbered by notions derived from previous reading or personal research. When she first played Ophelia, Ellen Terry visited a madhouse to study insanity at first hand. What she saw made a deep and powerful impression upon her, particularly the behaviour of two female inmates. However, and paradoxically, she found most of the lunatics too theatrical to teach her anything about Ophelia; the experience convinced her that 'the actor must imagine first and observe afterwards. It is no good observing life and bringing the result to the stage without selection, without a definite idea. The idea must come first, the realism afterwards.'[49] Similarly, in the case of Juliet she made the mistake (according to her) of reading everything written about the character and the way in which other actresses had played the part. Thus Juliet lacked 'original impulse', and it would have been much better if she 'had gone to Verona and just *imagined*'.[50]

Once the imagination had exercised its function upon the conception of a character, the detailed work of preparation and finally of rehearsal can begin. Yet the imagination must itself be sympathetic to the character. Ellen Terry disdained some of the characters she had to undertake at the Lyceum late in Irving's reign; she had strong likes and dislikes among the characters of drama and needed to find something in them that she could make her own. This included a sense of beauty which could be realized in performance. In a lecture upon Shakespeare she said, 'no interpretation entailing a sacrifice of beauty, whether to mirth or realism, can ever be satisfactory', a view exemplified in discussing the character of Portia. She represented Portia as a Venetian lady with a distinctive Aesthetic style quite *au fait* with current notions of art, decoration, and pictorial creation. This approach was one of five or six with which she experimented, and the one to which she always returned. Portia is a creature of the Renaissance, 'the child of a period of beautiful clothes, beautiful cities, beautiful houses, beautiful ideas. She speaks the beautiful language of inspired poetry. Wreck that beauty and the part goes to pieces.'[51]

The feeling for beauty was not only related to a particular character, but also to the whole concept of acting in the nineteenth century, a point already touched upon. Henry Irving said flatly that the ultimate aim of acting was beauty, and that 'to merely reproduce things vile and squalid and mean is a debasement of art'.[52] For Ellen Terry, it was clearly a necessary aspect of character and of playing the character, as well as being a general aim of theatrical performance. It was probably this feeling that led her to reject Ibsen's heroines (as Irving rejected Ibsen), despite the fact that they made splendid parts for a younger generation of actresses and despite the complaints of Shaw that she never undertook one. She said that she would not care to act in Ibsen since she considered herself 'very happy and fortunate in having nearly always been called upon to act very noble, clean characters, since I prefer that kind of part'. She loved Portia and Beatrice much better than Hedda, Nora, or 'any of those silly ladies'. She acknowledged the attraction of Ibsen's women, but believed this was because he was so easy to act, his characters being drawn 'in plain straight strokes'. They also converse naturally, which was easy for the actor; yet this superficial naturalness concealed an essential unreality, a lack of truth to nature.[53] It was a striking misjudgement and shows how out of sympathy with the new, psychological, 'unpleasant' characters she was;[54] her acting methods were also quite unsuitable for their portrayal. This kind of character lacked her definition of nobility, and no doubt of beauty as well. An actress who could say that Portia and all the ideal young heroines of Shakespeare ought to be thin, since thinness befits their ideality,[55] would hardly have found an ideal beauty in Hedda Gabler.

The strength of Ellen Terry's views about character made the assumption of a role, if she were playing a woman she admired, easier for her and more rewarding for the audience. Beatrice, for example, was one of her

15 Ellen Terry as Desdemona to Irving's Othello

best parts. Terry excelled in high comedy and playfulness, and was very good at falling in love on stage. In a journal from which she quoted during a revival of *Much Ado About Nothing* in 1891, she was pleased that she made Beatrice 'a nobler woman', the character being 'a gallant creature and complete in mind and feature'.[56] Although she fully developed the pathos of Desdemona's situation, she nevertheless did not think her weak or merely a pretty, innocent young thing. Desdemona is strong and would be best played by a great tragic actress with a strong personality and a strong method. Ellen Terry much admired her, declaring that she is 'more fitted to be the bride of Christ than the bride of any man'.[57] Imogen, in which role she so delighted her severest critic, Henry James, was praised for her dignity and unwavering love; she said it was her favourite part – 'she enchants me, and so I can find no fault in her'.[58] Here she was being thoroughly Victorian; Imogen always appealed for these very reasons. Henry Morley, reviewing Helen Faucit in the role at Drury Lane in 1863, was enraptured by her 'tenderness and grace of womanhood . . . the wife's

87

absolute love and perfect innocence'. For Morley, Imogen is 'the most beautiful of Shakespeare's female characters'.[59]

Beatrice, Desdemona, and Imogen were characters Ellen Terry thoroughly assimilated to herself; she absorbed them into her own personality rather than temporarily assuming theirs. Even Lady Macbeth received the same treatment: 'Adapt the part to my own personality'[60] is the best approach she can suggest, and it was the one she followed. She was not a protean like Beerbohm Tree, who could be virtually unrecognizable as himself from one part to another, nor did she have the range of Irving, a saint in one play, a devil in the next, and perfectly convincing as either. Her method was different; the task of the actress in approaching character was, as she saw it, 'to learn how to translate this character into herself, how to make its thoughts her thoughts, its words her words'.[61] She did not build a character from the outside in, by devising business and mannerism to define character; rather she entered the character and possessed it. In doing this she also entered that character's emotions and made them her own. As Ophelia she came off the stage in tears, and she cried real tears as Olivia in *The Vicar of Wakefield*. Not surprisingly she was quite opposed to Diderot and Coquelin in feeling that an actress could not move her audience unless she herself were moved. Even then she had that sense of double awareness an actor often has, of acting a part and being it, simultaneously. Graham Robertson tells the story of sitting off stage with Ellen Terry, quietly discussing business, as she waited for her last entrance as Rosamund in *Becket* – she runs down the steps from the cathedral choir to the dying Becket – when he received no answer:

I looked round and found Rosamund de Clifford beside me, pale and breathless. Her eyes fixed and full of a gradually growing horror, deaf and blind to everything but the mimic murder on the dark stage below. The dying words of Becket floated up – 'Into Thy hands, O Lord, into Thy hands' – she clutched my shoulder tightly, seeming to struggle for speech which would not come, until at last a long gasping cry broke from her lips as she tottered forward and began to run down the steps. Even as she ran the moment of identity with Rosamund passed, and Ellen Terry whispered back, 'Missed it again! I never can *time* that cry right.'[62]

One can be quite sure, however, that by the time she reached the stage she was Rosamund again.

This identification with, or rather possession of a character was especially strong in Shakespeare. It was noted that in Beatrice she came nearer than in any other part to playing Ellen Terry, and in Portia, as William Winter put it, she 'had only to be herself in order to make it real'.[63] Every actor, of course, has some special quality or qualities of manner, personality, and character which identify him in every part played, to a greater or lesser extent depending upon the desire and ability to change into another sort of person. Both Duse and Bernhardt had such readily identifiable qualities and exhibited them in a variety of characters. Terry, however, appears to have been different. It is hard to think of another nineteenth-century actor or actress who achieved such a great reputation playing himself or herself. Her own character was marked, at the least, by a fundamental innocence and sincerity, strong romantic feeling, strength of mind, an ability to endure suffering and hardship, an infectious gaiety and playfulness, and an indefinable beauty of personality that was everywhere recognized and appreciated. When she found a dramatic character containing some of these qualities – Portia, Desdemona, Imogen, Beatrice, Hermione, Olivia, Margaret in *Faust* – she did her best work in the theatre, not because she was *playing* or *impersonating* that character, but because she was playing herself, with the character's attributes subsumed into her own character and her own art. This distinctive method substantially contributed to her great popularity. Shaw summed up this special kind of appeal:

Although she was soundly skilled in the technique of her profession she never needed to perform any remarkable feat of impersonation: the spectators would have resented it: they did not want Ellen Terry to be Olivia Primrose: they wanted Olivia Primrose to be Ellen Terry . . . she had only to play a part 'straight', as actors say, to transfigure it into something much better than its raw self.[64]

Such an approach to character sounds instinctive rather than thought out, and no doubt it was; nevertheless the passage from instinctual conception to the development of the character's stage life was carefully planned as to idea, movement, speech, and gesture. Ellen Terry often looked to audiences as if she were not really acting at all, as if she were easily and spontaneously being someone else quite like herself. Behind this seeming artlessness – as is always true in acting of this kind – was a great deal of art and a great deal of thought. She prepared her role with much care and attention to detail. When asked what she remembered about the first ten years at the Lyceum, she replied 'work', and recalled that apart from rehearsing and acting, 'twenty-five reference books were a "simple coming-in" for one part'.[65] Her principal method, aside from contextual study, was to annotate her part in the play before and during rehearsals, not just in one copy but in several. In her working library she possessed four annotated copies of Wills's *Faust*, five of *Coriolanus*, and six of *Much Ado About Nothing*. Sometimes, as in the case of *Faust* and *King Lear*, they were texts privately printed by Irving for the benefit of his company, sometimes standard publishers' editions. Not all copies of the same play were equally annotated: one might be scribbled all over with notes and another might contain only textual deletions and the occasional comment. Such notes can be interpretive of character, instructions to herself on how to look, on how to say a line, laudatory or acidulous comments on other performances, questions about the meaning of words and lines, remarks on pace, mood, and climax – in short, just the sort of thorough annotation a hard-working actress would make in a copy of the text she was preparing, except that the annotation is clearly and characteristically by Ellen Terry and nobody else.

The best illustration of this method is to examine the way in which a part was prepared. Her observations on the characters of Macbeth and Lady Macbeth and her extensive notes on the latter, perhaps the most detailed commentary in any of her preparation books, have been quoted by Roger Manvell,[66] but a relatively unknown preparation book for *King Lear*, which came to light only in the last few years, is almost as good an example.[67] Ellen Terry played Cordelia at the Lyceum in 1892 and scored a personal success, despite Irving's inaudibility on the first night and the relative failure of the production. The copy of *King Lear* she used was Irving's first adaptation of the text, which he had printed and distributed to his cast. (A second privately printed adaptation followed, which became the acting text.) This copy is interleaved with blank pages, which are annotated in the margins and on the interleaves, mostly in pencil with ink occasionally written over the pencil.

Cordelia, the actress thought, 'is a most difficult part. So little to say, so much to feel!'[68] Her initial conception of the character, of whom she says very little in her *Four Lectures on Shakespeare*, is set down beside the *dramatis personae*:

Undemonstrative. Still: A singing voice – 'soft gentle & low' – About 25 years old I sh^d say: Nice looking, for the King of France took her without any Dowre for respect of her person and amiable virtues. The servants of the Court loved her – (The Fool 'pines away' when she marries and goes to France.) The Earl of Kent loved her dearly – she has a 'ripe lip'.

She is 'a good woman: a Lady: a Gentlewoman'. Her attitude to studying the part is a mixture of the conventional and the unusual:

First study the words: then say the words in imaginary dresses, this or that one may have thought about & _get the dress-maker to work_: (having decided) Then _think_ and _think_ (with the book & without it) by day at home or in the fields – at night in bed, about the character – & then try _aloud_ the various methods of producing it upon the public/what I intend to do.

Her costume must be 'all crinkly', 'purfled fabrics'. The setting of _Lear_ is 'a long time ago!! The Romans left many landmarks' – which accords with Irving's statement in his Preface that he accepted Ford Madox Brown's suggestion of 'a time shortly after the departure of the Romans, when the Britons would naturally inhabit the houses left'. Despite 'storms & cold nights', 'it is summer for our Play', and she insists at the beginning of the storm scene, '_Still_, it is summer, _summer_.'

In the first scene of the play, after Lear is seated on his throne, Ellen Terry instructs herself to 'arrange his cushions – attend to him – quite quietly all the time: still – & cold ['cold' crossed out] undemonstrative'. Cordelia's reaction to the protestations of love offered by Goneril and Regan is '_Disgust_: that's all she can do'. For 'What shall Cordelia do? Love and be silent', the actress notes, 'Shd like to say this _very_ quietly – so must be _alone_ apart – remote: or Lear's business will swamp Cordelia.' Before Lear's command 'Speak', she writes 'I'd like a pause – then Cor. to come up slowly & stand silently before L.' 'Shake the head first' is the instruction before 'Nothing, my lord'. (On 'Nothing will come of nothing' she remembers the 'grim humour alluding to the map – _C.K._, not the only reference to Charles Kean's 1858 Lear in the rehearsal copy.) For 'Obey you, love you, and most honour you', emotion is 'to be suppressed at once' on 'love you', and then 'most honour you' is to be said 'firmly'. The first phrase of 'So young, my lord, and true' bears the note 'slither over'; 'and true' is then to be heavily stressed. Surprise is expressed on 'Why have my sisters husbands?' After her rejection by Lear, Cordelia is to show 'no sign of extra emotion at the _property_ being given away'. During this scene Ellen Terry also notes aspects of Irving's Lear, or of what she would like Lear to do, such as 'L. sh^d rise to full height looking white and dangerous' on 'The bow is bent and drawn, make from the shaft'. From his 'Out of my sight' to 'On thine allegiance, hear me' there is 'a crescendo of passion on L's part', it being noted that 'C.K. worked this up very well.' However, Irving is deemed more effective: 'Great bustle – Climax: "on thine allegiance" up to "full height". A climax of QUIET. Much more powerful with H.I.'

For the remainder of the scene Ellen Terry is as concerned with other performances as her own. She does not care for the virtually simultaneous exit of Kent and entrance of Gloster (Irving's spelling), 'although it *is* S'. When he requests his dowry, Burgundy is described as 'smiling suave', and when Lear tell him 'But now her price is fall'n' there is 'Sensation! Burgundy leaves off smiling.' Her dislike of Burgundy is confirmed by her subtextual reading of

> Pardon me, royal sir;
> Election makes not up on such conditions.

as 'Oh excuse me – really – mm – I think that'. Throughout this, Cordelia stands stage centre; 'she sh^d show she loves France: & he her', and when she begins the 'I beseech your Majesty . . .' speech, 'she does not like it that France sh^d think ill of her & she speaks eagerly (for *her*) and asks for justification in his eyes'. Cordelia's farewell to her sisters can serve as an example of the way in which a speech is marked for delivery:

> I know you what you are//
> And, like a sister, am most loathe to call
> Your faults as they are nam'd. Love well our father:
> To your professèd bosoms I commit him:
> But yet//alas/stood I within his grace,
> I would prefer him to a better place.

The first line of this is marked 'aside', and in the margin by the rest of the speech is 'Spirit – Character'. Goneril and Regan are heartily despised. The former is described on the *dramatis personae* page as 'a brutish woman', the latter as 'a Cat, almost worse than her sister, more cruel', and at the end of the first scene are uncomplimentary drawings of them both. It is noted additionally in the text that Goneril has 'loose thick lips' and Regan 'sloping shoulders'.

The scene of Lear's awakening is fully annotated. To Irving's initial stage direction '*Enter* CORDELIA *and* KENT' Ellen Terry adds '& DOCTOR' and asks, 'Could the 2 be standing at Tent Entrance talking together. The Doctor bending over Lear: approaching them as he speaks: 2 men sitting on floor with Harps.' Cordelia's

> Was this a face
> To be opposed against the warring winds?
> My enemy's dog . . .

is to be said 'with great strength', and the opening of Lear's 'Pray do not mock me' speech must be 'Oh so quiet – *please* with *sense*'. At the end of this speech she remembers that 'K. [Charles Kean] "worked this up" to a point: I think it entirely wrong to do so. It sh^d be I think done *exactly opposite* to any *show* of emotion.' Cordelia's 'No cause, no cause' is to be spoken 'soothingly – she weeps at it'. Almost all critics and the general public agreed that this scene was most moving and intensely pathetic, the highlight of the production. Indeed, Lear's 'Pray you now, forget and forgive: I'm old and foolish' carries with it after the comment '*All quiet* – I hope' an exultant note, 'Oh Lord: We all shall cry together.' In Cordelia's final scene Lear's 'Come let's away to prison' speech is accompanied by the reflection that 'Lear here sh^d be very sane: & bright & happy & pathetic.' Already the actress is thinking of how she would look when carried on dead in Lear's arms, for she notes that 'I think I sh^d wear heavy serge (white) in this & next – *too long* – for falling in last act.' Since in this last scene the pages of the rehearsal copy are missing after Lear's line 'I've seen the day, with my good biting falchion . . .' we are deprived of any remarks she might have made upon the end of the play.

Ellen Terry's preparation for a role did not only include the study of character and lines to speak. We have seen how, with Ophelia, she undertook a preliminary examination of madness *in situ*, and with Juliet how (unrewardingly as it turned out) she read what criticism of Juliet she could find and accounts of other interpretations. When she first rehearsed Portia in 1875 she knew not only every word of her part, 'but every detail of that period of Venetian splendour in which the action of the play takes place. I have studied Vecellio.'[69] A contextual study of art and costume was quite appropriate to an actress educated in these matters by Godwin and steeped in the artistic values of the Aesthetic movement. It was also directly relevant to the playing of Portia, for, as she recalled, 'I played the part more stiffly and slowly at the Prince of Wales's than I did in later years. I moved and spoke more slowly. The clothes seemed to demand it, and the setting of the play developed the Italian feeling in it, and let the English Elizabethan side take care of itself.'[70]

Like any good actress Ellen Terry did not stop thinking about her performance after the first night. She was still reflecting on Portia years later, and Beatrice was the object of constant attention. Commenting in her diary upon the revival of *Much Ado About Nothing* – nine years after she had first played the part with Irving and eleven years after playing it on tour with Charles Kelly – she noted with satisfaction that she had made Beatrice 'a nobler woman'. Two days later, she 'played the Church scene all right at last. More of a *blaze* . . . The last scene, too, I made much more merry, happy, *soft*.' The next day she gave a more extended view of Beatrice and what should be done with her, characterized by the string of emphatic adjectives descriptive of character that one sometimes finds in the preparation books:

I must make Beatrice more *flashing* at first, and *softer* afterwards. This will be an improvement upon my old reading of the part. She must always be *merry* and by turns scornful, tormenting, vexed, self-communing, absent, melting, teasing, brilliant, indignant, *sad-merry*, thoughtful, withering, gentle, humorous, and gay, Gay, *Gay*! Protesting (to Hero), motherly, very intellectual – a gallant creature and complete in mind and feature.[71]

Ellen Terry faced particular difficulties in preparing and acting a role which remained with her all her life. She found it hard to manage a sustained effort in a single scene, and was relieved to act an Ophelia who can accumulate impressions and effects until the mad scene. The scene in *Cymbeline* where Imogen awakes to find a headless body was extremely trying, as she complained to Shaw; she was forced to cut her long discovery speech despite the loss of beautiful lines, 'for the emotional parts just kill me, and a sustained effort at that moment would probably make me mad. I should laugh – or die.'[72] With such a view of 'emotional parts' as that, it is hardly remarkable that Terry did not have the reputation of a tragic actress. Indeed, in her autobiography, admitting her lack of power to sustain, she declared, 'On the stage I can pass swiftly from one effort to another, but I cannot fix *one*, and dwell on it, with that superb concentration which seems to me the special attribute of the tragic actress. To sustain, with me, is to lose the impression that I have created, not to increase its intensity.'[73] Undoubtedly her other attributes of restlessness, vivacity, and quickness on stage worked against such a concentration.

Her other problem was forgetting lines, initially an aspect of first-night nerves, but later of genuine forgetfulness and increasing age. The great success of the first night of her Prince of Wales's Portia was, according to Clement Scott, 'Constantly threatened by a paralysis of nervousness which was resisted with extreme difficulty'.[74] Twenty-four years later she had trouble with her lines on the first night of *Robespierre*, and Max Beerbohm noted of the opening of *Captain Brassbound's Conversion* in 1906, in which she acted Cicely Wayneflete (the only time Shaw could persuade her to appear in one of his plays), that despite her vivacity she was very nervous, and 'often at a loss when it was most necessary that she should take her cue instantly'.[75] By 1906, however, Ellen Terry was nearly sixty and did not find it so easy to tackle new parts. Gordon Craig recalled that by the mid 1890s, when she forgot her words, she 'would click her fingers toward the prompt corner – ask for her line. She even did more – she would write out her part on pieces of paper and pin these up all over the stage – on a window-curtain, a chair-back, a lampshade – anywhere and everywhere.' Craig believed that the failures of memory in later years were mostly associated with new parts in indifferent plays which she disliked acting, such as Madame Sans-Gêne in Sardou's play of that name (1897) and Clarisse in *Robespierre*. She could not, said Craig, bring herself to learn bad lines properly, and did not improve matters by rewriting many of them to her own taste.[76]

If her memory was sometimes at fault, nobody in the audience or among the critics really minded. In the general and long-lasting chorus of praise that greeted Ellen Terry's acting, which the occasional detractor found monotonously repetitive, one of the words used over and over again to describe her performance is 'charm'; so frequently was it employed that she herself wearied of it. 'Charm' is elusive; as a critical term it tells us almost nothing about acting, and nineteenth-century English critics notoriously fail to define their terms in relation to what actually happens on stage. Not so the French, and it may be helpful to turn to Sarah Bernhardt's attempt to encompass the word's ambiguities in a single definition:

You must have this charm to reach the pinnacle. It is made of everything and of nothing; the striving will, the look, the walk, the proportions of the body, the sound of the voice, the ease of the gestures. It is not at all necessary to be handsome or to be pretty; all that is needful is charm, the charm that holds the attention of the spectator, so that he listens rapt . . . There is the charm that emanates from a feline grace made up of pretty movements, the charm that steals over you through the musical sound of the voice, the charm wafted from a person whose soul is clean and loyal, the charm not less taking of a subtle and elaborate brain, and the poetic charm that is the most delusive of all, for it is only a flimsy armour against the material blemishes of nature. Nevertheless, the charm of poetry in a woman is the most captivating of all. Then there is the charm exuded by a healthy and lively person, and that lasts the shortest time of all.[77]

Of these various types of charm Ellen Terry possessed the grace of movement (although 'feline' is not the right word for her), the music of voice, the 'clean and loyal' ('propre et loyale') soul – her much-praised innocence and devotion in love and adversity – and the poetry of womanhood, at first a sweet 'girlishness', then an admired 'womanliness'.

Not for a short time only, but for many years Terry captivated audiences with her youth and liveliness, and until late in her career always looked much younger on stage than she was. The charm of a 'subtle and elaborate brain' was not hers, but no English critic would have included this characteristic in any definition of charm. Bernhardt's list is difficult to transpose as a whole to the performance of nineteenth-century English actresses or to any one of them in particular, but it is striking how accurately and how usefully it accounts for much of Ellen Terry's appeal, if one can call that part of this appeal 'charm'.

She was not only 'charming' but also 'natural', another word that commonly recurs in descriptions of her acting. Of all critical terms since acting began, this is the hardest to define, for obviously what was 'natural' to the audiences of one period or one country is nothing of the sort to audiences of another period or another country. In Terry's case, however, we have already gone to the heart of the matter: she was 'natural' when, with the greatest of stage art, she was 'being herself', acting gracefully and with apparent ease, taking a character into her own personality rather than impersonating it. A typical remark which encapsulates this kind of 'nature' occurs in Clement Scott's description of her as Juliet in the scene of parting with Romeo, a scene 'instinct with charm and consistently natural. It was not acting at all, so true was it to the nature of such a Juliet at that moment.'[78] The terms 'natural grace' and 'natural beauty' frequently characterized her movement on stage – Scott used the former in this review – and even her voice was considered 'natural' in certain roles, Shakespeare not exempt. Gordon Craig said that when his mother spoke Shakespeare's prose 'it was as though she but repeated something she had heard at home, something said that morning. It seemed the easiest thing in the world to do, and the unskilful part of the world supposed that it was as easy as it seemed, and that, being easy, it could not be acting – it must be what is called "natural".'[79]

The trinity of critical vocabulary was made complete with 'graceful'. Grace, like charm, is 'irresistible' or 'unrivalled' or 'exquisite'. When one examines its use more closely, one sees that it usually refers to the actress's movements, 'the very poetry of motion' as Scott put it. Of her gestures on stage little is ascertainable, except that they were 'large', and specific descriptions of facial expressions are also lacking. But there is at least some evidence about stage movement. There are numerous photographs of Terry in character and many drawings published in magazines, but none of these gives any sense of motion upon the stage. Nor are the preparation books marked precisely for types of movement; all we find here are general directions for crosses, stage positions, and the occasional instruction like 'She, left behind – dazed – turn weary – faint & stagger to the throne – Alone – *Isolation*' at the end of the banquet scene in *Macbeth*. These instructions, however, do not tell us exactly *how* she moved, and without a cinematic record we will not know.

Nevertheless, Ellen Terry's contemporaries did try to describe the way she moved about the stage, and they resorted to analogies in order to do so. George Augustus Sala referred to 'the manner in which she floats rather than walks in exquisitely contrived draperies',[80] a word also employed by Clement Scott in a comment upon the lines on Beatrice:

> For look where Beatrice like a lapwing runs
> Close by the ground to hear our conference.

Scott asks, 'Is this not an exquisite description of the Ellen Terry movement which others so ludicrously attempt to imitate? She does not run off the stage, or skip up the steps of an Italian garden. She simply floats seemingly on the air. A more exquisitely graceful movement has never been seen from any other actress.'[81] Interestingly, Terry told Shaw, when he reproached her for fidgeting upon the stage, 'Do you know, I have no weight on the stage: unless I have heavy robes I cannot keep on the ground', and in connection with *Cymbeline* rehearsals wrote that 'though I may *seem* like myself to others, I never *feel* like myself when I am acting, but someone else, so nice, and so young and so happy, and always in-the-air, light and bodyless'.[82] Was this gaiety spun out of air, to paraphrase a felicitous metaphor of Bram Stoker's, a factor in making her movement appear so light and weightless? Was it the assumption of youth, happiness, joy, and love which contributed to her distinctive style of movement? If so, it was no mere matter of technique.

Some actors walk upon the stage in a way quite unlike their walk in daily life. Irving's walk, for example, was unrecognizable as soon as he stepped into a scene. Ellen Terry's stage movement was clearly related to her offstage walk. Before she started rehearsals at the Lyceum for *Hamlet*, Stoker noticed her 'fine form, the easy rhythmic sway, the large, graceful, goddess-like way in which she moved' – a somewhat rhapsodical description, but helpful. He also noted, when she was not playing a pathetic scene – and here the style of movement must necessarily have been heavier and slower – that her movement 'always gave one the idea of a graceful dance'.[83] The physical restlessness remarked by Shaw and others, and admitted by the actress herself, was an essential part of her style. Gordon Craig contrasted Irving, sometimes 'so still – seldom moving' with Terry; 'she was all movement . . . even with her head in a bag she would have captured the house. Tie her hands and ankles, and it would have been much harder. So it would seem as though much lay with her, in her movement – and indeed, an entrance with her was a gliding eager thing. She was very rapid in her light, long strides.'[84] Resorting to the familiar vocabulary, but also being analogically illuminating, Elisabeth Fagan saw her movement as through water:

Grace and Ellen Terry were one – graceful movement was as much a part of her as it is of running water. Of course, when the play required it she could be absolutely still and express everything without movement of either face or hands . . . she had, of course, this power, but when it was not needed she loved to move, to swim about the stage – not a human's swimming: a bird's, say a swan's – and when it was not essential to the play that she should be in any particular position, one never could be quite sure which exit she would take, or from which side she would address one.[85]

Floating, dancing, gliding, swimming – none of these words precisely pin down Ellen Terry's 'poetry of motion', and are inexact as analogies always will be. However, they do take us a long way into understanding at least the essence and quality of her movement, which was unique among actresses of her time.

More evidence survives for the sound of Ellen Terry's voice than for the look of her movement. Aside from the views of critics and associates, we have a good idea from the preparation books of how carefully she worked on the *sound* of her lines, their emphasis, tones, and pauses, and we can at least grasp from this evidence what she intended to do with them in performance. Her own advice on voice, recorded on a blank leaf of a manuscript lecture on Shakespeare's 'Pathetic Women', is remarkably close in attitude to her method of approaching a character: 'Get yourself into tune. Then you can let fly y^r. imagination & the words will seem to be supplied by yourself!!! Shakespeare supplied by oneself!!! Oh! . . . to Act, you must make the thing written your own – you must steal the words – steal the thought – convey these to others with great art.' She also recorded five speeches and parts of scenes from Shakespeare, so that it is possible to hear her voice and make observations based on certain evidence as long as two things are borne in mind: we do not hear what she said on stage, but studio recordings made in fairly primitive conditions by an actress quite unfamiliar with sound recording as it then was. Secondly, she was sixty-three when she made them; she was doing no stage work at the time, and her voice is recognizably elderly. Nevertheless, they are a great deal better than nothing, and tell us at least something about her vocal technique.

Sifting through the many remarks of contemporaries, we can establish general notions about Ellen Terry's voice. Clearly, the elocution lessons with her father and her early training with the Keans had been most valuable. She never had the slightest difficulty later in life making herself heard, and her voice seemed effortlessly to penetrate the furthest reaches of the gallery no matter how large the theatre. Mrs Kean would sit in the Princess's gallery until she was satisfied she could hear every word uttered by the child on stage. At the Princess's she was much impressed by the 'great beauty' of Charles Kean's voice, 'so soft and low, yet distinct and clear as a bell', with which Kean could keep a house spellbound.[86] The self-direction to keep her voice low frequently occurs in the preparation books, and although she by no means relied on voice alone to captivate an audience she must have absorbed something of the importance of beauty in acting from Kean. Her articulation, we are told, like Kean's, was perfect, her voice 'slightly veiled' (Shaw's description) and often, in scenes of pathetic emotion, 'deep' and 'choked'. She said herself that she sometimes spoke too loudly and that Irving used to stand in the wings and drop a handkerchief whenever she shouted.[87] Craig described her delivery as 'measured', and Sala mentioned the 'musical, albeit slightly monotonous cadence of her recitative'.[88] Her vibrato was not, by the evidence of the records, as strong as Bernhardt's, but it was marked, and reviewers did note a 'throb' in emotional speeches.

The recordings well illustrate both the vibrato and the musicality. They were made in America in 1911 when Ellen Terry was on tour with her Shakespeare lectures, and there are five altogether: the later part of Ophelia's mad scene in *Hamlet* (act IV, scene 5), with the actress also speaking Laertes's lines; what the Victorians called the Potion Scene in *Romeo and Juliet* (act IV, scene 3), where Juliet soliloquizes before taking the drug; Portia's 'The quality of mercy' speech from *The Merchant of Venice* (act IV, scene 1); the playful dialogue between Mamillius, Hermione, and her ladies from *The Winter's Tale* (act II, scene 1), and part of act II, scene 1 of *Much Ado About Nothing*, again with the actress speaking other lines besides her own as Beatrice. Both the *Winter's Tale* and *Much Ado* excerpts are conversational and quiet – or 'natural' – and the pace is relaxed and unforced, even casual, especially in *Much Ado*, although one is still aware of the elocutionary quality, the musicality of pitch, and the vibrato. 'The quality of mercy' is a formal declaration, a recitation rather than a plea, but it is hard to judge it, as it is hard to judge the other pieces, given in isolation as they are from all dramatic context. Certainly, despite some vibrato, there is no real sign of the 'tender and trembling accents' in the verse which Clement Scott heard upon the delivery of this speech at the Lyceum in 1879. In the Ophelia scene, the madness and the singing seem too refined and prettified to be dramatically convincing to the modern ear, but it is interesting to note the prolongation of the sounds of pain and grief. For instance, in 'O you must wear your rue with a difference' the 'O' is very long, the voice rising at the beginning of the vowel and descending at the end, converting a textual exclamation of no consequence into a mournful wail pregnant with sorrow. As in all the speeches the basic tendency is to linger on the longer vowels, pitch the voice musically in a kind of cadence, and indicate deep emotion by intensifying the vibrato; in spite of the age of the speaker the voice is sweet and melodious.

All these qualities are apparent and perhaps best illustrated in the most interesting excerpt, Juliet's soliloquy, which is fittingly given a much more emotional rendition than the other speeches and achieves a degree of fear and terror that contemporary critics did not on the whole believe Terry's Juliet managed in the theatre. Several examples can be offered. On 'No, no, this shall forbid it' the opening vowels are once again long, the first rising, the second falling. 'I fear it is, and yet methinks it should not' is spoken so that every word is lingeringly delivered and given on a different musical note. Even the 'Or' in 'Or, if I live' contains a long vowel, as does 'green' in 'bloody Tybalt, yet but green in earth'. The 'O' in 'O if I wake' is even stronger and longer than the equivalent exclamation in the line quoted from Ophelia's mad scene, and resembles Bernhardt's much resorted to wordless wails of grief. In 'Stay, Tybalt, stay' each 'stay' is measurably prolonged on the same note, so that the three words become an incantatory address. One sees what Sala means by using the word 'recitative'; there is something operatic about the voice, even early in the twentieth century, and there is no doubt about its musical beauty or the musical structure of the speeches. Whether it is dramatically appropriate to the content, or whether it might be judged somewhat formalized and

16   Ellen Terry as Juliet

detached from dramatic involvement can only be a modern point of view, which may or may not be correct by the standards of present-day acting, but which does not take into account the conditions of recording, the age of the actress, and the whole nature of nineteenth-century acting.

The preparation books document the study that went into the speaking of lines. Markings for voice are precise. We have seen evidence of this

17   Ellen Terry as Lady Macbeth

precision in the *King Lear* preparation book, notably Cordelia's reply to Lear in the first scene of the play. The *Macbeth* preparation books are detailed. On the line in Macbeth's letter, 'This I have thought good to deliver thee, my dearest partner of greatness', the word 'greatness' has the comment 'linger on this smiling'. With the arrival of the messenger, 'He brings great news./The raven himself is hoarse . . .' is 'Low – High: Breathless'. When Lady Macbeth chides Macbeth for cowardice, the voice is to be 'deep' and 'low', 'Low down voice always'; the lines

> And dashed the brains out, had I sworn as you
> Have done to this.

are notated 'Stirred–deep–slow'. A 'deep voice' is also to be used on the line 'Gentle my lord,/Sleek o'er your rugged looks.' At the end of the banquet scene

> Stand not upon the order of your going,
> But go at once.

is spoken with 'Voice choked–Alarm–Hurry. Convulsive fear'. The lines from the sleep-walking scene, 'Out damned spot, out I say! One – two – why then 'tis time to do't' are carefully marked. 'Damned' is high, followed by a pause; 'spot' is also followed by a pause; 'one – two' is low and long, and 'why then 'tis time to do't' is whispered.

The results of this meticulous preliminary breakdown of the structure of lines and their marking for stresses, pauses, tone, and pace were given life on stage in Ellen Terry's own style of delivery, combined of course with her expression of character and action by physical and visual means. Scott recalled how she delivered Beatrice's outburst, 'O God that I were a man! I would eat his heart in the market-place!' Scott held this to be an original reading, not the cry of a vixen or the scream of a shrew, 'but a sudden passionate sob of suppressed emotion'. He remarked a long pause after 'I would', as if Beatrice were too indignant to utter her thoughts, 'but soon, with a wounded cry, and with rage expressed in the scarcely suppressed tears' came the rest of the line.[89] The power of Ellen Terry's emotion much affected audiences. In the Lyceum *Faust* the despairing Margaret, betrayed and abandoned by Faust, her mother murdered by Mephistopheles's fatal draught, comes to pray to a statue of the Virgin, laying flowers at its feet. W. C. Wills's blank verse is not memorable, but serviceable for the occasion. The speech ends thus:

> These flowers I bring are watered by my tears.
> Oh, heal this bleeding heart – oh, rescue me

> From death and shame! Mother of many saviours!
> Have pity, oh, have pity – turn to me!

For the second line the note in the preparation book is 'More passion then burst out more passionately.' 'Mother of many saviours!' must be spoken 'with loving entreaty', and the instruction for the whole speech is 'Voice must be under cool control – must SING all this.' Annotation of this kind tells us something from the rehearsal point of view; it remains for a spectator to supply the audience point of view: 'The absolute truth of Miss Terry's acting . . . brought tears to the eyes of the most hardened in the audience. Her deep pleading voice – that wonderful voice of hers – half-choked with sobs that poured forth the pitiable lamentation' was deeply impressive; 'every word and every tone told upon the audience . . . Here was pathos drawn to its finest point.'[90] After the death of Valentine, Margaret again prays to the Virgin, a prayer that begins:

> Oh, who but thou canst know my agony?
> I have no refuge now but thee!

The note here is to dwell on 'agony', sing 'I have no refuge now' and '*press out*' the word 'thee'. In the final scene of *Faust* Margaret, who has gone mad, refuses to flee from her cell with Faust:

> To-morrow I must die,
> And I must tell thee how to range the graves.
> My mother the best place – next her my brother,
> Me well apart, but, dearest, not too far,
> And by my side my little one shall lie.

She delivered this speech with great feeling and dramatic power; the effect upon the audience and Clement Scott was overwhelming: 'The expression put into the words, ' "But, dearest, not too far", is beyond description. It went straight to the heart. This scene, acted with such mingled purity, pathos, and intensity, was the climax of one of the most beautiful and remarkable performances Miss Ellen Terry has ever given to the stage.'[91]

The actress's voice, then, would seem on balance to have been as significant an element in her art as her movement. It was particularly beautiful and expressive in scenes of high or light comedy, pathos, and romantic love. Commenting on what she alone could contribute to the English stage, Mowbray Morris said of Ellen Terry's Desdemona that in her appeal to the Duke for her husband, her plea for Cassio, and her sadness before Iago, 'We get what none other of her contemporaries can give . . . this seeming simple tenderness and grace, these "tears in the

18   Ellen Terry as Margaret in W. G. Wills's *Faust*

voice", as the French say – in a word this charm, for there is indeed no other word that can so fully denote this rare and delicate quality'.[92] The pathos of Desdemona, the 'piteous pleadings and remonstrances that went straight to the heart',[93] as another critic put it, showed the actress's power in scenes of this kind, scenes that were dependent for their effect upon the voice, gesture, and facial expression rather than movement. Margaret too was essentially a pathetic part, although also, like Desdemona, a woman in love – another of Terry's strong suits. William Winter declared that she was among the first actresses to show Portia as a lover, 'a woman knowing herself to be loved and radiant with happiness because of that knowledge'.[94] Her love-making was indeed much praised; it too was natural, at least in the sense she contrasted her own style with Bernhardt's. The Frenchwoman, she thought, was so extraordinarily decorative and symbolic on stage that she transcended personal and individual feeling; she played love scenes beautifully, but she was playing a *picture* of love, whereas her own style is 'a suggestion of the ordinary human passion as felt by ordinary human people'.[95] The pathetic predicament of Desdemona and Margaret is a consequence not only of love and tender trust, but also of innocence; it was not a coincidence that in significant scenes in each play Terry played both of them – and Ophelia, Cordelia, and Hermione – in white. It is also not surprising that she conveyed so convincing an impression of guileless girlishness; genuine innocence and sincerity would have been essential attributes of this girlishness, and these, from the standpoint of both technique and personality, the actress possessed in ample measure.

Ellen Terry's strength in playing innocence, romantic love, and pathos was, paradoxically, a weakness in the portrayal of characters requiring tragic force. The prime example of this weakness was Lady Macbeth. In her *Four Lectures on Shakespeare*, Terry classified her with Shakespeare's 'pathetic' women, a woman in love with her husband who does her best to satisfy his ambition and her own, but who finds herself in a pathetic situation when he becomes estranged from her. The sleep-walking scene she played effectively, but for pathos rather than haunted and broken grandeur. Gordon Craig concluded from this scene that 'you did not shudder at the thought beneath the words: "The Thane of Fife had a wife – where is she now?" You only felt: "Poor Ellen Terry – she is so sorry for the Thane of Fife's wife, and is wondering where she can possibly be now, poor, poor, dear. What a *nice* woman!"'[96] She did not conceive of the character as larger than life, noting in her preparation book beside the 'Come ye spirits . . . unsex me here' speech, 'She feels she has only a *woman's* strength & calls on "Spirits".' At the end of act I, scene 7 she wrote in large letters, 'She loved her babies & she could not kill the man who looked like her Father (*Woman*).' Of Lady Macbeth's fainting, she commented, 'That's *Just* like a woman.' One of her biographers greatly admired her appearance as Lady Macbeth in the splendid beetle-wing robes, and believed that any man would do the bidding of such a commanding and beautiful creature. Yet, 'she seemed to content herself with presenting an attractive, affectionate, and devoted wife . . . Despite her collusion in the series of cruel murders that were designed to clear the Thane of Cawdor's way to the throne, she was always feminine.'[97] Because she was so feminine her nature was frail, and it collapsed under the weight of guilt, remorse, and Macbeth's estrangement. If Lady Macbeth were a wife, a mother, and a Victorian woman, it is hard to see, even given the best efforts of the actress in the part (which were considerable), how the character could have possessed tragic, rather than merely pathetic stature.

The fundamental womanliness of this interpretation was repeated in a part which was probably even less suited to it, Volumnia in *Coriolanus* (1901), the last new part she undertook for Irving. Again, as for Lady Macbeth, the touchstone was Mrs Siddons, who played both with commanding authority, tragic dignity, and massive force. Ellen Terry, however, saw the part differently and placed Volumnia at the head of a domestic household. An article by Bram Stoker suggests a reason for the change:

The century which has gone has given woman a truer place in the organisation of the world than existed at its dawn, and with a wider tolerance of woman's ambitions and efforts comes a better understanding of her limitations. Neither women or men of to-day expect a strong man to take orders, no matter how imperiously the orders are given. 'Sweet reasonableness' has a part in the incitement to action, and especially in the persuasion to change.

Stoker went on to approve Terry's view of Volumnia. 'Without altering in meaning a single word of Shakespeare, she has vitalised his creation with her own nature. Her Volumnia is all woman; not weak woman, but woman in all her essential attributes.' The force of such a woman was in 'her silence as well as in her speech', and in 'the sweetness and common-sense of her domestic life as the mistress of a great household', as well as in her moments of authority and ambition for her son. Stoker plainly admired the sight of 'Ellen Terry sitting in her household as a true woman must, interested in the small affairs of daily life.'[98] We have seen how warmly the critics, artists, and audiences of the 1870s welcomed an actress who seemed in so many respects to incarnate the Victorian ideal of young womanhood. Yet this very femininity was a drawback when it came to tackling the larger tragic roles. Ellen Terry may not have possessed the technique necessary to make a tragic heroine out of Juliet or Lady Macbeth, but, more importantly, her personality and her *conception* of such parts prevented her; she was also, in a real sense, trapped in the Victorian ideal she had done so much to disseminate in performance. When she said that the Sargent picture of her as Lady Macbeth contained all that she meant to do, there was obviously another Lady Macbeth lurking within the Lady Macbeth she actually presented,[99] a hidden Ellen Terry who was rarely given a part in which she could 'come out'. Oscar Wilde and Martin-Harvey recognized this second Ellen Terry, but the critics and the audience did not, and doubtless would not have accepted her on the stage.

What Terry wanted to do with a part did not always coincide with her way of playing it. Lady Macbeth is a case in point; Desdemona is another. As has been mentioned, she believed that Desdemona is a strong character best played by a tragic actress with a strong method, a woman more fitted to be the bride of Christ than the bride of man. The actress saw her as another of Shakespeare's 'pathetic' women, but one who (like Ellen Terry herself) is unconventional and 'being devoid of coquetry behaves as she feels', 'genially expressive' rather than 'prim and demure'.[100] Love made a fool out of her, but a fool 'who is the victim of love and faith', not a simpleton.[101] The conception is one of strength of character in a fragile body (Terry thought that 'Othello towers over his fragile Desdemona'),[102] but this strength was not remarked by the critics. Even in the conception there is a paradox: the actress declared that on stage 'my appearance was right – I was such a poor wraith of a thing. But let there be no mistake – it took strength to act this weakness and passiveness of Desdemona's.'[103] To an actor this would be an acting problem and not a paradox, but Ellen Terry herself admitted a divergence between ideas and practice when, in writing of Mrs Siddons's conception of Lady Macbeth – but not her performance of it – as feminine and fragile, she said, 'It is not always possible for us players to portray characters on stage exactly as we see them in imagination . . . It is no use an actress wasting her nervous energy on a battle with her physical attributes. She had much better find a way of employing them as allies.'[104]

The critical reception of Terry's Desdemona is interesting in two respects. Firstly, it does not recognize her conception of the character in the playing of the part, or, to be exact, that aspect of it pertaining to strength and force, clearly perceiving the poor wraith rather than the bride of Christ. Secondly, it illustrates the problems of recreating an Ellen Terry performance from the fog of adjectives used to describe it. Of course the actress had the great disadvantage of playing opposite Irving and Edwin Booth, who alternated Othello and Iago: the critical focus was on these two actors, especially the former, and there is no shortage of fairly precise descriptions of what Irving was actually doing on stage at particular moments in the play. However, when the critics turned – always very briefly – to Desdemona from Othello and Iago, the inevitable adjectives appear and reappear: 'graceful', 'charming', 'delicate', 'natural', 'tender', 'pathetic', 'sweet', and 'exquisite'. In the critical response even her passion seems muted: 'The passionate expression of grief, when she sinks to the ground overwhelmed by Othello's cruel insult, had gained much in plaintive pathos. For the rest, she was a model of grace, beauty, and refinement.'[105] Typical of the emphasis on vaguely Aesthetic generalities was the comment of Dutton Cook, who said that Ellen Terry's Desdemona 'is now one of her most charming performances; very sympathetic, graceful, and picturesque'.[106] *The Times* found her womanly as well as graceful, tender, charming, gentle, playful, and exquisitely pathetic.[107] As has been suggested, it was never easy for Ellen Terry, playing with the dominating Irving for so many years, to get anything like the same critical attention and interest in specific moments of performance that he provoked. The reaction to her Desdemona shows this; yet it also shows (in addition to her evident lack of tragic power) the identification critics made with her Aestheticism – nobody said Irving was Aesthetic – and the difficulties they had in translating a very general understanding of her stage qualities into specific terminology.

It is true that Terry lacked the physical force necessary to attain the heights of dramatic power; Sala thought that she was not physically strong enough for Juliet's soliloquy in the potion scene; 'she simply lacks the *physique* to deliver with sustained force a soliloquy of agonized terror'.[108] The actress freely admitted that *sustaining* emotion was too much for her, and this may have been one reason why she sometimes failed in the great tragic speeches. Her lack of physical force was also noted in Tennyson's Camma; she captured the beauty, the poetry, the tenderness and the Aesthetic style of the part with relative ease, but as the vengeful and vindictive priestess she was unconvincing. She managed the love, gentleness, pathos and grace of the first half of the play, but not the impassioned frenzy of the second, where Camma seeks the death of her husband's murderer. The indignation and bitterness of Pauline in *The Lady of Lyons* also seemed beyond her reach, whereas she caught without difficulty the character's tenderness for and trust in her false lover. Dutton Cook, remarking in passing on the 'girlish grace' of the interpretation, noticed how Terry artfully avoided the rage and scorn in Pauline's reaction to her betrayal and instead emphasized her 'amiable characteristics', showing how Pauline 'is in truth tender, gentle, trusting, loving, and altogether womanly'.[109]

It was hardly Ellen Terry's fault that she excelled in playing those attributes of womanhood deemed perfect and desirable; indeed, she owed a great deal of her success to that ability, but it did limit her. Queen Katharine is undoubtedly a tragic figure, but when Terry played her – a role thought to be outside her range, as it was – what came over was the pathos and womanliness of the character rather than the desolation and the loss, although royal dignity was apparently convincingly enacted. William Winter made an instructive comparison between the two 'loveliest embodiments' of Katharine he had seen upon the American stage. Helen Modjeska, he said, was 'a perfect ideal of a patient sufferer subjected to cruel wrong'; Ellen Terry expressed 'with afflicting simplicity the grief of a heartbroken woman'. The 'supreme beauty' of the latter's performance 'was its intrinsic loveliness of womanhood'.[110] When she acted Hiordis in her son's production of Ibsen's *The Vikings at Helgeland* in 1903, a character whom the press variously described as 'a vicious vixen', a 'warlike and turbulent heroine', and 'a wild Scandinavian amazon', she was again out of her depth. She did attain, according to the reviews, an intensity of method and a dramatic power which were surprising, but one reviewer (with an image of Ellen Terry fixed firmly in his mind from which she would not be allowed to depart) believed that Hiordis was not a character 'to suit a radiant personality the whole and sufficient charm of which depends on temperamental high spirits and true womanliness'.[111] It is doubtful whether, at the age of fifty-six, and with a treacherous memory that did her performance no good at least on the first night, Terry could have really got hold of the fierce and formidable Hiordis. In his worst patronizing vein, Max Beerbohm buried her more deeply in what the critics found acceptable:

It is a melancholy thing to see Miss Ellen Terry, that incarnation of our capricious English sunlight, grappling with the part of Hiordis, and trying so hard not to turn it all 'to favour and to prettiness'. Now and again, she does contrive to break away from herself, but, even so, she is always a pleasant, English abstraction – a genial Britannia ruling unfrozen waves.[112]

The radiance, the sunlight, the high spirits, the womanliness – these were her strengths on stage, it is worth repeating, but they were also her prison, a prison from which she could only peep hesitantly into the light of a harsher and more glaring day.

The Vikings and *Much Ado About Nothing* at the Imperial Theatre represented Ellen Terry's only venture into management, which was financially disastrous. She had few talents as an organizer, a person of business or a producer, as shown by her unfortunate experience – from which she evidently had to be rescued at the final dress rehearsal by Irving – of co-directing Laurence Irving's *Godefroi and Yolande* on tour in Chicago in 1895. She had decided to go briefly into management in order to display the producing and designing talents of her son, Edward Gordon Craig, to the critics and theatre-going public who were almost entirely ignorant of his work. With herself on the stage, the critics and the public would *have* to attend, and in coming to see her acting would become absorbed in and impressed by his revolutionary talent. She took the Imperial in Westminster, an attractive theatre but tributary to the mainstream of theatre-going in Piccadilly, around Leicester Square, and along the Strand, a fact which did not help the box office. Money was spent on reconstructing the stage to accommodate Craig's scenic and lighting designs for *The Vikings*; the numerous properties were expensively made in wood and metal; and Craig's sister Edy had costumes to design for a cast of fifty-six. There were tensions between Craig and the actors, and between Craig and the business manager, with a harried Ellen Terry in the middle. The heavy expenses did not contribute toward a successful run. *The Vikings* opened in April 1903, and closed after only thirty performances. It may have been something of a *succès d'estime* for Craig, but the losses were heavy. The production was replaced after only a two-week interval for mounting and rehearsal by *Much Ado About Nothing*, which was done much more cheaply; Craig was not able to achieve with it what he really wanted. However, his mother recovered some of her losses by touring it successfully in the provinces; an American tour of both productions was considered but did not take place.

At least Ellen Terry's brief tenure of the Imperial offered her the second new part since she left Irving's company, the first being Mistress Page in 1902. As she grew older she became increasingly unsuitable for the younger roles in Irving's repertory, a fact of which she was well aware. She was really too old for Portia, although she continued to play it as well as a new part like Madame Sans-Gêne, but Sardou's play was not popular. Irving's repertory was itself limited by the fire of 1898 which destroyed so much of the Lyceum scenery, knocking plays like *Macbeth* and *Henry VIII* – in which she was certainly not too old for Lady Macbeth and Katharine – out of the repertory; it was just too expensive to remount them. *Faust*, however, was remounted for a revival in 1902, but Irving chose another, younger actress to play Margaret. Thus Ellen Terry's association with Irving and the Lyceum – now in the hands of a joint-stock company – had to end if she were to play any worthwhile parts at all.

The Lyceum in the period of Irving's sole management from 1878 to 1899 was the national flagship of the impressive fleet of playhouses under the captaincy of a group of actor–managers in the full late Victorian glory of their power and influence: Irving (the Admiral), Tree, George Alexander, John Hare, Charles Wyndham, Cyril Maude, Wilson Barrett, Squire and Marie Bancroft – the list is a long one. It was run on a repertory largely based on Shakespeare and romantic historical melodramas, many of them commissioned from living authors. Although the solid contributions of a number of long-serving secondary and tertiary actors helped to make Lyceum productions what they were, the theatre's box office was essentially dependent upon its star, Henry Irving, and his leading actress, Ellen Terry. The quality of Irving's productions and the social respectability of the Lyceum – Irving was the first actor to be knighted, in 1895 – also appealed to audiences. The Lyceum was a large long-run theatre with an acting, technical, and administrative staff of several hundred people. With a selection of his most popular pieces, all with full scenery and properties, Irving and the whole company regularly toured the provinces, visiting America eight times: profitable tours which became an absolute financial necessity in the later years when money was lost at the Lyceum itself. On almost all these tours Ellen Terry, who was paid far more than she was in London (much more than Irving himself), accompanied him.

Their partnership was remarkable by any standards. They had acted together for twenty-four years, in twenty-seven plays. It was not by any means a 'partnership' in the sense of equal managerial responsibilities. Irving was undisputed supremo of the Lyceum; he needed Ellen Terry, he paid her well, treated her handsomely, and listened to her advice. But he was solely responsible for hiring actors, choosing the repertory, assigning parts, directing rehearsals, deciding about music, lighting, scenery, costumes and properties. Without Irving and without the Lyceum, Terry would probably have played more comedy and a greater range of parts over twenty-four years, including her beloved Rosalind (Irving never produced *As You Like It*). Essentially, she was unambitious; with Irving and the Lyceum she enjoyed security, the highest standards of production in the contemporary theatre, American tours, and an established and unchallenged position in England's leading theatre. It is true that she had to play parts in a series of romantic and historical melodramas with which she was not always sympathetic, although she excelled in others – the Queen in *Charles I*, Olivia in *The Vicar of Wakefield*, Margaret in *Faust* – but she was also given Ophelia, Portia, Desdemona, Juliet, Beatrice, Viola, Lady Macbeth, Katharine, Cordelia, Imogen, and Volumnia: hardly a list to complain of. Before she joined the Lyceum, she was not, despite her Portia in 1875, a Shakespearean actress; Irving made her one.

Playing opposite Irving, whom Ellen Terry admired enormously (but not unreservedly) as a man and an actor, had its problems. In rehearsal Irving let her go her own way, relying on her talent and judgement, while he endlessly rehearsed lesser performers and the limelight men. As late as 1896 she complained about this to Shaw, who was writing her a series of letters brimming over with advice on playing Imogen (she received none from Irving), for which she was generally grateful:

You must understand I am the person at the Lyceum who is never advised, found fault with, or 'blackguarded' before the production of our plays! Henry finds fault with everyone, and rehearses and rehearses and rehearses and (da capo) them over and over and over again. Then our scenes (his and mine) come on, and he generally says 'Oh, we'll skip those scenes,' and I am to be found in the scene-dock doing it all by myself to myself, or being heard in the words by some girl or boy. Then Henry's scenes come on, and I watch those, and find fault with them (!), and this great advantage is lost *only* to me! . . . It is *frightful* not to be found fault with. Henry wont, cant find time, and the rest are silly and think me a very grand person indeed and would not dare.[113]

Rehearsals at the Lyceum were long and slow, and slowness was also a factor Terry had to take into account when on stage with Irving. He was, on the whole, a measured, deliberate actor, slowly building his effects, whereas his partner's natural tendency was to be quick, light, mercurial; they complemented each other well. She believed, for instance, that she should have been swifter as Beatrice, but had to slow down to accommodate Irving's more leisurely method as Benedick. *The Vicar of Wakefield* also suffered from slowness, in her opinion: 'That was often a fault there (the Lyceum). Because Henry was so slow, the others took their time from him, and the result was bad.'[114] Shaw was annoyed by the tent scene in *King Lear* when the waking Irving 'kept you waiting in an impossible pose for five minutes between "I will not swear" and "these are my hands"'. Irving 'cannot work out his slow, labored, self-absorbed stage conceptions unless you wait for him and play to him. This is a frightful handicap for you.'[115] Shaw was of course violently prejudiced against Irving, and it is most unlikely that this sort of thing was a 'frightful handicap'; a good actress could have adjusted to Irving's rhythms easily enough. Nevertheless, to do so must have meant at least some sacrifice of Ellen Terry's natural style and intention in a part. Perhaps the leading example of such a sacrifice came in *The Merchant of Venice*, where Terry had conceived a very quiet Portia in the trial scene. 'I saw an extraordinary effect in this quietness. But as Henry's Shylock was so quiet, I had to give it up. His heroic saint was splendid, but it wasn't good for Portia.'[116]

Aside from her contribution as an actress, Ellen Terry herself claimed that she brought 'taste and artistic knowledge' to the Lyceum which Irving's upbringing had not developed in him. This may well have been so; her taste in art, in colours, fabrics, and designs had been shaped in a good school. Probably she advised Irving on such matters, but the final decisions were his alone. More important were the sympathy, appreciation, understanding, and companionship she gave him over the years. Each was of benefit to the other. She believed that 'Henry could never have worked with a very strong woman, I might have deteriorated, in partnership with a weaker man whose ends were less fine, whose motives were less pure.'[117]

On a practical level, as a respected member of the Lyceum, Ellen Terry was a great deal of help to her colleagues, especially the younger members of the company. She said of Irving, 'I consider I have been a good deal of use to him as a buffer between him and his company',[118] and she was full of good advice for the other actors which must have been most helpful to Irving in the business of rehearsals. It is apparent from her complaint about *Cymbeline* that she commented on Irving's scenes; and Bram Stoker stated that 'when her own words had been spoken she would devote her whole powers to helping the work of her comrades on the stage'.[119] An interesting account of rehearsals for *Becket* records how she helped a young actor to understand the meaning of a passage and say it correctly, and shows Irving consulting her about the way William Terris as the King should jump over a table. She also looks at the costume sketches, suggests a change in blocking which much improves the scene, works on the music cues – asking the orchestra to play more softly in one scene because she believes that here the music must be subordinated to the action – and positions Rosamund's maid at the back of the stage for a song. At the first dress rehearsal she has a role in determining the proper colour balance for the lighting:

Miss Terry, clad in *Rosamond*'s (sic) magnificent robes, sits in the stalls and watches the effect of the lights upon each group. Sometimes a light is too blue, or too yellow, or too white, and in the first act the rehearsal is stopped several times on this account. When Miss Terry is on the stage, Mr Irving watches the lights; when Mr Irving is acting, she studies each flash.'[120]

Evidence of the careful thinking the actress did about other actors in rehearsal as well as her own role exists in the preparation books. In this respect her notes are of two kinds: points jotted down to pass on to Irving, and comments on what other actors should do. No doubt the annotation concerning the First Player in *Hamlet*, beside the 'Anon he finds him/ Striking too short at Greeks' speech, a withering 'Pretty attitude on a sofa – but *oh*!' would have come to Irving's attention, as would the opinion on the act III, scene 2 exchange between Hamlet, Rosencrantz, and Guildenstern, 'All this interestingly done but nothing meant by the great discovery he had just made.' Indeed, Ellen Terry obviously did not think much of some of the acting at whatever rehearsal stage of the 1878 *Hamlet* the preparation book dates from. Opposite Hamlet's first replies to Gertrude and Claudius is scribbled 'Ugly & flat. Looks a beastly tempered man – not a sad one.' After noting by the 'Angels and ministers of grace defend us!' speech that Hamlet 'shouts & then weeps' and then 'shouts defiantly', she asks 'Where is my gentle Hamlet.' Polonius's speech to Ophelia beginning 'That hath made him mad' is 'Awful', as is Hamlet's 'if his occulted guilt/Do not unkennel itself in one speech'. The 'To be or not to be' soliloquy is 'Jolly bad theatrically', and poor Irving's advice to the Players is also 'Jolly bad'. Whether or not all such vigorous views reached Irving's ears, it is significant that this was the *Hamlet* of her Lyceum début; even at this early stage Irving might well have been seeking the assistance of his new leading lady at rehearsals. The *Macbeth* preparation books also contain many notes on the playing of other parts, and Terry's copy of *King Lear* will serve as a good illustration of both kinds of comment. When Cordelia is not at all involved, the speeches of other characters are sometimes marked for stresses and pauses, exits and entrances are elaborated, and stage business supplied. Most, though not all, of her suggestions for interpretation and business relate to scenes in which Lear is not on stage. After his exit in the first scene of the play, Regan's 'That's most certain, and with you; next month with us' is to be said sharply, Regan 'dawdling up to the Throne: (appearing a casual action)'. Goneril is to accompany 'Pray you, let us hit together' by going slowly to Regan and 'resting on her shoulder'. Since their next appearances are 'a long time after' they must change gowns, 'for they are richer now'. Edmund's whole speech to Edgar, beginning 'O sir, fly this place' is marked 'simple and calm'; later, Oswald is to enter 'hands in belt, or pockets'. The exchange between Goneril, Regan and Lear in act II, scene 4 is frequently marked for stresses and interpretations. When Gloster takes Lear to shelter at the end of act III, scene 4, Ellen Terry's comments specify, 'I think Glos. sh^d give the torch to the Fool and begin to wrap Lear up with Cloak he has brought – good for many reasons – such a good exit sh^d be seen: Remember and exeunt quickly. Most remarkable effect.' After saying 'And I'll go to bed at noon' the Fool 'sh^d lie down quite done up'.

The fifth act receives detailed annotation of this kind. It is to open 'with *great* spirit', and when Goneril and Regan clash the note is 'The meeting of Amazons! Boadicea!' Particular attention is paid to Edgar's final confrontation with Edmund. After '*Third trumpet*' the added direction is 'Pause. All listen.' Edgar's accusation of treachery should not be shouted but spoken 'lower & vibrating – Agitate'; Edmund is to come in 'higher'. The page of printed text here, with other remarks, suggested alterations, and the restoration of some speeches cut by Irving, is covered by annotation, and at the top is a reminder to 'Speak to Henry'. These are hardly the comments of an actress noting what ought to happen in rehearsal for her own interest and pleasure, and look very like the work of a deputy standing in, at least temporarily, for the chief.

As an actress sitting in the stalls at rehearsal Ellen Terry must have helped Irving; as an actress on stage she was an essential and invaluable member of his company. Her own popularity was as great as Irving's; in fact it was greater, because her personality was more accessible to the public than Irving's and more attractive. The public respected and admired Irving, but they loved Terry. Today some find it hard to understand how she achieved the reputation she did. She was not a tragic actress like Bernhardt, and she did not distinguish herself in the modern repertory like Duse. Yet, as we have seen, in addition to her warmth and her sense of fun, qualities which radiated across the footlights, she had an image more substantial than that of a stage artist alone. She was a work of art and legend in an Aesthetic age, a symbol of femininity and womanhood in a domestic one, a picture of physical and sexual beauty and allure to those who chose to notice such things. She had such power over the press and the public that they quite overlooked her liaison with Godwin and her two illegitimate children, a surprising thing in a mid-Victorian England that insisted upon sexual morality in women, looked askance at actresses, and glorified marriage and home life for women. Her acting was much of this power, but not all of it. She had great style and great charm. Love, innocence, trust, tenderness, happiness, joy, and pathos were what she played best on the stage, all things that appealed strongly to her audiences. Her technique was broad without being melodramatic: bigger theatres and Shakespeare suited her better than small theatres and modern dramatists like Shaw and Barrie. Her range was limited, yet 'within that range, and at her best', as Mowbray Morris put it, 'no living actress of our stage can stand beside her'.[121] She took characters into herself and returned them to the audience as half Ellen Terry and half whatever woman she was playing. 'She spread herself,' said Gordon Craig, 'and encompassed the stage, the stalls, the pit, gallery, and somehow the air.'[122] She also encompassed the age, in a way no English actress had done, before or since.

19 Eleonora Duse as Anna in *La città morta*

Eleonora Duse

vvvvvvvvvvvvvvvvvvvvvvvvvvvvvvvvvvvvvvvvvvvvvvvvvvvvvvvvvvvvvvvvvvvv

SUSAN BASSNETT

ON 9 DECEMBER 1901 Eleonora Duse played the title role of Gabriele
D'Annunzio's new play, *Francesca da Rimini* in the huge Teatro Costanzi,
Rome's newest and biggest theatre. She was forty-three years old, Italy's
principal actress and, as the editor of the *Giornale d'Italia* noted, the whole
country had talked of little other than the première for weeks before the
event, such was her reputation and the expectations she could arouse.

Preparations for *Francesca da Rimini* had held public interest for some
time. D'Annunzio's plays had received mixed receptions so far in his
career, and the most recent D'Annunzio–Duse collaboration, *La città
morta*, which had premièred in March 1901, had only been a partial
success. The relationship between the writer and the actress, however, was
constantly in the public eye, and the publication in 1900 of D'Annunzio's
autobiographical novel about the doomed love affair between a talented
young poet and an aging actress, *La fiamma*, had turned their lives into
public property. Moreover, in an age when spectacle in the theatre drew
large crowds, preparations for *Francesca da Rimini* were even more
spectacular than average. Eleonora Duse herself provided the financial
backing, which is said to have exceeded 400,000 lire. Rehearsals had taken
place in the Teatro della Pergola in Florence, the city's opera house, and
no expense had been spared in the staging. D'Annunzio had originally
commissioned Mariano Fortuny, the painter, to design the sets, but he
withdrew two months before the opening and was replaced by Rovescalli.
Specialists in medieval art history were called in to assist with sets and
costumes, and an elaborate reconstruction of medieval siege weaponry was
designed for the battle at the end of act II. Duse, as financial backer and
director, might have been expected to play a large part in the process of
setting up the play, but from all accounts it was D'Annunzio who took
over the central organizational role. Mario Corsi comments that 'D'Annunzio turned himself into director, actor, designer, costume designer,
choreographer and master of arms.'[1] Intensive rehearsals lasted for two

119

20   Eleonora Duse as Francesca da Rimini

months and during that time tensions between D'Annunzio, Duse and the rest of the actors ran fairly high.

In a letter to Olga Ossani, Duse complained that:

I waited, on some occasions, *eight* hours . . . on some occasions 13 hours at the Costanzi – like that – waiting for *my hour*, grieving that all I could do was to sketch out a tiny fragment of the text . . . Tonight even *I do not know* which scenes we shall rehearse. I therefore think . . that you should ask Gabriele D'Annunzio yourself. He is directing – and we are quite at sea . . . I simply cannot tell you which way he is setting his sails.[2]

D'Annunzio's two prime concerns seem to have been the creation of powerful visual images and authenticity, in historical terms, of those images. The literariness of the production was noted by several critics, and in his biography of Duse, Cesare Molinari described the overloading of the stage with medieval paraphernalia and comments that: 'The whole thing became an undoubtedly committed but nevertheless pretentious piece of archaeological bric à brac, and Duse found herself turned into just another piece of that bric à brac.'[3]

D'Annunzio's ideas of directing were idiosyncratic. In search of authenticity of response, he attempted to organize rehearsals in the manner of shooting a film. According to Molinari, once the initial read-through had taken place, the actors were never told which scene they were going to rehearse and never knew what to expect at any time. Duse seems to have gone along with this method of working, though opinions of her final performance on the opening night were decidedly mixed. Adelaide Ristori's son, Giorgio, replying to a letter from his mother about the opening night that has unfortunately been lost, notes that:

Yesterday evening I read everything that there was about the famous first night in the *Popolo Romano*, the *Tribuna* and the *Patria*. Your opinion sums up everything that was written, and moreover all that I hear about Duse convinces me all the more that D'Annunzio has become her vampire and is slowly destroying her morally, physically and artistically. That she cannot see this for herself means that she must be in such a state of nervous depression that she is completely blind to it.[4]

Two days later, in her reply to Giorgio, Adelaide Ristori went even further:

Nobody would be surprised if it ended with a revolver. But keep that between ourselves. The *famous Francesca* cost her *two hundred thousand francs*! ! Costumes, music (that was so bad they had to cut it out!), sets, everything paid for by her. They tell me she is ruined! Poor soul!! Last night the show did not go on because one of the actors was ill. I believe they are going to perform tonight. But fortunately they did not send me a seat and I prefer to remain at home.[5]

Adelaide Ristori's negative opinions of D'Annunzio seem to have been shared by many others, but on the first night of *Francesca da Rimini* the audience response was by no means clear cut. Domenico Oliva, writing in the *Giornale d'Italia*, describes the mixed reception the play received, when it finally came to an end after six hours' playing time:

The contrasts were so many and so intense, the wild applause of some ladies and gentlemen in the audience was so mingled with the disapproval, the ironic laughter, the whistling that echoed round the elegant auditorium that one must conclude that the opinion of the public was decidedly uncertain.[6]

Luigi Pirandello, however, was quite sure of his views:

I believe I have never suffered so much in a theatre as I did at the opening night of *Francesca da Rimini* at the Costanzi in Rome. The artistic skills of the great actress seemed to be paralysed, indeed virtually shattered by the character depicted by the poet in such coarse strokes, in the same way that the action of the tragedy is impeded, crushed and shattered by the vast flood of D'Annunzian rhetoric.[7]

He further added that seeing Duse play D'Annunzio's roles evoked in him a sense of nostalgia for the past, for the roles belonging to the old tradition, often 'insignificant and mediocre as they were'. Duse, Pirandello claimed, had been a great actress but had never managed to find a writer who was able to allow her to develop the full potential of her inner resources.

Both the young critic and the grand old lady of the Italian theatre blamed the vehicle chosen by Duse for her failure to achieve success on the scale of some of her previous performances. Ristori's antipathy towards D'Annunzio shows up strongly in her letters, and Pirandello's own playwriting career was firmly based in his belief that D'Annunzio's theatre was sterile and overblown. Yet Duse herself was willing to invest large sums of money in D'Annunzio's work, to subordinate herself to his amateur directing technique, to give him a large portion of the take when *Francesca da Rimini* went on tour to Berlin and Vienna and then, finally, against all advice, to embark on a tour of the United States at the end of 1903 with an exclusively D'Annunzian repertoire. James Huneker, theatre critic of the New York *Sun*, tried to explain Duse's commitment to the plays of so controversial a writer:

The wisdom of her choice in selecting only D'Annunzio's dramas is not altogether apparent. She will listen to no advice; perhaps she is on a mission; perhaps she wishes to make known everywhere the genius of her young countryman, and to go back with the means to raise upon the border of Lake Albano a great independent theatre, the poet's dream of a dramatic Bayreuth.[8]

There has long been a tendency for some of the more romantically inclined Duse biographers to explain her passion for D'Annunzio's work in terms of her passion for the man himself. That Duse was in love with D'Annunzio, and that he treated her cruelly and caused her a great deal of suffering over many years is undoubtedly true, but it is hard to imagine Duse losing all sense of both the artistic and financial implications of her involvement with D'Annunzio. She had spent many years acquiring her pre-eminent position in the theatre both as actress and as manager, in charge of her own finances and her own repertoire, and had a strong sense of commercial exigencies. Nevertheless, from the outset, she seemed determined to perform D'Annunzio's plays regardless of their failure to win widespread public approval. As Huneker points out, she seems to have behaved like someone on a mission; a mission to extend the boundaries of theatre, to raise the level of taste in her audiences to one which she judged to be acceptable for them.

Early in the affair with Duse in 1897 D'Annunzio had argued for the creation of a Festival Theatre, 'a temple to the Tragic Muse' on the shores of Lake Albano, to the south of Rome, in which the ceremonial character of the drama would be recreated: 'What a distance will separate this Festival Theatre, built upon the serene hillside, from the cramped urban theatres' he proclaimed, those debased theatres in which actors perform 'amid a suffocating heat impregnated with all impurities, before a crowd of stupid imbecility . . .'[9] This dream of a pure theatre was an integral part of the beginning of their love affair, and it was in pursuit of that dream that Duse continued to tour in D'Annunzio's plays even though she must have recognized their failure as commercial ventures.

The meeting with Duse provided D'Annunzio with a physical presence on which to build his idea of the play. He began to write for her and later, as he astutely recognized the power of the box office, to write for other stars as well. Duse, on the other hand, met D'Annunzio when her career too was at a turning point. Dissatisfied with what she perceived as an inadequate repertoire available to her, she was eager to experiment with new roles and had long wanted to find a writer in whom she could put her trust. Both D'Annunzio with his lack of theatrical experience and Duse with her great wealth of it were also caught up in the whole ferment of experimentation with performance space in the last decade of the nineteenth century. From Wagner's Bayreuth to Strindberg's Adelsnas in Ostergötland, from Romain Rolland in France to Oberammergau and the

Festival of Vaux, ideas were in circulation for open theatres that would restore a sense of ritual and grandeur to performance, in direct contrast to the boundaries imposed by the naturalistic stage. Duse and D'Annunzio, in expressing their ambition for a modern Greek-style theatre, were following a clear line of development that was running throughout Europe. During their meeting with Rolland and his wife in 1900, Duse and D'Annunzio must have discussed Rolland's theories and compared notes for their dreams of a new people's theatre. In the Italian context, however, the desire for a Festival Theatre was linked to their desire to create a genuinely Italian art form that would express the greatness of both the new Italy and the older Italian tradition. Writing to her former lover, Arrigo Boito, in 1900, Duse expresses all her resentment at the failure on the part of Italian audiences to understand her attempts to extend her repertoire. 'There is nothing left for me (oh what a life!)', she writes, 'except an established name, bound hand and foot to the old bundle of works by Sardou and Dumas . . .' 'I want to *scream* my refusal, because I know I am right in this . . .'

In that same letter she talks of suicide, of her deep depression at what she sees as her fate:

what is left is the boredom, the discouragement, the dreadful effort that makes me feel sick of a Theatre *without Art*, the distress of my body, my disoriented soul, the sheer brutal tiredness of my nomadic life, Exile from city to city, and this unseen *Thing* that gnaws at me, this nostalgia – – A bedroom in a Hotel is all there is – that and my need for some kind of solution.[10]

So despite the reservations felt by so many of her contemporaries, Duse invested both her money and her talent in D'Annunzio's work because she saw, at a crucial point in her life, a possibility of change. The collapse of the affair, the public scandal caused by the publication of *La fiamma*, D'Annunzio's systematic betrayals of her both sexually and artistically (his one great theatrical triumph in 1904 *La figlia di Iorio* opened with Irma Gramatica in the title role, despite Duse's anguish over it) still did not defeat her belief in the superiority of his writing. Her sense of mission towards the Italian theatre did not falter even though her emotional life was devastated.

In his assessment of Eleonora Duse, Pirandello makes a very significant statement. He points out that D'Annunzio's technique is 'exterior . . . based on a massive formalism and extraordinary richness of language'. Duse's technique, on the contrary, is based on fluidity, on a physicalizing of dynamic internal processes:

In her everything is internally very simple, bare, almost naked. Her technique is the quintessence of a pure, lived truth, a technique that moves from the internal outwards . . . she has a very clear diction, which is the prime necessity for complete recreation of a verbal image. And if she only succeeds in reaching it through enormous tension, then that can only be an advantage for her performance. Hers is a technique of movement. A constant, gentle flowing that has neither time nor possibility of stopping, and certainly not of crystallizing itself into predetermined behaviour . . .[11]

What Pirandello seems to be suggesting is that far from providing Duse with the necessary vehicles in which to display her creative talents, D'Annunzio's concept of the drama could only serve to inhibit her still further and force her into modes of performance that were essentially alien to her. Certainly, in describing her as 'paralysed' in her movements as Francesca, Pirandello made his point quite clearly. He seems to have felt that Duse had a particular style of acting that she brought to the plays she chose to perform, whilst D'Annunzio's drama demanded of actors a specific performance that, in Duse's case, was at odds with her own. D'Annunzio's plays contain detailed stage directions for actors to follow, designed to ensure that his version of the stage picture was created on his terms. The death of Francesca and Paolo illustrates the details with which D'Annunzio worked out the version that the actors were to follow:

FRANCESCA. Let him go!
Let him go. Me, take me! Take me instead!

(Her husband lets go. Paolo leaps across the doorway and draws his dagger. The Hunchback backs away, draws his short sword and brings it down on him with terrible force. Francesca throws herself between them, but since her husband has flung himself forward with the force of the blow and cannot hold back, the steel goes through her breast. She sways, turns on herself towards Paolo who lets his dagger fall and clasps her in his arms.)

FRANCESCA. (*dying*) Oh, Paolo!

(The Hunchback pauses for a second. He sees the woman clasped in her lover's arms who seals her dying lips with his own. Mad with pain and fury, he thrusts another mortal stroke into his brother's side. The two entwined bodies sway, almost falling; they utter no sound; thus bound together they slide to the floor. The Hunchback bows his head in silence, painfully bends his knee and breaks the bloody sword across the other leg.)

The stage directions of *Francesca da Rimini*, as with D'Annunzio's other plays, are precisely worked out in order to ensure the recreation of specific visual pictures. *Francesca da Rimini* is structured around a set of images of rising and falling, of ascending and descending, and the stage directions indicating how a character should fall or bow, the sets that stress the use of staircases and split levels all reinforce the development of that group of images. D'Annunzio's technique is to create images that operate as leitmotifs throughout the play; the problem is that this is a technique that subordinates the actor to his will. Duse was therefore free to express Francesca only within the limits imposed by D'Annunzio.

The problem of limits for the actor is a vexed one, that resurfaces in different forms at different historical moments. D'Annunzio's concept of the actor who is the servant of the Master, and the Master who assumes the role of speaking for the Nation, was not unusual at the end of the nineteenth century, but can be viewed today for the proto-Fascist vision that it undoubtedly was. His was a hierarchical theatre: the Writer or Poet was pre-eminent; below him came the actors, there to do his bidding; and lowest of all came the audience, whose subservient position was perceived as an integral part of the Poet's task. He was to educate the illiterate, to raise their understanding of great art and in so doing to raise their patriotic consciousness. The task of the actor in this mission was therefore an ambiguous one. Though entrusted with a special role to play, the actor nevertheless had to be guided and instructed by the Master. The Poet was not content to merely write; he had to direct as well, hence his gradual intrusion into the practical process of theatre making.

But in that intrusion a fatal flaw emerged. D'Annunzio knew nothing at all about the practicalities of theatre, about problems of casting and rehearsing, about financial constraints and spatial ones. So *Francesca da Rimini* in its original version ran on until after 2 o'clock in the morning, and more care was spent in choosing the material of the gowns than in considering how to tackle practical problems of staging. The complex battle scene with its medieval machinery proved to be an anticlimax, the excessive smoke upset the audience and drowned the dialogue and the musical intermezzi, planned as a major innovation, proved disastrous. D'Annunzio was forced to remove them altogether, and to severely cut the show before it could go out on tour.

The photographs that remain provide evidence of the richly ornamented set and luxurious costumes. The starkness of the lighting on Duse as Francesca suggests that serious attempts were made to use lighting in a genuinely original manner. It is, of course, significant that the original designer was Fortuny, who, just one year later in 1902, in Paris, constructed his Cupola Fortuny. This lighting system projected white light onto bands of coloured silk, which acted as reflectors within a half-domed framework. Fortuny was obviously experimenting with indirect lighting in *Francesca da Rimini*. The chorus of women in the play is a deliberate revocation of ancient theatrical convention and the first entry of Francesca with her sister is an attempt to deconstruct the convention of the *prima attrice*'s grand solo entrance. The crowd scenes reflect an interest in spectacle theatre that had already emerged in *La città morta* and that was unusual in Italian prose theatre at that time. But despite these obvious attempts at theatrical innovation, despite the heavy influence on D'Annunzio of practitioners such as Wagner or the Duke of Saxe-Meiningen, D'Annunzio's theatre was primarily literary and general opinion seems to have been that Duse was constrained by his works, rather than enhanced by them.

The core of the problem lay not so much in D'Annunzio's lack of experience, although that was undoubtedly a factor of significance. Rather it lay in the situation in which the Italian theatre found itself at the close of the nineteenth century, with its antiquated touring company system, its convention of the *mattatore*, or star actor, who dominated every show, and its tradition of stereotyped roles in the manner of the old *commedia dell'arte*. D'Annunzio's concept of theatre was opposed to all such conventions; it required costly, large-scale staging, competent actors willing to experiment with alternative forms of performance beyond the stock types, a balance of skills spread throughout the company, with no one predominant. *Francesca da Rimini* had a large cast (twenty-six speaking parts, with archers, torch-bearers, musicians, etc.) and required elaborate scene changes and machinery. It was costly to stage and immensely costly to tour, and both the format of the play itself and D'Annunzio's authoritarian style of direction made great demands on the actors. In complete contrast to the old traditional Italian theatre, D'Annunzio's was not a theatre *of* actors or *for* actors; it was a theatre in which the actor was subordinate to other elements, to the richness of the linguistic and visual systems and to the design of the creator/director. But despite her co-operation with D'Annunzio, Duse, like the rest of the company, had trained in the old system and the *mattatore* principle was enshrined in them all. As Guido Noccioli points out in his Diaries, which give an account of Eleonora Duse's South American tour of 1906–7, she knew quite well that she was the star and refused to tolerate even the slightest hint of self-assertion on the part of any other actor:

This evening, the first performance for the general public of *La signora delle camelie*. A magnificent house. The ovation is even greater than on previous evenings. Acts II and IV especially arouse tremendous enthusiasm. The Signora acts with much feeling and gives a wonderful performance. There is, however, one lamentable incident this evening. At the end of act IV Orlandini slightly modifies the stage positions so that in the showdown with Armando the money is thrown quite by accident straight into the Signora's face. As soon as the curtain comes down, she gets up, livid with temper and as dangerous as any harpy, tearing at the veils around her throat and howling: 'Ah, dear God, have we come to this? How dare you attempt any such villainy with me? It is unspeakable . . . you base trickster!' Orlandini mumbles an apology: 'Forgive me, Signora . . . it was quite unintentional . . .' 'Ah! I thought as much! . . . Besides, you deliberately changed positions on stage without my permission. You are full of whims . . . You must have everything your own way . . . You continually disobey my instructions . . . but I will have you know I give the orders here!'[12]

Duse's acting style, however individually hers it might be, derived from the training she had received in playing the popular roles of her early career in the Italian theatre. She obviously had a strong sense of what suited her and a highly distinctive playing style, but she had also inherited many of the problems of the old system, of which the *mattatore* company structure was clearly one. D'Annunzio, however, was unconcerned with such matters. His aim was to create a great Italian lyric theatre that would be both a testament to the capacities of the new Italy and a monument to the greatness of the Italian past. In this respect, he can be described as a great innovator, since from the very start of his theatrical career in 1896 when he was working on *La città morta*, he was attempting to transcend the limits of the traditional prose theatre tradition.

The Duse–D'Annunzio collaboration, therefore, was founded on a misjudgement on both their parts. D'Annunzio, in his desire to revitalize the Italian theatre as part of his aim to revitalize Italian culture generally, had grandiose ideas and failed to recognize the limits of the raw material with which he was working. Duse, who had a keen sense of the commercially theatrical, nevertheless allowed herself to believe in D'Annunzio's vision, because it was seemingly so close to her own desire for change and innovation in what she had come to see as a tired repertoire. And whilst D'Annunzio was primarily a man of letters, extremely well read and open to influences from all sides, Duse for her part was an autodidact, since she had received almost no formal education in her childhood. As a result, she read voraciously but constantly needed a literary mentor. Her life-long friend Matilde Serao was a novelist; her first disastrous love affair with the man who fathered her short-lived baby son was with Martin Cafiero, a writer and director of the Neapolitan news-paper, *Il Corriere del Mattino*, who was also considerably older than she was. Her longest love affair was with another writer, also much older than her, Arrigo Boito, and their affair only ended when the relationship with D'Annunzio began. D'Annunzio may have been the younger (a detail that he emphasized strongly in *La fiamma*) but his intellectual bravura was exceptional. Duse does seem to have believed that in him she had found her ideal writer, and that his plays contained the seeds of greatness that would ensure them both a place in both literary and theatrical history. She may have been an astute judge of where to place an actor on a stage, of how to deliver a line or how to raise a hand at precisely the right moment, but she was unable to assess the quality of D'Annunzio's works, seeing them as she did through the rose-coloured lenses of her obsession for him and her high ideals of cultural renewal. All her life she seems to have carried those ideals, and the clearest evidence of her belief in the value of culture and education can be seen in the way she chose to bring up her daughter, Enrichetta, who was sent from boarding school to boarding school and kept as far away from the theatre as possible. Duse seems to have considered her work in the theatre as debased in comparison with her aspirations for her daughter's well-being. Her granddaughter, Sister Mary Mark, points out that she and her brother were forbidden to see their grandmother perform when she came to London.[13] Education, learning, art, in Duse's eyes, seem to have been idealized and located on a higher level than her own contribution to society.

All Duse's biographers have emphasized the impact on her formation as an actress and as a person of the financial hardship of her early childhood. She was born in Vigevano in northern Italy on 3 October 1858 in a room in the Albergo Cannon d'Oro. On her certificate of baptism her parents are recorded as Vincenzo Duse (though he was generally known as Alessan-dro), 'dramatic artist', and Angelica Cappelletto, an actress in her hus-band's company, but listed as being a lady of private means. The social aspirations of her parents are already apparent from these details on her birth records, and throughout her life Eleonora Duse seems to have felt an impulse to fulfil two quite different needs that, roughly speaking, corres-pond to the differing roles of both her parents. From Alessandro Duse derives the professionalism of the theatre, the commitment to acting as a way of life; from Angelica, who died young, when her daughter was only thirteen, derives a sense of propriety and a desire for financial stability and respectability. The Duse biographers recount how Angelica had to be given a pauper's funeral and how Eleonora could not afford to buy herself a mourning dress. Later, her determination to shield her own daughter from any kind of financial hardship and her decision to send her to the best schools in Europe show how anxious she was to avoid subjecting Enrichetta to some of the anxieties of her own childhood. That she rarely spent time with her daughter, due to her punishing touring schedule, seems to have been less important to her than the need to provide a respectable education suitable for a child of the middle class.

Although Angelica Cappelletto came from a poor family, with no theatrical background, she nevertheless acted in her husband's company and was *prima attrice* until too ill to continue. Alessandro, however, came from a theatrical family. His father, Luigi Duse, had been a famous popular actor in Padova, and all his brothers had followed their father onto the stage. One brother, Enrico, joined with Alessandro in setting up a company of their own and it was into that travelling group of players that Eleonora was introduced and first learned about performing. The legend much favoured by Duse biographers is that she first made her debut at the age of four, in Chioggia, playing Cosette in Hugo's *Les Misérables*. Some extend this story to include an account of how the little Eleonora was slapped or pinched in order to make her cry genuine tears on stage, and how the child's mother supposedly explained this treatment as necessary in order to entertain the public.

Whatever truth there may be in the anecdotes about her early life, Duse's beginnings in a small travelling company would seem to have been fairly typical. The company actors travelled extensively, often walking great distances carrying their props and costumes and performing to small semi-literate or illiterate audiences. Life was hard, but as the daughter of one of the founders of the company, Eleonora's lot was better than many, since she was virtually guaranteed leading parts as she grew up. But the problems of the small-scale touring companies were obvious – without a fixed base, without financial security of any kind, the actors were compelled to play popular pieces in the popular manner; there was no room at all for innovation, no time for rehearsal, and the need to keep a large range of plays in repertoire meant that the actors were spread thinly across a range of stock roles. The only hope of financial security for an Italian actor was to tour abroad, and when Adelaide Ristori accompanied by Cesare Rossi left for Paris in 1855 with the Reale Sarda company, she

set a precedent that was to last well into the twentieth century. International success furthered success within Italy, and Ristori, like Duse later
on, travelled continuously, punctuating her tours of Europe and America
with tours around Italy.

The state of the theatre in Italy in the latter part of the nineteenth
century was linked to the history of the unification. Through the years of
revolution in the first half of the century, theatre flourished in some
centres in certain forms – hence the strength of dialect theatre in places
such as Naples, Venice, or Sicily, the vast opera houses of Naples, Turin
or Milan, compared to the absence of similar traditions in the Papal States.
In the years leading up to unification, from the 1850s onwards, the
presence of Italian companies on the world stages was both an artistic and a
political statement. Some, like Ristori and Bellotti-Bon, her leading man
for a time after Rossi, tried also to revitalize the Italian theatre by
importing new plays and techniques. In 1859, with financial help from a
Trieste banker, Bellotti-Bon set up a new company and actively tried to
stimulate Italian writers to create new plays. For a time he was extremely
successful, so much so that he eventually set up three companies simultaneously, and both discovered and encouraged Giuseppe Giacosa, probably Italy's principal playwright of the late nineteenth century. One of his
actresses, Giacinta Pezzana, was eventually to give Duse her first big
chance at the Fiorentini in Naples in 1879. But the conditions of the
theatre, once the first wave of post-Risorgimento idealism died away,
remained unhealthy. The revolutionary ferment was replaced by bourgeois audiences who wanted a bourgeois repertoire. Bellotti-Bon began to
lose money, was forced to restrict his triple company structure, and finally
shot himself in despair in 1883. The years after 1870 for many were years
of great disillusionment.

Cesare Molinari gives some interesting statistics regarding the state of
the theatre in Italy in 1870. In that year the census shows 1,055 official
theatres in 775 town councils throughout the newly unified country, which
had a population of almost 29 million. In addition to this figure should be
added the unofficial playing spaces, the temporary performance areas both
indoors and outdoors that flourished in untold numbers. Attempting to
calculate the number of companies, he suggests that the official figure of
150 should be doubled at least, and points out that there were countless
very small companies working out in isolated rural areas. He notes that the
cost of tickets in Italy was exceptionally low, with prices from 50 centesimi

to 3 lire, so companies must have frequently collapsed and reorganized under financial pressures.

Survival of companies was through box-office returns. Nothing else counted. Some councils assisted theatres with grants, but what little money there was went towards opera, which had far more prestige and drawing power than straight theatre. Almost all the companies were itinerant ones, and the few small-scale fixed repertory companies were usually popular, dialect companies. There had been two major attempts to create large-scale fixed repertory companies, with the Milanese Vicereale and the Torinese Reale Sarda companies, but both were short-lived.

The format of the touring company was, as Molinari points out, a standard one, and reflected microcosmically the patterns of social order in the outside world, in its economics and its hierarchies. Co-operative companies were unusual; the general pattern was either a company structure in which all the members were joint stockholders, or one in which the leading actor was also the financial boss. Actors performed stock roles within the company, a long-standing tradition extending back through centuries. For some time it was supposed that this division of companies into stock roles derived from the *commedia dell'arte*; recently, in his major study of the *commedia*, Fernando Taviani has shown that this was not the case, since in fact the *commedia dell'arte* figure was based on the pre-existing stock roles of popular theatre.[14] Those stock roles can be broken down into two categories – the ones of primary importance and the secondary ones. Of primary importance were the *prima donna* and *primo attore* (leading lady and leading man), the *brillante* (comic lead), the character actor and the mother. Of secondary importance were the young *primo attore* and *prima attrice*, the *seconda donna* (second actress), the *promiscuo* (general utility) and the *generico primario* (a sort of second actor). Below these came a range of minor figures who played the secondary parts. The career structure within the company was clear-cut: a woman began as young *prima attrice*, moved on to *prima assoluta* (leading lady of the company) and finished up as the mother. When Duse joined the Pezzana company, she made the transition to *prima attrice* and Pezzana moved to the mother's role – hence Duse as Electra with Pezzana as Clytemnestra, Duse as Ophelia and Pezzana as Gertrude. Sometimes the pattern could be altered, when the *seconda donna* moved into the position of *prima* instead, and in the 1880–1 seasons, when Duse and her father joined Rossi's fixed company in Turin, she was taken on as a *seconda*. The transition for men followed a similar pattern – the young actor became the lead and eventually became the character actor, while the *promiscuo* could aspire to the position of *brillante*. But as in lyric opera, the male roles declined in importance in the nineteenth century and the principal box-office draw was quite definitely the leading lady by the time Duse was starting her career.

After Angelica Duse's death in 1875, Alessandro Duse's company disintegrated. Father and daughter joined the Pezzana–Brunetti company briefly, and then entered the more reputable Ciotti–Bozzo–Belli–Blanes company, where they are recorded in 1878 as being paid the sum of 14 lire. The company travelled to Naples, where they played in the city's leading theatre, the Teatro dei Fiorentini. The situation in Naples was an unusual one; as the capital city of the Kingdom of the Two Sicilies, it had been a centre of culture throughout the first decades of the nineteenth century and remained a leading city for dialect theatre. The unification and the change in status of Naples from capital city to southern marginal centre, combined with the economic crisis in the city itself, brought about all kinds of changes. On the one hand, the city was a centre of political activity, an exciting city full of energy and life, with a large community of artists and writers, but on the other hand, it was a city of great poverty and squalor. Hundreds of thousands died in the teeming slums during the great cholera epidemic of 1884, shortly after Duse had left the city and moved to the north.

During her two years in Naples, Duse's life changed in several ways. In personal terms, she suffered the first traumatic disillusionment in love, with her abortive romance with Martin Cafiero. She became pregnant and gave birth to a boy, who died almost immediately. Her close friend, the Neapolitan novelist, Matilde Serao, helped her through what must have been a devastating time, since Cafiero had abandoned her completely. Almost immediately after the child's death, she returned to work, storing her suffering away out of sight. It is pure speculation, but it is possible that when Duse gave such great moral help years later to Isadora Duncan, after the accident that killed both her young children, she was able to draw on her own horrific experience. Certainly she seems to have been the principal person to whom Isadora turned, and seems also to have given her a great deal of help and encouragement in persuading her to return to life and to work. This incident is worthy of note, since it raises an interesting question about Duse that successive biographers have never managed to explain. Duse's letters, the large number of testimonies relating anecdotes about her, Noccioli's diaries, D'Annunzio's companion–biographer Tom Antongini, all suggest to the reader that Duse was a woman who lived on her nerves, subject to periods of black depression and given to hysterical outbursts. She was neither an easy person to work with, nor an easy person to work for, and her emotional life was strewn with disasters. Yet despite all this, she seems also to have been a woman who inspired loyalty in other women; Matilde Serao was a close friend throughout her life; Isadora Duncan had nothing but good words to say for her. She kept in touch for years with good women friends; biographers who knew her such as Olga Signorelli and Eva Le Gallienne offer the picture of a very different kind of woman, a woman who internalized suffering, who was deeply maternal, who helped other younger women in their careers and who had a great sense of warmth. It would be unfair to discount either of these two conflicting portraits, since what emerges from them is a picture of a complex woman, better able to handle relationships with women than with men, yet constantly dealing with men both sexually and professionally and subordinating her impulses towards motherhood and bourgeois respectability to her work. She seems also to have avoided explicit links with the new feminism that was emerging in Italy, as in the rest of Europe throughout her lifetime, yet nevertheless in her choice of roles, particularly in her choice of Ibsen roles, she did a lot to change expectations about the theatrical image of women. As we shall see later, in considering some of her major roles, Duse offered audiences an alternative representation of womanhood and of femininity, and perhaps some of the strangeness of the language of some critics who seem to have been obsessed by a notion of 'spirituality' when discussing her performances derives from their attempts to adequately describe something entirely different in terms of the representation of women.

In 1878, Duse was twenty years old. During the year she changed companies four times; she worked for one month with the Pezzana–Brunetti company, leaving them at the end of January to join the Dondini–Piamonti–Drago company with her father. No sooner had they joined, than the company split into two, and Duse went with Adolfo Drago as *seconda donna*. By March, she was being billed as *prima attrice giovane*, due to the illness of the actress who had previously played in those roles, and in September she rejoined the Ciotti–Belli–Blanes company and went to Naples, where she accepted the offer of the post of *prima attrice giovane* in the new repertory company at the Teatro dei Fiorentini. Giacinta Pezzana, one of Italy's leading actresses, was the leading lady in the company and Giovanni Emanuel was the leading actor.

The Teatro dei Fiorentini competed strongly in a city where attracting audiences was a venture of some importance. It installed gas lighting in 1879, replacing the old oil lamps, and from Carneval to Carneval (the theatre seasons) advertised 256 performances, including 50 new plays and a fixed repertory company. Advertisements for the performers included the names of Pezzana, Emanuel and Eleonora Duse, an indication that she was considered something of a box-office draw already. The season began with a series of well-known plays, favourites by Dumas, Sardou and Alfieri, *Hamlet*, *Othello*, *The Marriage of Figaro* and Silvio Pellico's *Pia dei Tolomei*, to mention but a few of the many shows. Then on 26 July 1879 a new play was finally presented – a stage version of Zola's *Thérèse Raquin*, with Duse playing the title role of Teresa.

Teresa Raquin went through twenty performances, a number that indicates it must have been an enormous success, although apparently the play was not judged to be particularly successful as a piece of writing. What made the show successful were the individual performances and both Giacinta Pezzana and Duse acquired a reputation for their playing that was to endure in perpetuity, despite the fact that relatively few people actually saw them perform. Luigi Rasi, writing some time later, recalled the first night:

The success of that night will not be forgotten easily. I can still see her in her neat black gown, leaning against the little window, looking disconcerted, a stranger in that environment, living a lie, her life built on guilt, crime, horror, terror, disgust and hatred. When Teresa dressed in her white bridal veil is afraid, she clings to Lorenzo, whose love can no longer overcome her remorse. When the terrified woman sees the portrait of the murdered Camillo, she points it out to Lorenzo, wide eyed with fear, trembling, unable to speak. When, in the midst of reproaching her lover with the murder she hears the cries of Madame Raquin, she clutches her chair nervously; and in the last act, when love has turned to savage hatred and the paralysed mother smiles mercilessly at the agony of the two guilty lovers – she trembled, a shudder went through her whole being, and one felt so moved that one was actually unable to applaud. The old porter at the Teatro dei Fiorentini said to me that night:

'Yes sir, she's something special, that one is.'[15]

There is general agreement among Duse biographers that her perform-ance in *Teresa Raquin* marks the start of her rise to fame. She moved the Naples public in a very special way, and she seems to have acted with

Giacinta Pezzana in a totally successful manner. Pezzana had invested a lot of time and money in the play and was well-pleased with the result. What remains somewhat mysterious is exactly what Duse did that made her portrayal of Teresa so uniquely important and marked her as an actress whose career was destined to be a major one.

Giacinta Pezzana had taken exceptional care with the staging of the play, and Molinari suggests that her technique was reminiscent of that of Antoine a few years later. Certainly, the key to a reconstruction of *Teresa Raquin* lies in a notion of realism, both in terms of staging and in terms of performance. Duse's particular brand of psychological realism seems to have been developed to new levels in her performance, and marks a shift in her technique.

Italian realism, known as *verismo*, emerged as a literary and theatrical movement in the newly unified Italy of the 1870s and 1880s following French models. Nevertheless, there had been a tendency earlier in the nineteenth century to talk about 'realism' when describing the performance styles of some of the great Italian actors such as Ristori, Rossi and Salvini. The question that is difficult for a contemporary theatre historian to determine is quite what was meant by the use of that term 'realism' when applied to the performance styles of a range of actors across a period of some thirty to forty years. *Verismo* as such was a specific movement, closely linked to French naturalism, but the realism of acting seems to be related to a notion of psychological realism above all. Actors trained in the Romantic manner had the benefit of a series of manuals describing the stage poses that an actor might learn in order to express emotions. Ristori and then Duse, though obviously familiar with the conventions of stage expression of emotion, chose to devise alternatives to the familiar gestural modes. Duse's style in particular seems to have depended on nuance; in other words, her acting process seems to have been to pass through a series of stages – firstly, a stage of internalization, of relating to her part and experiencing it psychologically, then a stage of expressing her reactions through subtle signs rather than grand gestures. The effect of this technique was to draw attention through down-playing rather than over-playing, in much the same way as a very soft-spoken person can often control a conversation more effectively than someone with a loud speaking voice.

Adelaide Ristori gave her opinion on Duse's style to Leone Fortis, in an interview in 1897:

She has a subtle, slightly strident voice – and she has invented a manner of speech that is quite uniquely hers, very fast, very low, so that the voice cannot possibly be raised at all – and she makes a good job of imitating a harshness of timbre so that it seems to come from agitation of the spirit.

She is not really beautiful – but she is obviously one of the few women to have the sense to recognize this – and she has assumed an unusual, bizarre, eccentric appearance, extraordinarily pale . . . an appearance that one can easily take apart and reconstruct: an appearance that is imposing to the spectator the very instant she appears on stage, one which makes him focus his entire attention on her. She is thin – possibly a *fausse maigre*, as the French would say – but this enables her, in scenes involving love, seduction, abandonment, to give an impression of languor in her body, a dissolving of the senses that in her appears as passion and instantly wins over the sympathies of the audience.

Being as she is, Duse is an artist that one admires greatly with one's intellect rather than feeling her in one's heart; she imposes herself, she holds her public in thrall, she communicates her nervous over-excitement to that public, so that even when they have left the theatre they are still aware of it.

These virtues and these vices of Duse make her powerful in stage exchanges, when her face, together with the trembling of her whole person testify to an expression of nervousness that is the main secret of her effectiveness.

Sometimes she abuses that expression of nervousness.

She has a rather curious manner of gesture that has an automated quality, a certain stiff letting go of her arms down her sides with her body tired and drooping, a certain angular way of lifting her arm, holding it in a rather mechanical stiffness, a certain way of raising her open hands with all five fingers pointing outwards that would be unutterably intolerably baroque were any other actress to try to imitate her, but which in her produces an effect that holds one's attention fixedly. From all this I draw the conclusion that Duse is an actress of great skill, of great ingenuity, but that she is by no means an artist of truthfulness, as some of her over-enthusiastic admirers are wont to suggest.

Duse has created her own style, she has created for herself a sort of convention that is quite hers, through which she effectively becomes the woman of modern times, with all her complaints of hysteria, anaemia and nerve trouble and with all the consequences of those complaints; she is, in short, the fin de siècle woman, and with great astuteness she has assembled a repertory which consists of a complete collection of that sort of abnormal woman with all their weaknesses, quirks, unevenness, all their outbursts and languors, from *Marguerite Gautier* to *Fedora*, from *la femme de Claude* to the central character in Sudermann's *Heimat* from *Francillon* to Pinero's *Second Wife*.

But the greatest defect in Duse is that there is only one original type of character.[16]

Ristori's analysis of Duse takes up many of the points that critics refer to throughout her career – the use she made of arm and hand movements, the sense of nervous excitement, the intellectualizing process. What distinguishes Ristori's views, however, is her emphasis on the technique required for Duse to achieve these effects. Whereas many critics described what they saw in terms of Duse's lack of artifice, Ristori stresses the artificial devices she used in order to create that efect. Above all, Ristori insists on the fallacy of 'truthfulness' or 'realism' in Duse's acting.

Contemporary theatre anthropology has begun to examine the ways in which the western theatre has become focused around concepts of psychological realism in the training of actors, to the detriment of alternative forms.[17] Psychological realism calls for emphasis on character as a primary consideration; the actor must first analyse the character in terms of closeness or distance to his or her own experience and then study ways of reaching that character through mutations of his or her own personality. The technique is like the shedding of skins and the assumption of a fresh new colouring, a new identity. The actor gradually begins to merge with the role, to look for ways of reshaping movement through the identity of the character, rather than alternatively bringing that character to life through conventions of movement and diction that derive from other sources than the search for 'truth'. Duse's career in the theatre spanned the period of transition, when western actors were gradually moving towards the centralizing of notions of psychological realism away from the old conventions of stylized mimetic performance. Audiences were beginning to demand realism as part of the act of perceiving in a theatre; hence the dying Marguerite Gautier came increasingly to be played as a consumptive, with the pale face and coughing of a sick woman rather than to be played as a tragic heroine *per se*. In the latter part of the twentieth century, conditioned as we are to realism in performance, it is difficult to reconstruct the perceptual system of other times, when audiences seemed to have a totally different set of parameters for reading performance, but what does seem clear is that the latter part of the nineteenth century marked the period of shift towards the conventions of seeing that we have today. Hence Duse's dying Marguerite, hunched on her small truckle-bed, could be appreciated by audiences who might also appreciate Bernhardt's obvious male disguises. Realism, in the early stages of its development in nineteenth-century acting, does not seem to have been used to evaluate negatively alternative modes of play.

On 14 January 1884 Duse appeared as Santuzza in the première of Verga's play *Cavalleria rusticana* in Turin. She had left Naples in 1880 and joined Rossi's company based in Turin, where she was taken on as *seconda donna* with Giacinta Pezzana as *prima*. When Pezzana left the company in 1881 there was a brief hiatus and then Duse was elevated to the coveted *prima donna* position. Her rise to seniority in the company seems to have been due to the fact that she managed to succeed where Pezzana had failed. Pezzana had played in Dumas's *La Princesse de Bagdad*, but the play had received bad notices. Duse revived it in Venice in April 1881, working alongside Flavio Andò, who was to be her leading man and lover for several years, and this time it was a great success. It was typical of Duse that she would try to make something succeed that was universally judged to be a failure; throughout her life she seems to have been motivated to try to impose her views of what ought to be successful on others. This personality trait obviously accounts in part for her insistence on performing D'Annunzio's works despite initial public hostility, and accounts also for her determination to rival Bernhardt, even to the extent of appearing in London, in 1895, in Sudermann's *Heimat* (as Magda), a role that Bernhardt was also performing in the same city at the same time. It was this confrontation between the two actresses that Shaw describes in his piece in *The Saturday Review*, emphasizing Bernhardt's technique and 'peach-bloom complexion from the chemist's' and contrasting it with Duse's 'moral charm' and ability to produce 'the illusion of being infinite in variety of beautiful pose and motion'.[18]

The need to be compared and compared favourably, possibly at the expense of a rival claimant, was not exclusive to Duse. It was a quintessential feature of the *mattatore* system and often leading actors would assemble a whole company of inferior performers around themselves and construct the kinetics of stage movement in such a way as to give themselves the maximum possible limelight. But in reconstructing the history of Duse's performances and rise to international fame, there is a strong combative element that comes across quite clearly. She seems to have felt a need to prove herself publicly and this, together with her determination to raise the standard of Italian theatre, was a powerful motivation.

Duse's Santuzza was a triumphant success and is generally acclaimed as a turning point in her career. Prior to *Cavalleria rusticana* she had been building a name for herself in Rossi's company, though increasingly irritated by her repertoire of (predominantly French) plays. On 28 October 1882, she had written to Ernesto Somigli in Florence:

In the Rome season I played 7 *Odettes*, 4 *Frou-Frous*, 2 *Lady of the Camelias*, 2 *Fernandes*, 3 *Scrollinas* and, as of today, 6 *Femmes de Claude* and with this absolutely *wild* success we'll close the season, playing this work right up to the last night, though (in confidence) Rossi didn't want me to do it at all and I had to impose it on him for an evening. Last night, the 27th, I did a *fourth* performance of *Frou-Frou*. I took 1400 and the applause was loud and *intelligent*.[19]

21 Eleonora Duse as Odette

The letter to Somigli reveals several points about Duse's attitude to her work. The tone is that of a schoolgirl asking 'haven't I done well?' and expecting praise for all her efforts. But there is also the business woman, noting the size of the take, the seasoned performer forcing Rossi to do what she wanted and being proved right, the would-be creative artist noting the intelligence of the audience alongside its vociferousness. Something of this shrewdness, combined with a belief in the strength of Verga's play, led Duse to oppose Rossi and insist on doing *Cavalleria rusticana*. As with *La Femme de Claude*, her judgement was sounder than his.

Cesare Molinari points out that all the early portrayers of Santuzza created a low-level character, with no striking physical or vocal character-istics, a character whose restraint revealed almost a feeling of repression. He suggests that since Duse created the role and made it hers, she must also have established a mode of performance that others took up and followed. The downbeat portrayal of the betrayed Sicilian woman whose hopes of happiness are destroyed forever and who is responsible for the murder of her beloved Turiddu by the wronged husband of his mistress obviously gave Duse an opportunity to establish her own realist style of playing to complement Verga's *verista* plot and dialogue. A succession of critics, both Italian and others (including Arthur Symons), have attempted to describe what Duse did with the role of Santuzza. Her restraint is emphasized, together with the final explosion of rage that leads ultimately to the tragedy through a series of small, but highly significant gestures. Symons notes the almost unconscious way that Duse allowed her hand to rest on her beloved's wrist, a device that Molinari suggests was a frequent one of hers. She tended to touch her partners and fellow performers, giving an impression of spontaneity that brought audience attention back fully onto herself when she did so, precisely because of the apparently innocuous, unconscious movement. Hermann Bang recalls the image of Duse twisting a handkerchief in her hands, back against a wall, a physical though silent embodiment of inner anguish.

Again and again in criticism of Duse's performances we find evidence of an impression of restraint, of the unconscious working its way to the surface, of an inner performance that catches and holds everyone who watches it. Luigi Rasi, who acted with her, suggests that the basis of her acting was the creation of *la faccia convulsiva* (the distorted face), which is normally associated with mental illness:

Her eyes were agitated by imperceptible quiverings, they flickered rapidly from side to side; her cheeks went from blush to pallor with incredible rapidity; nostrils and lips trembled; her teeth were clenched violently and every smallest portion of her face was in motion . . . Then her body, to round off the portrayal of this type of person, had serpentine shifts of weight or profoundly languorous gestures and moved in perfect accord with the action and counterbalancing action of her arms, hands, fingers, torso and counterpart activity of her face. And so, perhaps, the great actress was able to outclass everyone in her portrayal of characters with *hysterical temperaments*.[20]

The photographic record of *Cavalleria rusticana* emphasizes the costumes. This is hardly surprising, since the verisimilitude of the costumes had been a major feature of the rehearsal period, with Verga taking Duse's measurements down to Sicily to obtain an authentic Sicilian peasant costume for her to wear. But from remaining photographs and drawings (including Orens' caricature), one clear feature emerges: the emphasis on head, neck and shoulders of Duse as Santuzza. Allowing for conventional posing and photographic constraints, the variations in the use of shawls and scarf-headdresses, together with the angles at which her neck is tilted suggest that Duse did make this part of her body the focal point of her performance. The photographs of *Denise* or *La Femme de Claude*, for example, roles which also date from her period with Rossi, show a completely different carriage of the head and shoulders. What Duse seems to portray in her Santuzza is indeed neurosis and repression, and she does it through a dislocation of the neck muscles (which also inhibits the pelvis, site of sexual desire which causes poor Santuzza such problems) and subsequent rigidifying of the chest muscles and shoulders. The effect of this is to provide contrast between apparent rigidity of the torso and the mobility described by Rasi and others of flickering facial expressions. She would also probably have breathed shallowly into her chest cavity and the famous Dusian ability to blush at will, something that caused critics worldwide to marvel at, would then be a simple technical device of holding her breath and keeping the tension in the chest which would cause a rush of blood to the face and head.

Duse seems to have conspicuously avoided the grand gesture, with its heightened arm movements and dramatic poses, in favour of more contained gestures. She frequently used draped garments, shawls and cloaks that drew attention to her hands, and her device of playing with things – handkerchiefs, small bunches of flowers, rings – is recorded time after time. Her particular type of realist acting, therefore, derived from a technique that placed emphasis on separate parts of the body, rather than

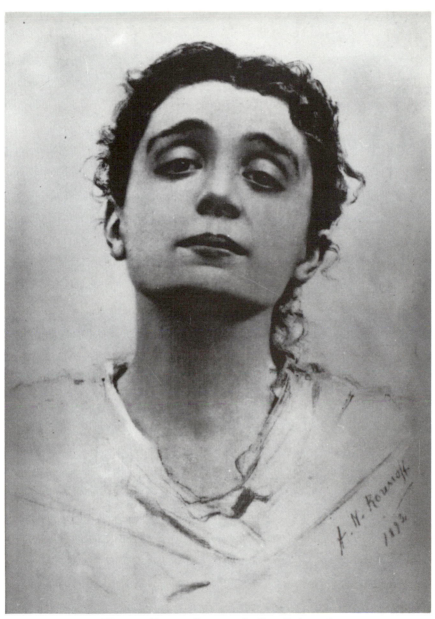

22   Eleonora Duse as Santuzza in *Cavalleria rusticana*

23   Eleonora Duse in *La Femme de Claude*

on a notion of wholeness embodied in the grand gesture style of playing. This technique enabled her to maintain careful control, whilst giving the impression of being totally at one with her character. It was a technique that she seems to have developed early. In 1873 she played Juliet in the amphitheatre in Verona, and she gave a detailed account of how she had used the device of a bunch of roses in her performance to Count Primoli, who was writing an article on her in 1897. The same story appears also in D'Annunzio's novel, *La fiamma*, when La Foscarina tells her lover about that great moment in her young life:

You know, when I heard Romeo say: 'Ah, she could teach the torches to be bright' I actually felt myself light up, I was all aflame. I had bought a huge bunch of roses with my pittance in the Piazza delle Erbe, under the fountain of Madonna Verona. Those roses were my only ornament. I mixed them with my words, my gestures, every move I made; I let one fall at Romeo's feet when we met, I threw one over the balcony onto his head, and I covered his dead body with them in the tomb. I was entranced by their scent, by the light and the air. My words flowed on with a strange facility, almost involuntarily, as in a delirium; and I could hear them through the constant beat of the pulsing of my veins . . . Every word before I uttered it seemed to pass right through the heat of my blood . . . I was Juliet.[21]

In 1881, in an article in *Nuova Antologia*, the Marchese D'Arcais attempted an analysis of Duse's acting style, and tried to explain her phenomenal success in the Italian theatre. Arguing that she was breaking with tradition in totally unforeseen ways, he also pointed out the long period of delay in her rise to stardom: 'She went unnoticed and untouched alongside leading men who yelled like wild beasts and leading ladies who waved their arms epileptically around the stage, among character actors afflicted with a perpetual tremor and open-mouthed serving girls.'[22] Certainly, by 1885, when the Rossi company set sail for South America for an extensive tour, Duse was a major star in Italy, and a big box-office attraction. The South American tour was an attempt on her part to widen her fame, but it was by no means an easy period in her life. She had married Tebaldo Cecchi, an actor in the Rossi company, in 1881, and her daughter Enrichetta was born in 1882. But during the South American tour Duse began a relationship with Flavio Andò, who was to become her leading man for several years, and Cecchi refused to return to Italy with her, deciding to remain in Buenos Aires. Duse found herself having to cope as a single parent and to deal with the possible negative criticism of a public still vehemently opposed to divorce.

A year later, in December 1886, Duse gave her final performance in the

Rossi company and from 1887 started out in a company of her own. The Compagnia drammatica della Città di Roma was the realization of her ambition for independence; despite the years working with Rossi, there had been some disagreements between them and she wanted a free hand in controlling the roles she played. Moreover, as emerges from her correspondence, she felt strongly that it was her duty as a mother to provide well for Enrichetta. As ever in Duse, artistic ambition was fused with bourgeois social aspirations.

The Duse company, with Flavio Andò as leading man and Giovannina Aliprandi as *seconda donna*, proved to be a success, though Duse's repertoire hardly enlarged at all for several years. She still played the ticket-selling roles – La Femme de Claude, Fedora, La Locandiera, Denise, Froufrou, Marguerite Gautier, etc. But although she had succeeded in obtaining financial independence and control over her own company, the sameness of her repertoire was still a source of concern. Earlier, in 1886, she had written to Francesco Garzes, husband of a close friend, expressing her hopes for the new company:

My dream, my ideal is to realize in practical terms everything I think and feel about the moral advantage of the art form to which I belong.

I want to set up a large company with completely modern intentions and send back to the attic (oh, yes, I really do) all the old trickeries of our blessed organization.

I want to bring a revolution (I do) in terms of staging as well, both in terms of setting up the stage and in terms of the final combination . . . etc. . . . . etc. . . . . I want to surround myself with everything that is most signif . . . etc. etc. . . . .[23]

Her great hopes for a truly innovative theatre were encouraged by her meeting with Arrigo Boito, in 1887. She had met him previously, in 1884, briefly, but when they met for the second time they embarked on a lengthy, intense love affair that lasted until Duse fell in love with D'Annunzio in 1897. Duse in 1887 was twenty-eight years old, Boito was forty-five. She was enormously popular in Italy, hoping for international stardom through her considerable touring programmes, and Boito was at the peak of his success as a writer, having provided the libretto for Verdi's *Otello* in that same year. The pattern in the Duse–Boito relationship was a familiar one; Duse fell in love with a man who could guide her intellectually and professionally, someone she could learn from and turn to in times of difficulty. They were to remain close despite Duse's passion for D'Annunzio, and Boito seems to have loved her until his death in 1918.

Since Duse travelled almost continuously, and most of the time abroad, in order to keep the company solvent, she and Boito maintained a frequent correspondence. Writing to him on 8 October 1887, a few months after the start of their affair, Duse mentions her own ambition for a new role:

I worked that night – I felt my own strength like I never did before – I saw the Vision up above – and do you know? I said to myself: I must go through this before I reach the greatest height of Cleopatra – I enjoyed it and suffered too – You saw yourself last night how physically exhausted I was – but .. . I worked well, really well . . . and I *applauded myself* . . . myself . . . – Can you forgive me? – But if I don't tell you all these dark feelings, who can I tell?

I have already stayed silent so often in my life – and I have never lost the TRUE REASON for my silence! Yes, it was a *fever brought on by art*! – but it was useful to me, to help me measure my flight – useful to the masses – perhaps – I don't care about that. You'll see! You'll see! I love you! If I stay well, I hope to *see the Vision* every night – You'll see! – You'll see me reach Schespeare (sic) now you hold me in your arms![24]

Boito translated *Antony and Cleopatra* for Duse, and the play premièred in Milan, at the Teatro Manzoni, on 22 November 1888. Preparations took a year, and Duse allocated 9,000 lire for the set and costumes, designed by Alfredo Edel, who had also done the costumes for Verdi's *Otello*. Details of the careful, precise planning and rehearsing of the play are preserved in some of Boito's letters. He clearly intended *Antony and Cleopatra* as a vehicle for Duse and in his letters he details some of the reasons for the cuts he made to Shakespeare's text. The final scene, with Cleopatra's death coming only after several other poignant deaths, should be pared down so that the audience's attention focuses on Cleopatra. Moreover, there was the question of the absence of a good leading man (in a letter of January 1888, Boito points out that Shakespeare wrote for Burbage, his brilliant leading actor, and Duse does not have Burbage in her company). After the opening night, which was badly received by the Italian critics, Boito wrote apologetically to Duse, admitting he had made a mistake in cutting so much of the original text: 'We only thought about one thing and that was: taking from this powerful poem all the divine essence of love and pain and we shut our eyes to everything else. That was a mistake.'[25]

The Italian reviews were almost universally bad. Duse was attacked for her inability to play great tragedy, while Boito's translation was condemned for bowdlerizing Shakespeare. The play did badly on tour in Italy, and in the following year Duse performed almost exclusively abroad, putting the unfortunate memory of her Italian Shakespeare behind her. Nevertheless, the play did well on tour abroad, particularly in Germany and Russia, and she kept it in her repertoire for several years.

24   Eleonora Duse as Cleopatra

William Archer's analysis of Duse's Cleopatra, written in 1893, is scathing in its attack:

It is said that Signora Duse understands no English; and this fact, if fact it be, is the explanation and excuse of her Cleopatra. If she could read Shakespeare's *Antony and Cleopatra* she would either drop the part altogether from her repertory or act it very differently. She would realize that the play is not a badly-constructed domestic drama in outlandish costumes, but a glorious love-poem, portraying and celebrating that all-absorbing passion for which the world is well lost.

Archer goes on to criticize the Italian version for its prosaicness and lack of beauty in the language. Having done so, he changes the direction of his attack, and concentrates on Duse's lack of passion:

There is nothing in the least voluptuous, sensuous, languorous about her performance. Her very embraces are chilly, and she kisses like a canary-bird . . .

Signora Duse's Cleopatra is never for an instant that incarnation of love and luxury, of all that is superb and seductive in womanhood, which has haunted the minds of men for nineteen centuries. She is simply a bright little woman, like her Nora or her Mirandolina. She is not Cleopatra, but Cleopatrina, Cleopatrinetta.[26]

Archer's criticism, which is more sharply focused than many of the negative reviews of 1888, reveals an interesting aspect of Duse's performance.

He maintains that she was lacking in sensuality, that she was too ordinary and everyday in her performance to rise to the expected heights of a tragic queen. What makes Duse's obvious failure as Cleopatra significant is that the role was so enormously popular with a number of other actresses of the *fin-de-siècle* period, and Cleopatra was a figure who aroused the popular imagination. It is with Cleopatra that we seem to see the limits of Duse's acting techniques. Highly skilful at the small gesture that could transform the mood of a scene, Duse was later to become equally skilful at the statuesque rendering of intense inner pain when she played D'Annunzio's heroines. But she was not languorous, her movements were not pliable and voluptuous. And if we consider the photographic record of Duse's many roles, this fact becomes fairly clear to determine. Duse's body line is variable, but she tends towards the backward curve for repressed characters who try to fight back (Santuzza, La moglie ideale, Denise, La femme de Claude, Rebecca West, Hedda Gabler, Francesca da Rimini), and the forward curve, with hunched shoulders, for characters in pain, contemplation or thought (Marguerite Gautier, Froufrou). What she does not do is the off-centre displacement of the body that emphasizes the pelvis and consequently arouses images of sensuality. The existing photographs of her *Cleopatra* show magnificent costumes and headdresses, but curiously passive poses, many with Duse reclining but even here less in languor than in meditation.

Another additional difficulty with Cleopatra could have been that Duse's great strength was in the representation of characters with a strong inner life and often with a contradictory outer life. Cleopatra, on the other hand, is a character whose inner emotions burn through into her public, outer existence. There are no clear boundaries between the two, unlike the tormented heroines of Duse's early repertoire or even the D'Annunzian and Ibsenian heroines of her later repertoire. Politics and passion combine in Shakespeare's Cleopatra, and they combine on the surface. Bernhardt was therefore much more able to take on board the Cleopatra role, whereas Duse's emphasis on smallness of gesture and nuance of feeling was lost on the part.

Luigi Rasi took it upon himself to defend Duse against the attacks on her lack of 'anima tragica' (tragic soul), but his defence is ambiguous. Although he categorically denies the accusation, he does nothing to disprove it except to cite examples of the practical problems of staging the play. He points out that Boito's translation is a travesty of the original, and lacks a sense of the tragic in its skeletal reduction of Shakespeare. But he also notes that the play makes heavy demands on staging; Duse's company abroad consisted of only ten or twelve actors and in *Antony and Cleopatra* this meant that at least half of them were playing two or even three parts. Moreover, there were thirty-eight scene changes, all of which involved elaborate technical apparatus, so the play was complex to put on and gave an impression of fragmentation.[27] Boito obviously geared the play for Duse, reshaping it primarily as a vehicle for her, and it suffered as a result. Audiences abroad, particularly in Russia, liked the production because it was spectacular and because Duse was by then a huge selling point, but in terms of Duse's character it taught her a salutary lesson. In her continued search for an extended repertoire, she henceforth stayed with contemporary writers and did not venture back into the world of Shakespeare, the writer with whom she was so poorly acquainted that she had problems in actually spelling his name.

Boito tried to introduce Duse to Shakespeare and was unsuccessful. He also tried to put her off Ibsen, which was an even greater failure. On 9 February 1891 Duse presented Ibsen's *A Doll's House* at the Teatro Filo-drammatici in Milan. It was the first Ibsen production in Italy and it marked the start of a new impulse in Duse's enlargement of the repertoire.

Duse's passion for Ibsen – and it seems fair to describe her relationship with his work as a passion – lasted for the rest of her career. Lugné-Poe tells a story, which may well be apocryphal, of how Duse tried to meet Ibsen in 1906 when she was playing in Oslo. When she learned that Ibsen was too old and ill to receive visitors, she stood in the street outside his house and waited for a chance glimpse of the great man at a window. Whatever the truth of this anecdote, Duse's involvement with Ibsen was quite as intense as her involvement with D'Annunzio's plays, and lasted a great deal longer. Writing in 1907, during the company's tour of South America, Guido Noccioli comments:

The Signora also attends today's rehearsals, and the rehearsal of *Rosmersholm* alone lasts for almost three hours. La Duse's passion for Ibsen is unbelievable. Hers is a true apostolate. Her diction in this play reveals such genius, such a wealth of ideas and depth of vision!

The other actors, naturally enough, end up by loathing Ibsen. They are not accustomed to having to analyse their roles to this extent. Their Latin temperament rebels. And as for the public, it is certainly not sophisticated enough to appreciate this type of play.[28]

Describing Duse's performance in *Rosmersholm*, G. A. Borghese, the Italian critic commented that 'no one on the Italian stage today is so resolutely avant-garde in matters of stage technique'.[29] He praised her 'statuesque poses and moments of silence', which he claimed were almost more significant than the spoken lines themselves.

Duse continued to add plays by Ibsen to her repertoire throughout her career. After *A Doll's House* in 1891, she waited seven years to add *Hedda Gabler* in 1898 (though this was not the first time the play had been performed in Italy, since it had been presented by Italia Vitaliani in 1892). Then, after the break with D'Annunzio, she worked with Lugné-Poe and presented *Rosmersholm*, designed by Edward Gordon Craig, followed later by *John Gabriel Borkman* (1921), *Ghosts* (1923), and *The Lady from the Sea*, which became one of her finest roles. In 1916 she tried hard to set up a film version of *The Lady from the Sea*, going so far as to examine locations and work on the script. But the project collapsed through lack of funding, and though Duse kept on trying for a time, even approaching Claudel to see if he would collaborate with her, the film was never made.

Molinari points out that Nora, the protagonist of *A Doll's House*, is an abbreviation of Eleonora, a significant detail that Duse may well have noted.[30] Moreover, it is striking how many of Duse's early roles involved women who have been betrayed – by lovers, husbands or by society, and in some cases (notably Denise) had lost a child. Obviously to some extent parallelisms of this kind may have been coincidental, but with Ibsen's Nora, Duse played a woman who strikes out for her own independence against the overt moralizing (that manifests itself as oppression) of a man. It is tempting to speculate that in playing Nora, Duse was striking a blow for her own liberation from the over-protectiveness of Boito and his dominance of her artistic development. Certainly, the choice of first Nora and then Hedda does show a break from the kind of heroines she had previously made her stock in trade. Nor can this choice be attributed to any change of opinion on Duse's part regarding the emancipation of women; she was far too steeped in bourgeois ideology to see herself in any way as a feminist. Yet she chose to play these two controversial roles at a time in her life when she was struggling to find something different, looking for a way forward in her career even whilst apparently enjoying the satisfaction of a profound relationship and the glories of international stardom.

There is some evidence that Duse chose roles that struck a personal chord for her. In 1892, when she added Sudermann's *Heimat* (known in Italian as *Magda*) to her repertoire, she wrote to the author:

Your Magda worked for 10 years.

The writer of this letter – has been working for 20 years. The difference is enormous if you think that you are dealing with a woman – unlike Magda – who is counting the days until she can leave the theatre.

Magda was 17 years – *in her own house*.

The writer of this letter has nothing like that. At 14 years of age they put her into long skirts – and told her: 'YOU HAVE TO act.'

There is some difference between these two women.

And, of course, Magda belongs to you as your creation, while the other woman is alive, wears clothes like the rest of the world.[31]

Magda, in fact, is the heroine who rebels against the ideal of home, as determined by her tyrannical father, and manages to make a career for herself on the stage when her father has thrown her out. In this respect she is similar to Ibsen's Nora, for both embody the spirit of revolt on the part of the modern woman. Bernard Shaw described Duse's performance as Magda in 1895 as infinitely superior to Bernhardt's, who uses predictable techniques and effects, and he summarized Duse's skills in the following terms:

Duse produces the illusion of being infinite in variety of beautiful pose and motion. Every idea, every shade of thought and mood, expresses itself delicately but vividly to the eye; and yet, in an apparent million of changes and inflexions, it is impossible to catch any line at an awkward angle, or any strain interfering with the perfect abandonment of all the limbs to what appears to be their natural gravitation towards the finest grace. She is ambidextrous and supple, like a gymnast or a panther; only the multitude of ideas which find physical expression in her movements are all of that high quality which marks off humanity from animals, and, I fear, I must add, from a good many gymnasts. When it is remembered that the majority of tragic actors excel only in explosion of those passions which are common to man and brute, there will be no difficulty in understanding the indescribable distinction which Duse's acting acquires from the fact that behind every stroke of it is a distinctively human idea.[32]

Nora, Magda, and Hedda were all heroines representative of the New Woman, tormented in a society that marginalized her and unable to see a positive way forward except through overt statements of rebellion. Von Hofmannsthal's famous article on Duse as Nora focuses on the way in which her portrayal went beyond the naturalistic representation of a woman with unique personal problems:

It seems that in 'Nora' Duse did not seek to portray the story of the soul of a little woman; and what she played was the vast symbolizing of an ethical and social accusation. She merely played the part of an individual and we felt it as typical. It was

25   Eleonora Duse as Hedda Gabler

in this way that the sacred Player, of whom chronicles relate, must have interpreted the Mystery of the Passion of Our Lord Jesus Christ: as a tormented man, beyond our help, 'and yet everyone was aware that beneath this was the Son of God.'

She played cheerfulness that was not happiness and laughed brightly to portray the dark void hidden behind that laughter; she played I-don't-want-to-think-about-it and I-must-think-about-it; she played at being a squirrel and a lark and her timid wildness aroused a physical sense of fear; when, with a sudden gesture she threw herself into the frenzied rhythm of the tarantella in the stiffening sense of mortal terror, she turned pale, cast down her chin, and her tormented eyes screamed at us in silence.[33]

In playing Ibsen, at least in the first plays added to her repertoire, Duse seems to have tried to develop her naturalistic acting techniques to produce effects beyond the melodramatic. The early roles of her rise to greatness were played naturalistically in an attempt to rouse the pity and stir the emotions of her audiences, whilst the note she seems to have been striving for in her Ibsen parts was that of arousing indignation. Yet even here there were striking personal quirks that conditioned her response to the parts. Lugné-Poe recounts how Duse insisted on having certain revisions made to the Italian version of *Hedda Gabler*, removing all references to Hedda's possible pregnancy from the script. Lugné-Poe suggests that: 'Duse revolted against the thought of possible motherhood (she revolted against it, just as Hedda did!) – and would not even allow the formal indications of it, as written by the author.'[34]

Motherhood presented Duse with very special problems. On the one hand was her direct experience of it, first with the dead child by Martin Cafiero and then with her daughter, Enrichetta, who lived a life of boarding schools, distanced from her mother, and eventually married a Cambridge don and turned wholeheartedly to the Catholic Church. On the other hand was the crisis that motherhood created in the life of a woman dedicated to art, and to an art that involved touring the world without a firm home base. All the crisis of Duse's bourgeois expectations must have been focused on her role as mother; for here the anti-bourgeois nature of her life as an actress could not be denied. The best she could hope for was to have the child raised by other people, in another system, and trust that there might still be a basis for a relationship with her from time to time. In a letter to Boito of 2 August 1891 she had written cryptically: 'The joys of motherhood!!!! Yes! some people love to sing about them . . . provided they've never actually been through it!'[35] It is hardly surprising that she should have had very mixed feelings about her own capacities as a mother, and although Lugné-Poe later persuaded her to reintroduce the references to Hedda's pregnancy after 1905, the role remained a crucial one for Duse, highlighting her own ambiguous feelings about sexuality and motherhood in particular. Throughout her career, Duse seems to have steered a course well away from representations of sensuality for its own sake, and it is interesting to speculate on how Duse forced audiences to rethink their received notions of femininity in her portrayal of women in different kinds of pain. D'Annunzio could write in his novel about La Foscarina being imaginatively possessed by the men in her audiences, but Duse seems to have constantly stressed, in one way or another, the immense gap between expectations and secrecy, between outer and inner lives. Critics of all nations return over and over to their attempts to describe how Duse portrayed inner struggle, how she rejected make-up and corsets and tinted hair in favour of natural physical decay and change, how she emphasized the pause and the infinitesimal movement rather than the wide gesture. In all these ways, the unspoken statement is that Duse was insisting on representing a femininity that had nothing to do with artifice, a femininity that accepted the existence of untapped inner depths that could not be controlled or described. But that femininity had little to do with feminism. Silvio d'Amico records in his diary in 1921 that when he suggested to Duse that *The Lady from the Sea* was 'the drama of the female spirit', she replied 'No! The drama of everyone . . .'[36]

Duse's relationship with Ibsen splits into two distinct parts. The first stage, in the 1890s, is that of her discovery of Ibsen, her playing of Nora and Hedda and, in her private life, of her movement away from Boito and beginning of the great passion for D'Annunzio. When she returned to Ibsen in 1905, it was after the relationship with D'Annunzio had taken its toll and transformed both her personal life and acting style.

The relationship between Duse and Gabriele D'Annunzio has tended to become the focus of attention for biographers and critics, often at the expense of a consideration of the rest of Duse's theatrical career. In fact, their relationship lasted only seven years, from 1897 to 1904, when it finally ended with immense bitterness on Duse's part. From the start, they had tried to combine their passionate affair with their ambition to revitalize the Italian theatre and create a new, more elevated, truly Italian art form, but D'Annunzio's infidelities (both sexual and professional) clashed with Duse's need for security and commitment. The final blow came in 1904, when D'Annunzio's *La figlia di Iorio* opened at the Teatro Lirico in Milan, with Irma Gramatica in the role of Mila, Duse's part.

D'Annunzio had written *La figlia di Iorio* in one month, whilst holidaying with Duse at Anzio in 1903. The role of Mila was conceived for her, and she planned to perform it the following February, when the play was due to open. However, the years spent trying to maintain a company that could perform D'Annunzio's plays, which were singularly unsuccessful in commercial terms, meant that she had to tour extensively abroad in order to keep financially afloat. Reluctantly, she agreed that the new play should be presented by the Talli–Gramatica–Calabresi company, a young group trained by Virgilio Talli, but that she would rejoin them to play Mila, handing on the part to Irma Gramatica at the end of the proposed Italian tour.

None of Duse's plans for herself came to pass. Exhausted by the winter tours, Duse was too ill to perform on the opening night of 2 March 1904. D'Annunzio was moreover now emotionally involved with another woman and Duse's distress was becoming more apparent. Matilde Serao recounts the famous story of how Duse, on her sickbed, recited the whole of *La figlia di Iorio* while the actual performance was taking place in Milan.[37] Next day the reviews were wildly enthusiastic, and for the first time D'Annunzio had a theatrical success on his hands. That the success had finally happened, after years of failure, and happened without Duse, was a bitter blow. The day after the opening night she wrote to him, in the anguished tone that characterizes most of her letters to him at this period:

> *The victory is yours . . .*
> Your burning desire for art feeds my whole life!
> Everything is fine. Everything is fine. Everything is fine.
> You did not feel anything and I died and was cured.
> My soul will never *touch* yours again.
> Never again that instant that I see in your eyes – and is life.
> I will never find your soul in me again.
> We are two – but I – am dead.[38]

The artistic collaboration between Duse and D'Annunzio had begun in 1897, when she appeared in his *Il sogno di un mattino di primavera*. This was not the first play he had written (*La città morta*, written with Duse in mind and performed later, pre-dated his other plays) but it was the first to be performed. Duse premièred it in Paris, on 15 June 1897 and took it on to Italy, to the Teatro Rossini in Venice, on 3 November 1897. It was performed with one of Duse's most popular roles, Goldoni's *La locandiera*, and the audience applauded the Goldoni comedy as enthusiastically as they refrained from applauding the D'Annunzio. *Il sogno* offered Duse the possibility of playing a madwoman, La Demente, who has witnessed the brutal murder of her lover by her own husband and has consequently lost her mind. The horrific story of the murder is recounted by La Demente during the course of the play, and Duse had a series of powerful monologues, together with scenes of madness that recall Lady Macbeth's sleep-walking scene and Ophelia with her flowers. Molinari has pointed out that the prompt-copy shows heavy underlining of a stage direction in the third scene: 'She touches her hair at the back of her neck and on her forehead with a shudder; then stares at her hands.' He suggests that the emphasis on this stage direction shows the way in which Duse was seeking to interpret D'Annunzio through some of her own preferred techniques, such as the nervous touching of her hair that characterized her perform-ance of the last act of *The Lady of the Camellias*. She had also written 'all the perfumes of Arabia', in the margin alongside the stage direction, referring herself back to Shakespeare.[39]

Molinari does not develop this point, but he seems to be suggesting that Duse was unsure about the best way to perform D'Annunzio's play. She had acquired a huge international reputation by 1897, had a sizeable repertoire, even though she was not entirely happy with it, and had developed her own style of performance. But that particular playing style was characterized by a quality that reviewers struggled to describe as *spiritual, internal, profound, subtle, soulful, mystical* or, approaching it from a different angle, *neurotic*. Arthur Symons describes her performing technique as 'the antithesis of what we call acting', and adds that her greatest moments 'are the moments of most intense quietness'.[40] Through the smallness of her gestures, her hesitations, her pauses that seemed to imply the presence of an internal struggle going on, Duse came to portray for an entire generation the ultimate in realism, because her acting did not appear to be acting at all. Symons sums it up well:

Duse's art . . . is like the art of Verlaine in French poetry; always suggestion, never statement, always a renunciation. It comes into the movement of all the arts, as they seek to escape from the bondage of form, by a new, finer mastery of form, wrought outwards from within, not from without inwards. And it conquers almost the last obstacle, as it turns the one wholly external art, based upon mere imitation, existing upon the commonest terms of illusion, triumphing by exaggeration, into an art wholly subtle, almost spiritual, a suggestion, an evasion, a secrecy.[41]

This type of acting could be used with great effect in many of the roles of the naturalistic theatre that Duse took on and developed, and it could also be used in Ibsen's plays. But it was not suited to D'Annunzio's works, which were very definitely structured around a series of strong external features. The visual element was important to D'Annunzio through the grand gesture, the frozen moment of extreme emotion, the tableau, and so also was the powerful effect of poetic language. His was a theatre totally removed from realist modes, and required completely different acting and staging techniques. As he became more involved in the theatre, through his work with Duse, D'Annunzio took enormous pains with lighting his productions, with costumes and stage design. The cost of his productions was high because of his insistence on creating the perfect moment; costumes took a huge part of the production budget, for example, and in *La città morta* Duse wore cloth of gold, designed by Worth in Paris. D'Annunzio's enthusiasm for creating effects in the theatre led him also to introduce an innovation into the Italian theatre of the time: the elimination of footlights. Teresa Rasi, writing in her diary, quotes D'Annunzio as saying that he would personally smash the footlights himself if they were not extinguished. She adds: 'And he actually started to put his threat into practice. He was so persuasive they went dark at once. But how on earth will the public react to the darkness tomorrow?'[42] They reacted badly in fact, and the *Corriere della Sera* of 10 December 1901 described *Francesca da Rimini*, the production without footlights, as a long, morningless night.

D'Annunzio's personal involvement in the staging of his plays led Duse to the brink of financial ruin, but more significantly, perhaps, it also changed her style of performing. Unable to use the minutely nuanced acting style of her previous playing, Duse had to devise alternative methods to deal with the radically different material of the plays and with the changes in staging. D'Annunzio's passion for effect led him to insist on precise historical accuracy of props and costumes, to experiment with costly materials to see what kind of effect could be created under different lighting conditions, to light the productions in totally new ways, to arrange the actors spatially in accordance with the effects he wanted and to insist on a particular form of diction when speaking his lines. So in *La città morta*, for example, Duse was placed a long way away from the front of the stage, and the photographs show her right at the back, distanced from her audience by a great expanse of empty space.

D'Annunzio also demanded a special way of speaking from his actors, claiming that the poetry of his lines required a conventionalized, non-naturalistic mode of playing. Critics complained about the artificiality of this performance style, but as Molinari points out[43] a feature that recurs in reviews of Duse's D'Annunzio performances is the emphasis on positive changes in her voice:

The actress's voice had renewed itself, had discovered more classical resonances and previously unknown tones. She had learned how to 'scan and shape' the prose of *Sogno* and how to make the lines of *Francesca* rhythmical (to the point of monotony, as many felt) but she never reached the sonority of chant and tended eventually to deny herself and fade off into nothing. Now that she had found her poet, Eleonora no longer had to struggle with words, trying to find something inside herself to say or exhausting herself behind the urgency of speaking, but she was afraid of overwhelming the divine words, afraid that the means of performing it would prevail over the work itself and so instead of exposing it, she concealed it. But on the other hand, she could not escape from the pain of alienation: the divine words that she had been looking for all her life were not her own.[44]

Poor Duse was caught in a double bind. As a self-educated woman with aspirations of creating great art, she nevertheless saw herself as an instrument rather than as an initiator. The experience with Boito had been fulfilling personally but had not helped her a great deal in the pursuit of her goal; her attempts to do Shakespeare, though a source of her success in Russia, were generally judged to be a failure, and Boito had advised her against Ibsen, the one certain successful writer in her repertoire. D'Annunzio, however, who was prepared not only to write but to collaborate in practical terms with putting a play on the stage, came closer to her ideal figure. He joined in enthusiastically with Duse's views on the poverty of the Italian theatre and the need to create something new, learning from her whilst purporting to be teaching her everything she needed. Looking back on the lengthy documentation of the love relationshp and professional collaboration between them, as it appears in the letters, diaries, memoirs of their own and other people, what appears most strikingly is not so much the case of a woman approaching forty who falls in love with a younger man, nor even of two deeply neurotic, creative people who were fundamentally unsuited to each other. Instead, we can see how D'Annunzio's dreams of a golden age of Italian culture together with his personal arrivism so typical of his petit bourgeois background came close to Duse's very similar dreams and very similar social aspirations. The basis of their romantic and working relationship, therefore, was not in the real world that each was managing to inhabit very successfully, but in the world of their imagination, and consequently neither can ever really have met the other on a significant level.

It was this fundamental non-communication that could lead Duse to exhaust herself financing D'Annunzio's schemes and not to complain about D'Annunzio's continued nagging over her (to him) inexplicably petty economies. And likewise, it led Duse to go against her training and instincts and allow herself to be directed by a man with no experience who used the filmic technique of rehearsing in fragmented bits, never giving actors a clear indication of the overall shape of the production. But undoubtedly, the seven years together helped each of them enormously in different ways. D'Annunzio learned how to write for the theatre, and Duse learned another type of performance style. Placed at the back of a dimly lit stage, in lavish costumes, speaking words that demanded rhetorical power and overt displays of energy, Duse had to change her introverted nuanced approach. What she developed was in some ways an extension of her earlier work, in some ways a departure from it. In terms of voice, if the many reviewers are to be believed, she found a deeper resonance and spoke more from the whole body rather than from the head (the nasal quality of her voice is often commented on in her early years). In terms of gesture, she was constrained to open out into larger patterns of movements, to occupy space differently, more coherently and with greater weight. The photographs of *La città morta*, *Francesca da Rimini* and *La gioconda* all testify to this. The hunched shoulders are gone, and so are the little props – the handkerchief, the bunch of flowers. In their place, what we see are more open movements, wider arms, heavy use of draped materials for a statuesque effect, hands used almost as a dancer would use them. Duse's hands, the focal point of many of the photographs from this period, fascinated D'Annunzio, and the dedication of *La gioconda* is 'To Eleonora Duse of the beautiful hands'. But as ever with D'Annunzio, his consciousness of Duse's beautiful hands was not without ambiguity. The protagonist of *La gioconda*, fighting for her sculptor husband against his mistress, saves his greatest statue and loses her hands in the process when it falls on her. Her reward for fidelity and belief in his art is abandonment when he returns to his mistress and the loss of her greatest beauty, her hands.

In choosing to cut off the hands of his protagonist in the one play dedicated to Duse, D'Annunzio shows the profound insecurity of his own position. Forced to use actors, he nevertheless despised them and, like Pirandello, who called all actors traitors, disliked the loss of control that happened whenever a play of his was staged. In 1899, when Duse was abroad on tour, an interview with D'Annunzio appeared in *La Stampa*, castigating Italian actors for their incompetence and stupidity. What a poet needed, he claimed, was a company made up of 'virgin souls, ready to be shaped by the images' he could create. The only way forward for actors was for poets like himself to show them how to work:

I think that if we set out to try and find them, inspire them, arouse them, we'll be able to overcome their reluctance. And then we would be able to perform our works wholly and perfectly in the eyes of the world, those works which have hitherto been cut off and reviled by that accursed race of actors.[45]

D'Annunzio's attack on actors provoked hostile reaction, and a telegram from the Duse–Rasi company who were performing in Bucharest was sent immediately, demanding an explanation, since they were about to return to open in *La gioconda*. He had always demanded particular qualities from his actors, insisting on Flavio Andò being part of the company formed for *La città morta* (Andò refused nevertheless, and Ermete Zacconi took over instead) or using actors straight from the Florence Dramatic School on the grounds that he could better shape their style of performance if they were young and untried. He seems to have been satisfied that Duse had the qualities he wanted from an actor, whatever they might be, but his contempt for actors in general, combined with his lack of financial foresight and his idealistic notions of staging, meant that rehearsals were fraught with tension and the actors had a hard time of it.

After the break with D'Annunzio, Duse continued working as energetically as ever, but with certain crucial differences. Her health had begun to give way and in 1903 she had worked very little, travelling only to Switzerland, Germany and London, where *Francesca da Rimini* failed to please. The cost of touring D'Annunzio's plays was astronomical, both in terms of staging expenses and the number of actors required. She contracted a huge debt for *La figlia di Iorio* which was paid by one of her friends, Robi Mendelssohn from Berlin, the man who was to be her financial manager until his death ten years later. Primoli tells how Duse told him that she had been forced to go back to the old box-office successes, such as *The Lady of the Camellias*, to try to make ends meet. The dream of a new theatre had collapsed under economic constraints.

When the relationship with D'Annunzio ended and Duse emerged from the black depression – suicidal, according to close friends – she went to Paris and began the search for more plays. She commissioned Adolfo de Bosis to translate Maeterlinck's *Monna Vanna*, which she opened in Milan

26   Eleonora Duse as Rebecca in *Rosmersholm*

at the Teatro Lirico in May 1904 to great public acclaim and critical uncertainty. Then she toured Germany with a predominantly Ibsen repertoire. Several years later she commented that: 'Germany is the country where I like best to perform Ibsen, because it is the country in which the great tragic writer revealed himself to me; I understood him for the first time thanks to German actors, and they taught me how to love him.'[46]

Meanwhile, she was planning a return to Paris, and signed a contract with Lugné-Poe to appear at the Nouveau-théâtre with her company, alongside Lugné-Poe's own Oeuvre company. She may have met Lugné-Poe earlier through Romain Rolland, but their new-found collaboration was a successful one and seems to have given Duse back her self-respect and will to continue working. Lugné-Poe organized her tour of Scandinavia in 1906 and of Latin America in 1907, and during her collaboration with him she added Gorki's *The Lower Depths* to her repertoire and tried unsuccessfully to set up a production of von Hofmannsthal's *Elektra*. Lugné-Poe describes life as a co-worker with Duse in *Sous les étoiles*, and from his book, together with Noccioli's diaries of the 1906–7 tour, we have some idea of the conditions under which she worked at that time. What emerges from both accounts is Duse's shrewd financial sense and very professional attitude to her work in terms of the precision she demanded from her actors. What also emerges, however, is the portrait of a woman often in poor health, certainly very temperamental, who could never be relied on to perform unless she felt like it. Encouraged by Lugné-Poe she took artistic risks and increased her Ibsen repertoire, adding in particular the two plays that were to be her trademark for the rest of her life, *Rosmersholm* and *The Lady from the Sea*.

For Rosmerholm, Duse finally found her ideal collaborator, Edward Gordon Craig. She had seen his designs for Von Hoffmansthal's *Elektra* and been deeply impressed, and in 1906 the two met and discussed working together. Details of their collaboration are recorded in Isadora Duncan's autobiography, *My Life*. She claims that since Craig had neither French nor Italian and Duse had no English, she became the interpreter between them. Craig started work on the designs for *Rosmersholm*, and Duse enthusiastically supported them. On the opening night at the Pergola in Florence, on 5 December 1906, she made a speech to the actors, announcing that it was her destiny to have found 'this great genius', and that only through him 'will we poor actors find release from this monstrosity, this charnel-house which is the theatre of today'.[47]

General opinion of Ibsen in Italy was that the environment of the plays was a crucial component. The austerity and coldness of the Rosmer household was therefore considered to be an essential feature for an understanding of the play. Craig, on the other hand, rejected a realistic interpretation and argued that the play was a statement on Ibsen's part of his detestation of realism:

The words are the words of actuality, but the drift of the words, something beyond this. There is the powerful impression of unseen forces closing in upon the place: we hear continually the long drawn-out note of the horn of death . . . We are not in a house of the 19th or 20th century built by Architect this or Master builder that, and filled with furniture of Scandinavian design. That is not the state of mind Ibsen demands we shall be in. Let us leave period and accuracy of detail to the museums and to curiosity shops.[48]

What Craig created was a symbolically structured set, in tones of blue and violet. Corradini describes it:

The stage was transformed, truly transfigured, enormously high with a new architecture, with no wings, all in one colour somewhere between green and pale blue, simple, mysterious, compelling, worthy in short to receive the most profound life of Rosmer and of Rebecca West . . . The stage is a representation of a state of mind.[49]

The photographs of Duse as Rebecca West show a more mature figure, less ethereal than in the flowing draperies of her D'Annunzio roles, more solid and substantial, her head wreathed in heavy braids of hair. It seemed that she had finally found a way forward, both in terms of new parts and in terms of a young man of talent whose views of the need to restore the theatre from within came close to her own. As the symbol of life in *Rosmersholm*, Duse was affirming her own determination to continue and to move into new areas of performance. During her years with D'Annunzio, she had learned how to adjust her performance style to cope with the competition from the staging itself, so working with Craig was not a problem. What was still unresolved, however, was the structure of the company with which she performed.

The notice in the 1907 *Almanacco del Teatro Italiano* described Duse's newest company as 'a collection of mediocrities'.[50] Leo Orlandini was now her leading man, and Noccioli records how all the actors were chosen on the basis of personal recommendation. But the *mattatore* system was still strongly in operation, and despite Duse's search for new plays, directors and designers, she was as culpable as any of maintaining that system in operation to enhance her own playing. Numerous testimonies record how erratic she was in attending (or calling) rehearsals and how she could never be relied upon to perform until the last minute. With this kind of attitude (though in all fairness, it must not be thought that Duse was unusual in her behaviour) it is hardly surprising that she could not gather round her a strong permanent company. Moreover, she does not seem to have spent much time training her actors, no doubt expecting them to acquire the skills she required in much the same haphazard way as she had learned them for herself at the start of her career.

Nor did the collaboration with Craig last long either. In 1907 he started work designing *The Lady from the Sea* for her, but they clashed violently in Nice early that year, when Duse's touring production of *Rosmersholm* played in a small theatre and the stage staff cut the set down to make it fit. Craig complained to Duse that his art had been massacred and henceforth collaboration between the two of them broke down. Later, both claimed that the breach between them had been healed, but the episode of *Rosmersholm* was decisive. It also points to something else; that despite her theoretical pleas for a new theatre, Duse had no clear idea of how to go about making it, and seems not to have been too concerned with the destruction of Craig's set, telling him 'what has been done to your decor is simply what people have been doing to *my* art for years'.[51]

The post-D'Annunzio years have been described by some biographers in terms of Duse's 'mysticism'. There may be some basis in this idea, since Duse apparently became more religious in later life, as her daughter Enrichetta certainly did (both Enrichetta's children joined religious orders in England), but she also continued to be difficult as a working partner and to have increasing bouts of illness and depression. Writing to Lugné-Poe when she had spent some time with Isadora Duncan, trying to help her deal with her desperate grief after the death of her two young children in 1913, Duse comments:

I do not understand, dear friend, how that woman dares to want to RECONSTRUCT her life!

Nothing that is *irreparable* is understood by that magnificent, dangerous creature. Her generosity is as great as her error of judgement.

The irreparable, which nevertheless elevates the tone of life – no – she cannot see it at all and she wants to throw herself back into life, the life which bleeds – and see again – what? The smile of her dead child *in another* smile of another child that will be hers!

Dear friend, you may regret my pettiness but I understand nothing of *that kind of will*, that madness, that supreme wisdom. Isadora Duncan has supreme force on her side – something greater than life itself.[52]

The subtext to this letter is a statement by Duse about her own life and suffering. After the pain of the break-up with D'Annunzio, she seems to have considered herself as a being destined to suffer, and to have conceived a romantic notion of the eternally suffering artist. Part of her survival strategy after the humiliations of the collapse of the great love of her life (at one point she even wrote to D'Annunzio's latest mistress asking to be allowed to share him) was to focus intensely on her work, and since by 1904 she was forty-six years old she was also well aware of the need to move on from playing parts more suited to younger women. But whilst Isadora seems to have still clung to a belief in an eventual possible happiness, Duse had no such illusions. Pain and the representation of pain had been for so long a quintessential part of her life and work that she could not imagine any other state of being.

On 25 January 1909, Duse performed *The Lady from the Sea*, one of her favourite roles, in Berlin and retired from the stage. She had been acting since the age of four, almost half a century, and had come to the point of exhaustion. She remained in retirement for several years, though during that time there were various plans for a return to the stage, plans involving Rilke at one point, who tried for two years to find ways of working with her, and Yvette Guilbert with whom Duse hoped to work, though nothing came of it. In 1916 she made her one and only film, *Cenere*, and after the end of the Great War she returned once again to the stage. But in the years from 1909 to 1921, when she made her come-back, she seems to have kept some distance between herself and the theatre. Instead, she seems to have tried to work out certain unresolved matters in her private life, in particular those relating to her daughter Enrichetta and her female friends.

Weaver in his biography discusses Duse's close friendship with Lina Poletti, the lesbian feminist poet, but dismisses any suggestion that the two women might have had an affair. The few surviving letters, he suggests, prove nothing one way or another, and Duse's tendency to develop close female friendships was always noteworthy. Nevertheless, the years of retirement from the theatre were by no means years of seclusion. Duse had plans to set up a support centre for women in the theatre, and in 1914 she opened her Libreria delle Attrici (Library for Actresses) in Rome. The purpose of this enterprise was to provide a meeting place for women, somewhere they could not only study and encounter one another to exchange views, but also occasionally find a place to stay. It was an innovative project, and despite the derisory way that contemporaries and later biographers have discussed it (Weaver is dismissive, Molinari is contemptuous) it was a genuinely feminist initiative on Duse's part and very much in keeping with her phase of re-examination of her female roles.

Besides the relationship with Lina Poletti, biographers have noted the number of other, younger women including Ellen Terry in Duse's life at this time, and tended to describe them all as 'surrogate daughters'. This notion of the surrogate daughter is a curious one, since Duse would appear to have encountered these women at a time when she was strongly seeking to develop her relationship with her own daughter and also since often these other relationships ended in extraordinary bitterness and hostility. Moreover, it is precisely during this period that Duse made several overt statements about her attitude towards feminism, revealing herself as a woman who took a middle position, arguing against a feminism based on separatism.

It is a matter of speculation for future Duse biographers as to whether she finally found a new way forward outside the love of men in her menopausal years. The signs, on the basis of a few remaining letters and testimonies, are ambiguous, but it would make a great deal of sense in assessing Duse's life and career to recognize the strength of her attachments to women and her commitment to changing the image of women in the theatre. Rather than seeing her third phase as one of mysticism, it would be more appropriate to see it as a feminist phase, when she introduced new roles into the Italian theatre that showed women as strong, forceful and positive, as survivors rather than as victims. Her earliest roles portray women as trapped by the norms of a society that ranks men in the highest position; her D'Annunzian roles portray women as victims precisely because they possess depths and qualities that men cannot understand or reach, and so receive the full force of male sadomasochistic oppression. It is in the third phase that Duse began to play women who celebrate their Otherness and who impose their will upon the world around them. Woman may still suffer, but she survives and is a source of life and energy.

The Library ran into financial trouble and eventually failed. Duse gave the books to another library, run by the National Committee of Italian Women, in 1915 and six years later, in 1921, returned to the stage when her savings ran out (her German financial adviser had invested some money in German banks, and the devaluation of the mark hit her hard).

She made her return on 5 May 1921 at the Teatro Balbo in Turin. The play she chose was the one in which she had made her farewell performance more than a decade earlier: Ibsen's *The Lady from the Sea*. When he saw her perform the role of Ellida Wangel in this play in London in 1923, James Agate wrote:

This play is a godsend to a great actress whose *forte* is not so much doing as suffering that which fate has done to her. With Duse, speech is silver and silence is golden . . . The long second act was a symphony for the voice, but to me the scene of greatest marvel was the third act. In this Duse scaled incredible heights. There was one moment when, drawn by every fibre of her being to the unknown irresistible power of the Stranger and the sea, she blotted herself behind her husband and took courage and comfort from his hand. Here terror and ecstasy sweep over her face with that curious effect which this actress alone knows – as though this were not present stress, but havoc remembered of past time. Her features have the placidity of long grief; so many storms have broken over them that nothing can disturb again this sea of calm distress. If there be in acting such a thing as pure passion divorced from the body yet expressed in terms of the body, it is here. Now and again in this strange play Duse would seem to pass beyond our ken and, where she has been there is only fragrance and a sound in our ears like water flowing under the stars.[53]

In her final years of performance, Duce continued to innovate, introducing Ibsen's *Ghosts* in 1921 and a new play by Tommaso Gallarati Scotti, *Così sia*. She was working with Ermete Zacconi, and Silvio d'Amico records how she was full of ideas for other works, including Yeats and Synge. She did, however, refuse to play a role written specially for her by Luigi Pirandello, that of Donn'Anna in *La vita che ti diedi* (*The Life I Gave You*) in 1923, for reasons that remain mysteriously unresolved. She claimed poor health; d'Amico suggested that the subject matter of the play was offensive to her. An undiscussed reason might also have been her reluctance to embark on working with a playwright whose views about actors were so close to D'Annunzio's and so antagonistic.[54] The significant roles of her return to the theatre remained her Ibsen performances, together with Marco Praga's drama of adultery, *La porta chiusa*. For her American tour of 1923 she took five plays: *The Lady from the Sea*, *Ghosts*, *Così sia*, *La porta chiusa* and D'Annunzio's *La città morta*.

Duse had always had a love–hate relationship with the United States. She had first toured in 1893, when the impression she created was one of mixed feelings, a combination of lavish praise and scepticism about her talent. Then in 1896 came a second, more successful tour, though the ground won during that period was lost again in 1902, when she toured the United States with a solely D'Annunzian repertoire and alienated audiences as a result. In 1915 she was involved in negotiations to go out to California to work on a film with Griffiths, but she did not return until the 1923 tour. On 21 April 1924, in a hotel in Pittsburgh, she died of pneumonia after an increasingly difficult tour during which she was constantly afflicted with ill-health. She was sixty-seven years old, and died as she was born – on the road, in a place where she had no sense of belonging.

Assessment of Duse's career is necessarily a patchy affair. Her daughter destroyed a large number of her letters, but in any case documentary evidence still does not help in trying to reconstruct what she did on stage and how she did it. It is undeniable that she had an enormous impact on audiences across a period of sixty years, and that in trying to explain what it was that they thought they had seen, people fell back constantly into a language of allusion, suggestion and quasi-mysticism. Duse, the general consensus of the late nineteenth and early twentieth centuries seems to have been, was the supreme actress of the spirit, in contrast to other actresses, such as Bernhardt, who embodied the supremacy of the physical. This obscure language of criticism, together with the carefully posed photographs are not very helpful to us today, particularly when we consider that the terminology of then and now are two entirely different concerns.

Nevertheless, two things do come through clearly. The first is that Duse must have employed physical strategies to obtain the effects that she did, and those strategies can be determined to some measure. Secondly, Duse must have so refined her technique (as Ristori said she did) that her strategies became second nature to her. In other words, where so many actors are conscious of *acting* a role, of building it and developing it, Duse focused her mental energy on the creation of a role, but when interpreting it physically, she was able to bring into play all the techniques that had by then been incorporated into her body–mind responses. The ability of actors to do this, to so train their bodies that the process of using those bodies becomes almost unconscious, is something that has existed for centuries in the Oriental theatre (one thinks of actors training themselves for months to acquire exactly the right effect by the movement of a single finger or the rolling of the eyes) and in the past twenty years it has become an aspiration of laboratory theatres throughout the world. What Eugenio Barba tries to define as a search on the part of actors for the state of pre-expressivity from which to begin working, rather than from a state of conscious construction of a role, must have been part of Duse's schema.[55]

Duse clearly sought parts that she could relate to within herself, without having to make a conscious effort to work herself into alien personalities. In this respect she obviously tried to bring the role into herself, rather than seeking for a way into it. And because her starting point was not a deliberate search for psychological realism, but rather that of looking for a means through which she could offer the role her own feelings about it in physical terms, she managed to create the impression of extraordinary sincerity and bravura combined. The price she paid for this kind of performing was high, as her fraught private life and constant neurotic illnesses testify, but she was most certainly ahead of her time in her method of working.

The irony is that her individuality which resulted in her powers also meant that she left no school of followers. The interiority of the Duse mode of performance could not be imitated, and although some actresses may have adapted some of her mannerisms, the essential uniqueness of her work died with her.

Notes

vvvvvvvvvvvvvvvvvvvvvvvvvvvvvvvvvvvvvvvvvvvvvvvvvvvvvvvvvvvvvvvvvvvvvvvvv

Introduction

1 'Image and Reality: The Actress and Society' in Martha Vicinus (ed.), *A Widening Sphere. Changing Roles of Victorian Women* (London: Methuen, 1977), p. 94.
2 Ernst Gombrich, *Art and Illusion* (New York: Bollingen Series, 1961); Umberto Eco, *A Theory of Semiotics* (London: Macmillan, 1977), p. 204.
3 Gombrich, quoted in Eco, *A Theory of Semiotics*, p. 205.
4 *The Stage*, 17 May 1900, p. 15.
5 *What is Theatre?* (London: Methuen, 1969), p. 42.
6 *Around Theatres* (London: Rupert Hart-Davis, 1953), p. 81.
7 Michael R. Booth, *Victorian Spectacular Theatre 1850–1910* (Boston, London and Henley: Routledge and Kegan Paul, 1981).
8 Martin Meisel, *Realizations, Narrative, Pictorial and Theatrical Arts in Nineteenth-Century England* (Princeton, New Jersey: Princeton University Press, 1983), p. 11.
9 Havelock Ellis, *Man and Woman* (London: Walter Scott, 1894), p. 325.
10 Francisque Sarcey, *Quarante ans de théâtre* (Paris: Bibliothèque des Annales, 1900), vol. III, p. 230.
11 *Bibliothèque de Mme Sarah Bernhardt*, 2 vols. (Paris: H. Leclerc, 1923), pp. 35–6.
12 Sarah Bernhardt, *The Art of the Theatre*, trans. H. J. Stenning (London: Geoffrey Bles, 1924), p. 144.
13 Ellen Terry, *The Story of My Life*, 2nd edn (London: Hutchinson, 1908), p. 218.
14 'A Chat with Sarah Bernhardt', *Westminster Gazette*, 2 November 1894.
15 Reynaldo Hahn, *Sarah Bernhardt* (London: Elkin Mathews and Marrot, 1932), p. 88.
16 'The Legend of Duse' in Ian Fletcher (ed.), *Decadence and the 1890s*, Stratford-upon-Avon Studies 17 (London: Edward Arnold, 1979), p. 154.
17 Martin Buber, 'Die Duse in Florenz' in M. Friedman (ed.), *Martin Buber and the Theatre* (New York: Funk and Wagnalls, 1969), p. 10.

Sarah Bernhardt

1 See Laurence Senelick, 'Chekhov's Response to Bernhardt' in Eric Salmon (ed.), *Bernhardt and the Theatre of Her Time* (Westport, Connecticut and London: Greenwood Press, 1984), pp. 165–81.
2 See Matthew Arnold, 'The French Play in London', *The Nineteenth Century*, August 1879, reprinted in R. H. Super (ed.), *The Complete Prose Works of Matthew Arnold*, 11 vols. (Ann Arbor: University of Michigan Press, 1960–77), vol. IX, 1973, pp. 64–85; and Henry James, 'The Comédie Française in London', *The Scenic Art* (London: Rupert Hart-Davis, 1949), pp. 125–61.

3 Arthur Symons, 'Modernity in Verse', *Studies in Two Literatures* (London: Leonard Smithers, 1897), pp. 188–9.
4 The historical determinants of Bernhardt's 'image' are discussed in my 'Aspects of Bernhardt', *Yearbook of English Studies*, vol. II (London: MHRA, 1981), pp. 143–60.
5 *Gazette des Tribuneaux*, 19, 20, 26 June 1880. The case was reported in full, with a special report on previous contract breakers on 19 June. The archives of the Comédie Française contain many of Bernhardt's contracts from 1862 onwards and chart her steeply rising salary. They also contain her contract as a *sociétaire* of 24 March 1875.

The fine was to be paid in 3 instalments: 30,000 francs immediately, 35,000 by 30 July 1883, 35,000 by 30 December 1883. The Comédie Française has correspondence with lawyers revealing the great confusion about what was and what was not paid, through to 1892. The debt was eventually annulled when Bernhardt lent her theatre to the company in 1900 after a fire.
6 Louis Verneuil, *La Vie merveilleuse de Sarah Bernhardt* (New York: Brentano's, 1942), pp. 126–7.
7 Jacques de Plunkett, *160 ans de théâtre. Fantômes et souvenirs de la Porte Saint-Martin* (Paris: Ariane, 1946), p. 297; Verneuil, *La Vie merveilleuse*, p. 147.
8 *Entr'acte*, May/June 1888.
9 Unidentified cuttings at the Bibliothèque de l'Arsenal, September 1884. The case, which was farcical and long drawn out, hinged upon the validity of the Damalas' marriage, which had taken place in England.
10 Ernest Pronier, *Une Vie au théâtre: Sarah Bernhardt* (Geneva: Editions Alex Jullien, n.d.), p. 258.
11 Edouard Noël and Edmond Stoullig, *Les Annales du théâtre et de la musique* (Paris: G. Charpentier et E. Fasquelle, 1883), p. 254.
12 Unidentified cutting dated 2 May 1883, Collection of the Association de la Régie Théâtrale (ART), Bibliothèque Historique de la Ville de Paris (BHVP).
13 Unidentified and undated cutting, BHVP (ART).
14 Unidentified cutting dated 2 May 1883, BHVP (ART).
15 Unidentified cutting dated 14 October 1882, BHVP (ART).
16 Unidentified cutting dated 15 October 1882, BHVP (ART).
17 Verneuil, *La Vie merveilleuse*, p. 177; Pronier, *Une Vie au théâtre*, p. 259.
18 William F. Apthorp, 'Paris Theatres and Concerts. III – The Unsubventioned Theatres and Orchestral Concerts', *Scribner's Magazine*, April 1892, p. 484.
19 *La Chronique Parisienne*, 31 October 1884.
20 Information from Noël and Stoullig, *Annales*, 1884–8.
21 Sardou in a letter to Pierre Berton dated 1 January 1886, quoted by Verneuil, *La Vie merveilleuse*, p. 189.
22 *Ibid.*, p. 206.
23 Report by A. Loyau, *ingénieur civil*, filed under 'Théâtre de la Renaissance. Administration 1838–1909', Arsenal.
24 Apthorp, 'Paris Theatres', p. 484.
25 'A Chat with Sarah Bernhardt', *The Sketch*, 27 June 1894, p. 458.
26 Edward John Hart, 'Illustrated Interviews. No. XI – Sarah Bernhardt', *Strand Magazine*, May 1895, p. 535.

27 *Le Temps*, 13 November 1893.
28 Catulle Mendès, *L'Art au théâtre*, 3 vols. (Paris: E. Fasquelle, 1897–1900), vol. I (1897), p. 338.
29 Noël and Stoullig, *Annales*, 1895, p. 178.
30 Verneuil, *La Vie merveilleuse*, p. 227.
31 *Ibid.*, p. 229.
32 Information from *Le Gaulois*, 23 November 1898, and *Le Figaro*, 26 November 1898.
33 Alfred Delilia, 'Le Théâtre Sarah Bernhardt', unidentified cutting, Arsenal. The interview must have been conducted in December 1899.
34 Félix Narjoux, *Paris. Monuments élevés par la ville 1850–1880*, 4 vols. Ouvrage publié sous le patronage de la ville de Paris. (Paris: A. Morel, 1883), vol. III, *Edifices consacrés aux beaux-arts* (1882), p. 2.
35 Delilia, 'Le Théâtre'.
36 For financial details of *L'Aiglon* see Stoullig, *Annales*, 1900, p. 200 and Emile Faguet in *Journal des Débats*, 23 January 1899.
37 *Le Théâtre du peuple* (Paris: Librairie Fischbacher, 1904), pp. 35–6.
38 Details of the 1909 lease renewal application are taken from the minutes of the Deuxième Commission du Conseil Municipal de Paris, 30 June 1909; of the 1921 application from the *Bulletin Municipal Officiel*, 31 December 1921. From the start of Bernhardt's tenancy all the lease applications, which took the form of lengthy hearings at the Hôtel de Ville, were widely reported in the press: see in particular *Commoedia*, *Le Figaro*, *Le Gaulois*, *L'Information*, *Le Journal des Débats* and *Liberté*. For concerted attacks on her and Verneuil's style of management in the last years see the left-wing newspaper *Bonsoir* from November 1921. Bernhardt eventually felt compelled to serve *Bonsoir* with a writ.
39 8 April 1923.
40 *Bonsoir*, 26 November 1921.
41 For a reconstruction of the 1879 *Hernani* see Anne Ubersfeld, *Le Roman d'Hernani* (Paris: Mercure de France, 1985).
42 E. H. Yates, 'Mdlle. Sarah Bernhardt in the Avenue de Villiers', *Celebrities at Home*, 3rd series (London: Office of *The World*, 1879), pp. 168–9.
43 See Gerda Taranow, *Sarah Bernhardt. The Art within the Legend* (Princeton, New Jersey: Princeton University Press, 1972), pp. 10–12.
44 Alb., 'How to make an actor. No 1. A lesson at the Conservatoire', *Time*, May 1879, p. 233.
45 Alb., 'A Rehearsal at the Française', *Time*, June 1879, p. 350.
46 *Daily Telegraph*, 10 June 1879. Also see *Morning Post*, 10 June 1879 and *The Times*, 11 June 1879.
47 *The Sunday Chronicle*, 1 April 1923.
48 'PHEDRE. To Sarah Bernhardt', *Complete Works of Oscar Wilde* (London and Glasgow: Collins, 1966), p. 777.
49 'Le Naturalisme au théâtre' in *Oeuvres Complètes* (Paris: Cercle du Livre Précieux, 1968), vol. II, p. 369.
50 Perrin is quoted by Félix Duquesnel in 'A Propos de *Théodora*', *Le Théâtre*, February 1902, p. 3.
51 Taranow, *Sarah Bernhardt*, p. 154.

52 See for example Edouard Gerspach, *La Mosaique* (Paris: Bibliothèque de l'Enseignement des Beaux-Arts, 1881); Charles Bayet, *L'Art Byzantine* (Paris: Bibliothèque de l'Enseignement des Beaux-Arts, 1883). But for criticism of Sardou's accuracy see Alfred Darcel, 'L'Archéologie au théâtre: Théodora', *La Chronique des Arts*, 3 January 1885, pp. 4–5 and 10 January 1885, pp. 10–12.

53 Frimousse, 'Théodora', *Les Premières Illustrées*, 1884.

54 The point is confirmed by the discussion that followed *Théodora*. For example: Henry Houssaye, 'L'Impératrice Théodora', *Revue des Deux Mondes*, 1 February 1885, pp. 568–97; and Paul Radiot, 'Notre Byzantinisme', *La Revue Blanche*, February 1894, pp. 110–25. Also see Philip Stephan, *Paul Verlaine and the Decadence, 1882–1890* (Manchester: Manchester University Press, 1974), p. 19 and p. 144.

55 Further excellent visual evidence is provided by the special numbers produced to accompany revivals, in particular *Le Théâtre*, February 1902, and *L'Illustration Théâtrale*, 7 February 1907. There are illustrations of costume designs for *Théodora*, probably intended for the 1902 revival, along with many other items relating to Bernhardt in the 'Catalogue of Theatre, Ballet and Music-Hall Material' for the sale held at Sotheby's on 23 October 1980.

56 The compiling of a *livret de scène* is described by Paul Ginisty in *La Vie d'un théâtre* (Paris: Les Livres d'Or de la Science, 1898): 'During the final rehearsals the stage-manager will have recorded the *mise-en-scène* on a manuscript destined for the theatre's archives, with precise indications which, if the play is ever revived, will considerably reduce the preparatory work. He will have drawn a plan of each scene, with its exact proportions; he will have followed the movements of every character and made a note of every grouping.' The *livret* was also invaluable when a production went on tour.

57 'The Diseases of Costume', *Critical Essays*, trans. Richard Howard (Evanston: Northwestern University Press, 1972), p. 46.

58 Reynaldo Hahn, *Sarah Bernhardt*, trans. Ethel Thompson (London: Elkin Mathews and Marrot, 1932), p. 92.

59 Jules Lemaître, *Literary Impressions*, trans. A. W. Evans (London: Daniel O'Connor, 1921), p. 285.

60 Baronne de Beaulieu, 'Le Chic', *Panurge*, 4 February 1883, p. 7.

61 *Our Theatres in the Nineties*, 3 vols. (London: Constable, 1948), vol. II, p. 261.

62 *The Sketch*, 27 June 1894, p. 458.

63 'A M. Cuvillier-Fleury', *Théâtre complet avec préfaces inédits* (Paris: Calmann Lévy, 1890), vol. V, pp. 171–223.

64 *L'Homme-Femme: Réponse à M. Henri D'Ideville* (Paris: Michel Lévy, 1872).

65 See René Doumic, *De Scribe à Ibsen* (Paris: Librairie Paul Delaplane, 1893); Auguste Ehrhard, *Henrik Ibsen et le théâtre contemporain* (Paris: Lecène, Oudin et Cie, 1892); A. Dikka Regne, *Trois auteurs dramatiques scandinaves: Ibsen, Bjornson, Strindberg, devant la critique française, 1889–1901* (Paris: Librairie ancienne Honoré Champion, 1930).

66 For the complicated story of Racine's reputation in the nineteenth century see Emile Faguet, 'Racine et Sarcey', *Propos de Théâtre*, 5 vols. (Paris: Société Française d'Imprimerie et de Librairie, 1903), vol. I, pp. 306–21. For *Phèdre* in particular see Maurice Descotes, *Les Grands Rôles du théâtre de Jean Racine* (Paris:

Presses Universitaires de France, 1957); Béatrix Duzzane, *Reines de théâtre, 1633–1941* (Lyon: H. Lardanchet, 1944); Claude Francis, *Les Métamorphoses de Phèdre dans la littérature française* (Quebec: Editions du Pélican, 1967).

67 Francisque Sarcey, *Quarante Ans de théâtre*, 8 vols. (Paris: Bibliothèque des Annales, 1900–1902), vol. III, 1900, p. 283.

68 *Ibid.*, p. 222.

69 *Ibid.*, p. 135.

70 *Ibid.*, pp. 178–90.

71 'La Semaine dramatique', *Journal des Débats*, 26 November 1893. The same thesis is extended in Jules Lemaître, *Jean Racine* (Paris: Calmann-Lévy, 1908).

72 Adolphe Brisson, 'Phèdre et Mme Sarah Bernhardt', *La Revue Illustrée*, 1 July 1895, pp. 33–43.

73 Roland Barthes, *S/Z*, trans. Richard Miller (London: Jonathan Cape, 1975), p. 169.

74 Brisson, 'Phèdre et Mme Sarah Bernhardt', p. 36.

75 *Ibid.*, p. 40.

76 *Ibid.*

77 *Ibid.*, p. 42. The 'tu le savais' is also described, in rather different terms, by Reynaldo Hahn, *Sarah Bernhardt*, pp. 46–7. Comparisons with Rachel's delivery of the same line were standard.

78 Maurice Maeterlinck, 'Le Tragique Quotidien' in *Le Trésor des Humbles* (Paris: Société du Mercure de France, 1896).

79 *La Plume*, 15 October 1900, p. 728.

80 Christiane Issartel, *Les Dames aux camélias de l'histoire à la légende* (Paris: Chêne Hachette, 1981), p. 71.

81 'A propos de la dame aux camélias', *Théâtre complet avec préfaces inédits*, vol. I, p. 26.

82 Sarcey quoted in Victor Mapes, *Duse and the French* (New York: The Dunlap Society, 1898; reissued New York: Benjamin Blom, 1969), p. 24.

83 Unidentified clipping in BHVP (ART).

84 André Antoine, *Le Théâtre* (Paris: Les Editions de France, 1932), p. 337.

85 Noël and Stoullig, *Annales 1896*, pp. 217–19.

86 'The Lady of the Camellias' in *Mythologies*, trans. Annette Lavers (London: Jonathan Cape, 1972), p. 103.

87 James T. Boulton (ed.), *The Letters of D. H. Lawrence. Vol. I 1901–13* (Cambridge: Cambridge University Press, 1979), p. 58.

88 *The Scenic Art*, p. 317.

89 The controversy was prolonged. See three articles by George Barlow: 'Talent and Genius on the Stage', *The Contemporary Review*, September 1892, pp. 385–94; 'Mr Irving and the English Drama', *The New Review*, December 1892, pp. 655–65; 'French Plays and English Audiences', *The Contemporary Review*, August 1893, pp. 171–81.

90 *The Contemporary Review*, September 1892, p. 388.

91 *The Star*, 1 February 1889.

92 *Our Theatres in the Nineties*, vol. II, p. 145.

93 E. H. Mikhail (ed.) *Oscar Wilde, Interviews and Recollections*, 2 vols. (London: Macmillan, 1979), vol. I, p. 249.

94 'Some Misconceptions about the Stage', *The Nineteenth Century*, October 1892, p. 671.

95 See *Plays, Acting and Music* (London: Duckworth and Co., 1903).

96 *The Sunday Chronicle*, 1 April 1923.

97 For examples of Fay's enthusiasm for French acting see Robert Hogan (ed.), *Towards a National Theatre, The Dramatic Criticism of Frank J. Fay* (Dublin: The Dolmen Press, 1970).

98 W. B. Yeats, 'Notes', *Samhaim*, October 1902, p. 4.

99 See Forrest Reid, *Pound/Joyce* (London: Faber and Faber, 1968), p. 53.

100 For Agate in general see James Harding, *Agate* (London: Methuen, 1986). For his French obsession see the *Ego* series *passim*.

101 *Rachel* (London: Gerald Howe Ltd, 1928).

102 For the history of Lewes's famous passages see my 'Rachel's "Terrible Beauty": An Actress among the Novelists', *English Literary History* (Winter 1984), pp. 771–93.

103 *Bull Fever* (London: Longmans, Green and Co., 1956), pp. vii–viii.

104 *Observer*, 24 March 1957.

105 *Sunday Times*, 24 March 1957.

106 *L'Information*, 12 April 1923.

107 *Le Théâtre Français*, 10 April 1923.

Ellen Terry

1 Ellen Terry, 'Stray Memories', *New Review*, April 1891, p. 334. Doubtless these were dress rehearsals.

2 *Ellen Terry* (New York: Stokes, 1900), p. 26; pp. 17–18.

3 *Ibid.*, p. 20.

4 T. Edgar Pemberton, *Ellen Terry and Her Sisters* (London: Pearson, 1902), p. 304.

5 'The Gardner's Daughter', *The Poems of Tennyson*, ed. Christopher Ricks (London: Longman, 1969), p. 514.

6 *Theatrical Notes* (London: Lawrence and Bullen, 1893), p. 51.

7 'Mr Henry Irving's Production of *Cymbeline*', *Harper's Weekly*, 21 November 1896.

8 'The London Theatres', *Scribner's Monthly*, January 1881, p. 361.

9 *Harper's Weekly*, 21 November 1896.

10 *Plays, Acting, and Music*, 2nd edn (London: Constable, 1909), p. 53.

11 John Parker Towse, *Sixty Years of the Theatre* (New York: Funk and Wagnalls, 1916), p. 311.

12 *Ellen Terry and Her Impersonations* (London: George Bell, 1898), pp. 266–7.

13 *Saturday Review*, 26 March 1906.

14 *The Autobiography of Sir John Martin-Harvey* (London: Sampson, Low, and Marston, 1933), p. 29. Martin-Harvey later became a member of the Lyceum company and played Osric in revivals and tours of *Hamlet* while Ellen Terry was still playing Ophelia.

15 Hiatt, *Ellen Terry*, pp. 113–14.

16 *Four Lectures on Shakespeare*, ed. Christopher St John (London: Hopkinson, 1932), p. 165.

17 *Characteristics of Women*, new edn, 2 vols. (London: Saunders and Otley, 1858), vol. I, pp. 256–7.

18 *The Works of Oscar Wilde*, ed. G. J. Maine (London: Collins, 1948, repr. 1952), pp. 766–7.

19 *Ellen Terry's Memoirs*, ed. Edith Craig and Christopher St John (London: Gollancz, 1933), p. 234. She also said of Lady Macbeth that 'the whole thing is Rossetti – rich stained-glass effects' (p. 233).

20 'Porphyria's Lover', *Browning: Poetic Works*, 1833–1864, ed. Ian Jack (London: Oxford University Press, 1970), p. 399.

21 Quoted in Ellen Terry, *The Story of My Life*, 2nd edn (London: Hutchinson, 1908), p. 115.

22 *The Works of Oscar Wilde*, p. 766.

23 *Time Was* (London: Hamish Hamilton, 1931), p. 55; p. 154. Another artist, Burne-Jones, was much struck by Bernhardt's portrayal of Phèdre: 'Sarah's pale face with its shadowed eyes and slow, mystic smile, the hieratic pomp of her golden robes, stiff with jewels, her garlands of jewelled flowers, her girdles of turquoise, opal, and agate, seemed to come straight from the wonderland of romance which the artist loved to paint' (p. 124).

24 'The London Theatres', *Galaxy*, May 1877, p. 670.

25 'The London Theatres', *Nation*, 12 June 1879.

26 *Saturday Review*, 27 April 1901.

27 For a discussion of the relationship and the paintings, which are all reproduced, see David Loshak, 'G. F. Watts and Ellen Terry', *Burlington Magazine*, November 1963, pp. 476–85.

28 *Truth*, 13 January 1881.

29 'The Art of Acting: Harvard 1885', *The Drama: Addresses* (London: Heinemann, 1893), p. 63.

30 *Scribner's Monthly*, January 1881, p. 361.

31 Robertson, *Time Was*, pp. 54–5.

32 *Theatre*, October 1880, p. 217.

33 For a further development of the Victorian theatre's production of Shakespeare, see Michael R. Booth, *Victorian Spectacular Theatre 1850–1910* (London: Routledge and Kegan Paul, 1981).

34 Jameson, *Characteristics of Women*, vol II.

35 *Ibid.*, p. 340, 343.

36 *Ibid.*, pp. 168–9.

37 *Ellen Terry* (London: John Lane, 1907), p. 83. She had played Hermione for Tree in 1906, not Irving.

38 Hiatt, *Ellen Terry*, p. 155. The comment is not actually Hiatt's, but George Wedmore's in an undated issue of the *Academy*.

39 *Ibid.*, p. 120. Ellen Terry first played the role at the Princess's in 1875, and at the Lyceum in 1879, the latter being the performance alluded to.

40 Knight, *Theatrical Notes*, pp. 51–2.

41 *Scribner's Monthly*, January 1881, p. 143.

42 Hiatt, *Ellen Terry*, p. 115. Henry Labouchère, reviewing *Hamlet*, compared Terry's appearance as Ophelia to that of a medieval Madonna (*Truth*, 9 January 1879).

43 *Saturday Review*, 17 July 1897. Characteristically, Shaw went on to attack the Lyceum for this very pictorialization: 'And here you have the whole secret of the Lyceum: a drama worn by age into great holes, and the holes filled up with the art of the picture gallery.'

44 *Henry Irving* (London: Chapman and Hall, 1893), p. 130. The great picture in the Louvre is 'The Marriage at Cana'.

45 Knight, *Theatrical Notes*, p. 305.

46 *Nights at the Play* (London: Chatto and Windus, 1883), p. 393.

47 *The Drama of Yesterday and To-Day*, 2 vols. (London: Macmillan, 1899), vol. I, p. 587.

48 Terry, *The Story of My Life*, p. 39.

49 *Ibid.*, p. 155.

50 *Ibid.*, p. 209.

51 Terry, *Four Lectures on Shakespeare*, p. 116. Christopher St John believed that Ellen Terry interpreted Portia through her sense of beauty rather than through her intellect. 'Ellen Terry', *Stars of the Stage*, ed. J. T. Grein (London: Bodley Head, 1907), p. 35.

52 'The Art of Acting: Edinburgh, 1891', *The Drama: Addresses*, p. 163.

53 Ellen Terry, 'Stray Memories', *New Review*, June 1891, pp. 503–4.

54 In her manuscript lecture on 'Pathetic Women' in Shakespeare, Terry jotted down the note 'Realism *only* of lowdown things.'

55 Terry, *The Story of My Life*, p. 106.

56 *Ibid.*, pp. 229–30.

57 Terry, *Four Lectures on Shakespeare*, p. 129.

58 *Ibid.*, p. 159.

59 *The Journal of a London Playgoer* (London: Routledge, 1866), pp. 346–7.

60 This is a marginal comment on an essay by G. Fletcher in the *Westminster Review* in 1843, on the relationship between Macbeth and Lady Macbeth. It is quoted by Laurence Irving, *Henry Irving* (London: Faber and Faber, 1951), p. 500.

61 Terry, *Four Lectures on Shakespeare*, p. 80.

62 Robertson, *Time Was*, pp. 153–4.

63 *Shakespeare on the Stage*, First Series (London: Unwin, 1912; repr. New York: Benjamin Blom, 1969), p. 219.

64 *Ellen Terry and Bernard Shaw: A Correspondence*, ed. Christopher St John (London: Constable, 1931), pp. xix–xx.

65 Terry, *The Story of My Life*, p. 159.

66 *Ellen Terry* (London: Heinemann, 1968), pp. 192–3, 356–62.

67 It passed from Lynn Fontanne to the Theatre Museum in 1977.

68 Terry, *Four Lectures on Shakespeare*, p. 156.

69 Terry, *The Story of My Life*, p. 101.

70 *Ibid.*, p. 106.

71 *Ibid.*, pp. 229–30.

72 *Ellen Terry and Bernard Shaw*, p. 52.

73 Terry, *The Story of My Life*, p. 95.

74 Scott, *The Drama of Yesterday and To-Day*, vol. I, p. 587.

75 *Saturday Review*, 26 March 1906.

76 *Ellen Terry and Her Secret Self* (London: Sampson, Low, and Marston, 1931), pp. 149–50.
77 *The Art of the Theatre*, trans. H. J. Stenning (London: Geoffrey Bles, 1924), pp. 23–4.
78 *From 'The Bells' to 'King Arthur'* (London: John Macqueen, 1896), p. 241.
79 *Henry Irving*, 2nd edn (London: J. M. Dent, 1938), p. 187.
80 *Living London* (London: Remington, 1883), p. 109. Sala's critical vocabulary is typical: 'She cannot choose but to be always winning, trusting, and charming.'
81 Scott, *Ellen Terry*, pp. 15–16.
82 *Ellen Terry and Bernard Shaw*, p. xii; p. 80. Mrs Patrick Campbell, never noted for her tact, told Shaw that Duse had leaden feet and that perfect people walked on air, 'like Ellen Terry' (p. 449).
83 *Personal Reminiscences of Henry Irving*, 2nd edn (London: Heinemann, 1907), p. 362; p. 126.
84 Craig, *Ellen Terry and Her Secret Self*, p. 165.
85 *From the Wings* (London: Collins, 1922), p. 11.
86 'Stray Memories', *New Review*, April 1891, p. 337.
87 *Ellen Terry's Memoirs*, p. 329.
88 Sala, *Living London*, p. 109.
89 Scott, *The Drama of Yesterday and To-day*, vol. II, pp. 95–6.
90 Scott, *From 'The Bells' to 'King Arthur'*, p. 292.
91 *Ibid.*, pp. 294–5. Critics recognized Terry's Ophelia in her Margaret, and apparently she used the same methods.
92 *Essays in Theatrical Criticism* (London: Remington, 1892), p. 116. Morris declined to define 'charm' in an actress and claimed it was only spiritually discernible.
93 Fitzgerald, *Henry Irving*, p. 168. Fitzgerald remarked of these pleadings and remonstrances that 'nothing more natural could be conceived' in contrast to the tempest raging all around her.
94 Winter, *Shakespeare on the Stage*, p. 218.
95 Terry, *The Story of My Life*, p. 218.
96 Craig, *Ellen Terry and Her Secret Self*, p. 158.
97 Pemberton, *Ellen Terry and Her Sisters*, p. 267.
98 'The Art of Ellen Terry', *Playgoer*, October 1901–March 1902, p. 47.
99 In one of her *Macbeth* preparation books, Ellen Terry had instructed herself to say 'Think of this good peers/But as a thing of custom' 'Sweetly but with a ghastly mouth – the *mouth* tells all, the pain & the effort & the madness.' This is the mouth in Sargent's painting.
100 Terry, *Four Lectures on Shakespeare*, p. 130.
101 Terry, *The Story of My Life*, p. 205.
102 Terry, *Four Lectures on Shakespeare*, p. 123.
103 Terry, *The Story of My Life*, p. 207.
104 Terry, *Four Lectures on Shakespeare*, p. 163.
105 *Illustrated London News*, 14 May 1881.
106 *Nights at the Play*, p. 463.
107 *The Times*, 5 May 1881.
108 Sala, *Living London*, p. 109.

109 Cook, *Nights at the Play*, p. 378.
110 Winter, *Shakespeare on the Stage*, p. 563. J. R. Towse described Terry's Katharine as lacking 'the sombre touch of tragedy that should ennoble it, but it was womanly to the core' (*Sixty Years of the Theatre*, p. 300).
111 *Illustrated London News*, 25 April 1903.
112 *Saturday Review*, 25 April 1903.
113 *Ellen Terry and Bernard Shaw*, p. 80.
114 Terry, *The Story of My Life*, p. 235.
115 *Ellen Terry and Bernard Shaw*, p. 299.
116 Terry, *The Story of My Life*, p. 163.
117 *Ibid.*, p. 305.
118 *Ellen Terry's Memoirs*, p. 270.
119 Stoker, *Personal Reminiscences of Henry Irving*, p. 364.
120 G. B. Burgin, 'The Lyceum Rehearsals', *Idler*, March 1893, pp. 123–41.
121 Morris, *Essays*, p. 115.
122 Craig, *Ellen Terry and Her Secret Self*, p. 166.

Eleonora Duse

1 Mario Corsi, quoted in Olga Signorelli, *Vita di Eleonora Duse* (Bologna: Cappelli, 1962), p. 143.
2 Letter to Olga Ossani, November 1901, Venice, Fondazione Cini.
3 Cesare Molinari, *L'attrice divina. Eleonora Duse nel teatro italiano fra i due secoli* (Rome: Bulzoni, 1985), p. 197.
4 Giorgio Capranica del Grillo to Adelaide Ristori, 12 December 1901, in *Teatro Archivio*, 8 September 1984, p. 175.
5 Adelaide Ristori to Giorgio Capranica del Grillo, 14 December 1901, in *ibid.*, p. 175.
6 Domenico Oliva, quoted in Signorelli, *Vita*, p. 143.
7 Luigi Pirandello, 'The Art of Duse', in *The Columbian Monthly*, vol. I, no. 7 (New York, 1928).
8 James Huneker, quoted in William Weaver, *Duse. A Biography* (London: Thames and Hudson, 1984), p. 247.
9 Gabriele D'Annunzio, quoted in Weaver, *Duse*, p. 199.
10 Eleonora Duse to Arrigo Boito, 1 February 1900, in Raul Radice (ed.), *Eleonora Duse–Arrigo Boito. Lettere d'amore* (Milan: Il Saggiatore, 1979), p. 950.
11 Pirandello, 'The Art of Duse'.
12 Guido Noccioli, *Duse on Tour. Guido Noccioli's Diaries, 1906–07*, ed. Giovanni Pontiero (Manchester: Manchester University Press, 1982), entry for 15 August 1907, pp. 120–1.
13 Private letter to the author from Sister Mary Mark, 1985.
14 Fernando Taviani and Mirella Schino, *Il segreto delle commedia dell'arte* (Florence: La Casa Usher, 1983).
15 Luigi Rasi, *La Duse*, ed. Mirella Schino (Rome: Bulzoni, 1986), pp. 29–30.
16 Adelaide Ristori to Giuseppe Primoli (published in *Le Gauloise*, Paris, 26 May 1897 in French, entitled *La Duse jugée par la Ristori*) in *Teatro Archivio*, 8 September 1984, p. 163.

17 See N. Savarese, *Anatomia del teatro* (Florence: La Casa Usher, 1983).
18 Bernard Shaw, 'Duse and Bernhardt', *Our Theatres in the Nineties*, vol. III (London: Constable, 1932).
19 Quoted in Signorelli, *Vita*, p. 45.
20 Rasi, *La Duse*, p. 27.
21 Gabriele D'Annunzio, *La fiamma* (Milan: Treves, 1919), pp. 447–8.
22 D'Arcais, quoted in Molinari, *L'attrice divina*, p. 104.
23 Signorelli, *Vita*, pp. 55–6.
24 Duse–Boito, *Lettere d'amore*, p. 81.
25 *Ibid.*, p. 290.
26 William Archer, review of *Antony and Cleopatra*, 28 June 1893, reprinted in *Theatrical World for 1893*.
27 Rasi, *La Duse*, p. 95–6.
28 Noccioli, *Duse on Tour*, p. 99.
29 *Ibid.*, p. 105.
30 Molinari, *L'attrice divina*, p. 142.
31 Rasi, *La Duse*, p. 69.
32 Shaw, 'Duse and Bernhardt', pp. 83–4.
33 H. von Hoffmansthal, *Eleonora Duse: Eine Wiener Theaterwoche* in *Werke. Prosa*, vol. I (Frankfurt-am-Main; Fischer, 1936).
34 Lugné-Poe, *Sous les étoiles* (Paris: Gallimard, 1933), p. 98.
35 Duse–Boito, *Lettere d'amore*, p. 801.
36 Quoted in Weaver, *Duse*, p. 342.
37 Matilde Serao, quoted in L. Ridenti, *La Duse minore* (Rome: Casini, 1966), p. 65.
38 Letter to D'Annunzio, quoted in Molinari, *L'attrice divina*, p. 202.
39 Molinari, *L'attrice divina*, p. 182.
40 A. Symons, *Eleonora Duse* (New York/London: Benjamin Blom, 1969; first published 1926), p. 6.
41 *Ibid.*, p. 7.
42 Teresa Rasi, quoted in Rasi, *La Duse*, p. 212.
43 Molinari, *L'attrice divina*, p. 178.
44 *Ibid.*, p. 179.
45 D'Annunzio, quoted in Rasi, *La Duse*, pp. 215–16.
46 Duse, quoted in Molinari, *L'attrice divina*, p. 204.
47 Duse, quoted in D. Bablet, *The Theatre of Edward Gordon Craig* (London: Methuen, 1981), p. 87.
48 Programme for *Rosmersholm*, Teatro della Pergola, Florence. Quoted in Bablet, *Theatre of Edward Gordon Craig*, p. 88.
49 Corradini, quoted in F. Marotti, *Gordon Craig* (Bologna: Cappelli, 1961), p. 85.
50 Quoted in Noccioli, *Duse on Tour*, p. 145.
51 Duse, quoted in Signorelli, *Vita*, p. 88.
52 Letter from Duse to Lugné-Poe, *Sous les étoiles*, p. 288.
53 James Agate, *Red Letter Nights: A survey of the post-Elizabethan drama in actual performance on the London stage 1921–1943* (London: Cape, 1944), pp. 71–2.
54 For a discussion on the Duse–Pirandello project, with correspondence, see: 'Rendezvous manqué. Eleonora Duse et Luigi Pirandello', *Théâtre en Europe*, no. 10 (April 1986), pp. 98–105.
55 See E. Barba, 'Antropologia teatrale' in Savarese, *Anatomia del teatro* pp. 13–42.

Select bibliography

vvvvvvvvvvvvvvvvvvvvvvvvvvvvvvvvvvvvvvvvvvvvvvvvvvvvvvvvvvvvvvvvvvvvvvvvvv

Sarah Bernhardt

There are innumerable lives of Bernhardt. Among the more modern are Joanna Richardson, *Sarah Bernhardt* (London: Reinhardt, 1959); André Castelot, *Sarah Bernhardt* (Paris: Le Livre Contemporain, 1961); Cornelia Otis Skinner, *Madame Sarah* (London: Michael Joseph, 1967); William Emboden, *Sarah Bernhardt* (London: Studio Vista, 1974); Philippe Jullien, *Sarah Bernhardt* (Paris: Editions Balland, 1977); Joanna Richardson, *Sarah Bernhardt and Her World* (London: Weidenfeld and Nicolson, 1977). Still valuable is Ernest Pronier, *Une Vie au théâtre: Sarah Bernhardt* (Geneva: Editions Alex Jullian, n.d.), particularly useful for its appendices which give details of Bernhardt's repertoire over the years. Less reverential than its title might suggest is Louis Verneuil, *La Vie merveilleuse de Sarah Bernhardt* (New York: Brentano's, 1942). Verneuil, a playwright, was briefly married to Bernhardt's grand-daughter and his book has a good deal of inside information.

Bernhardt's own memoirs, *Ma double vie* (Paris: Charpentier et Fasquelle, 1907), have been many times reprinted, most recently as 'une édition féministe de Claudine Herrmann' (Paris: Editions des Femmes, 1980).

Even in recent books the emphasis invariably tends to fall more upon Bernhardt's exploits off the stage than upon it, a fact for which she must bear a good deal of the blame herself. There is one major exception: Gerda Taranow, *Sarah Bernhardt. The Art within the Legend* (Princeton, New Jersey: Princeton University Press, 1972), a notable instance of modern scholarly methods applied to nineteenth-century theatrical technique. Taranow is particularly expert on the origins of Bernhardt's delivery and she amplifies and explains the otherwise rather opaque descriptions provided by Bernhardt in her own *L'Art du théâtre* (Paris; Editions Nilsson, 1923). Taranow also includes a discography. Commercial record companies occasionally reissue the various cylinders that Bernhardt made, and transcriptions of the originals can be heard at the Phonothèque division of the Bibliothèque Nationale. Attempts to view her films in France are likely to be more protracted.

The historian of the French theatre in the nineteenth century has in the main to rely upon the critics, most of whom eventually produced collected editions of their work. Two major figures who frequently refer to Bernhardt are Emile Faguet, *Propos de théâtre*, 5 vols. (Paris: Société Française d'Imprimerie et de Librairie, 1903–6) and Francisque Sarcey, *Quarante ans de théâtre*, 8 vols. (Paris: Bibliothèque des Annales, 1900–2). There are also some essential sources for purely factual information, in particular Edouard Noël and Edmond Stoullig (from 1899 Edmond Stoullig only), *Les Annales du théâtre et de la musique* (Paris: G. Charpentier and E. Fasquelle up until 1896, then P. Ollendorf, 1897–1914/15); Arthur Pougin, *Dictionnaire historique et pittoresque du théâtre et des arts qui s'y rattachent* (Paris: Firmin-Didot, 1885); and a short but fascinating introduction to the practicalities of theatre: Paul Ginisty, *La Vie d'un théâtre* (Paris: Les Livres d'Or de la Science, 1898). James Brander Matthews, *The Theatres of Paris* (New York: Charles Scribners and Sons, 1880) is another contemporary guide. Marvin Carlson, *The French Stage* (Metuchen, New Jersey: The Scarecrow Press, 1972), is full of basic information.

Among French libraries the Bibliothèque de l'Arsenal has the richest collection of theatrical material: for Bernhardt, the cuttings books are full of surprising and forgotten details. The theatrical holdings of the Archives Nationales, though crucial in that they include plays submitted to the Censor, can be disappointing for the late nineteenth century. The library of the Comédie Française has some material specifically relating to Bernhardt in the meticulous records of its history.

Special mention must be made of the unique collection of the Association de la Régie Théâtrale which is preserved by the Bibliothèque Historique de la Ville de Paris. This has pictures, cuttings and designs from many areas of French theatre, and, in the case of Bernhardt, some invaluable *livrets de scène*.

Ellen Terry

Much of the writing on Ellen Terry has consisted of straightforward descriptive accounts of her roles: these can provide useful information but too often convey almost nothing specific about acting style. The standard biography is Roger Manvell, *Ellen Terry* (London: Heinemann, 1968); this has the merit of career coverage and of reprinting much of the actress's annotation upon the role of Lady Macbeth, but it goes little into the acting. Ellen Terry's approach to Shakespearean roles is best treated in Alan Hughes, *Henry Irving, Shakespearean* (Cambridge: Cambridge University Press, 1981); an older descriptive approach to these roles and to her other performances on Lyceum first nights until 1895 is that of Clement Scott, *From 'The Bells' to 'King Arthur'* (London: John MacQueen, 1896). The best sources of contextual information about the Lyceum and Terry's position in the company are those in Bram Stoker, *Personal Reminiscences of Henry Irving* (London: Heinemann, 1906), *The Autobiography of Sir John Martin-Harvey* (London: Sampson, Low, and Marston, 1933) and Laurence Irving, *Henry Irving* (London: Faber and Faber, 1951). Her own autobiography, *The Story of My Life*, 2nd edn (London: Hutchinson, 1908), is perhaps the best of Victorian acting autobiographies, full of valuable insights into her own acting and that of Irving. The notes added to the same book in *Ellen Terry's Memoirs*, ed. Edith Craig and Christopher St John (London: Gollancz, 1933) are helpful, as are her own *Four Lectures on Shakespeare*, ed. Christopher St John (London: Hopkinson, 1932) even though only two chapters are relevant, 'The Triumphant Women' and 'The Pathetic Women', and these are accounts of character rather than performance. The correspondence with Shaw, which began in 1892 and was mostly concluded by 1900, is contained in *Ellen Terry and Bernard Shaw*, ed. Christopher St John (London: Constable, 1931).

Of other accounts and criticisms of Ellen Terry's acting, W. Graham Robertson, *Time Was* (London: Hamish Hamilton, 1931) is written by an artist and valuable for that reason; Edward Gordon Craig, *Ellen Terry and Her Secret Self* (London: Sampson, Low, and Marston, 1931) is occasionally penetrating and illuminating if eccentric; and

Henry James's essays on the London theatre from the 1870s to the 1890s, usefully collected in *The Scenic Art*, ed. Allan Wade (New Brunswick: Rutgers University Press, 1948), contain, on the whole, a refreshingly dissenting view of the acting.

Eleonora Duse

There are a great many books, articles and reviews on Duse, together with a myriad of references to her in the autobiographies and diaries of many of her contemporaries. The present bibliography includes some of the best-known works on Duse, several of which also contain further bibliographies.

Bordeaux, Jeanne, *Eleonora Duse. The Story of Her Life*, New York: Doran, 1925
Corsi, Mario, *Le prime rappresentazioni dannunziane*, Milan: Treves, 1928
Fuseo, Clemente, *Eleonora Duse*, Milan: dall'Oglio, 1971
Guerrieri, Gerardo, ed. *Eleonora Duse nel suo tempo*, Milan: Quaderni del Piccolo Teatro, 3, 1962
    Eleonora Duse e il suo tempo (catalogue) Treviso: Canova, 1974
    Eleonora Duse. Tra storia e leggenda (catalogue), Rome: publication for Ente Festival di Asola, Mostra dedicata a Eleonora Duse, Rome, Palazzo Venezia 6 June–6 July 1985
Harding, Bertita, *Age Cannot Wither. The Story of Duse and D'Annunzio*, London: Harrap, 1949
Knepler, Henry, *The Gilded Stage*, London: Constable, 1968
Le Gallienne, Eva, *The Mystic in the Theatre. Eleonora Duse*, London: The Bodley Head, 1965
Mapes, Victor, *Duse and the French*, New York: The Dunlap Society, 1898
Matthews, J. F., ed. *Shaw's Dramatic Criticism 1895–98*, Westport, Connecticut: The Greenwood Press, 1959
Molinari, Cesare, *L'attrice divina. Eleonora Duse nel teatro italiano fra i due secoli*, Roma: Bulzoni, 1985
Nardi, Piero, ed. *Carteggio D'Annunzio–Duse*, Florence: Felice–Le Monnier, 1975
Pontiero, Giovanni, *Duse on Tour. Guido Noccioli's Diaries 1906–07*, Manchester: Manchester University Press, 1982
    Eleonora Duse. In Life and Art, Frankfurt: Bern and New York: Peter Lang, 1986
Radice, Paul, *Eleonora Duse – Arrigo Boito. Lettere d'amore*, Milan: Il Saggiatore, 1979
Rasi, Luigi, *La Duse*, Rome: Bulzoni, 1986 (with a useful essay by Mirella Schino)
Ridenti, Lucio, *La Duse minore*, Rome: Casini 1966
Schino, Mirella, 'La Duse e la Ristori', *Teatro Archivio*, 8 September 1984, pp. 123–82.
    'Ritorno al teatro. Lettere di Eleonora Duse a Ermete Zacconi e a Silvio d'Amico, *Teatro Archivio*, 8 September 1984
Setti, Dora, ed. *Eleonora Duse and Antonietta Pisa*, Milan: Ceschina, 1972
    La Duse com'era, Milan: Pan editrice, 1978.
Signorelli, Olga, *Eleonora Duse*, Milan: Silvana, 1959
    Vita di Eleonora Duse, Bologna: Cappelli, 1962
Stubbs, Jean, *Eleanora [sic] Duse*, New York: Stein and Day, 1970
Symons, Arthur, *Eleonora Duse*, New York and London: Benjamin Blom, 1961 (first edition 1927)

Weaver, William, *Duse. A Biography*, London: Thames and Hudson, 1984

Winwar, Frances, *Wingless Victory*, New York: Harper and Bros., 1956

Wings of Fire. A Biography of Gabriele D'Annunzio and Eleonora Duse, London: Alvin Redman, 1957

Index

vvvvvvvvvvvvvvvvvvvvvvvvvvvvvvvvvvvvvvvvvvvvvvvvvvvvvvvvvvvvvvvvvvvvvvvvvvvvvv

187